CONSPIRACIES
(DECLASSIFIED

THE *SKEPTOID*® GUIDE TO THE
TRUTH BEHIND THE THEORIES

A Critical Analysis by Brian Dunning
Creator of the *Skeptoid*® Podcast

Adams Media

New York   London   Toronto   Sydney   New Delhi

Adams Media
An Imprint of Simon & Schuster, Inc.
57 Littlefield Street
Avon, Massachusetts 02322

First Adams Media trade paperback edition June 2018

ADAMS MEDIA and colophon are trademarks of Simon & Schuster.

For information about special discounts for bulk purchases, please contact Simon & Schuster Special Sales at 1-866-506-1949 or business@simonandschuster.com.

The Simon & Schuster Speakers Bureau can bring authors to your live event. For more information or to book an event contact the Simon & Schuster Speakers Bureau at 1-866-248-3049 or visit our website at www.simonspeakers.com.

Interior design by Katrina Machado

Manufactured in the United States of America

10 9 8 7 6 5 4 3 2 1

Library of Congress Cataloging-in-Publication Data
Dunning, Brian, 1965–, author.
Conspiracies declassified / Brian Dunning, creator of the *Skeptoid*® podcast.
Avon, Massachusetts: Adams Media, 2018.
Includes bibliographical references and index.
LCCN 2018003627 (print) | LCCN 2018005579 (ebook) | ISBN 9781507206997 (pb) | ISBN 9781507207000 (ebook)
LCSH: Conspiracies--History.
LCC HV6275 (ebook) | LCC HV6275 .D86 2018 (print) | DDC 001.9--dc23
LC record available at https://lccn.loc.gov/2018003627

ISBN 978-1-5072-0699-7
ISBN 978-1-5072-0700-0 (ebook)

Dedication

This book is dedicated to the many supporters of my nonprofit, Skeptoid® Media, whose generosity has made this work possible.

Acknowledgments

My thanks to a plethora of colleagues with whom I've spent much of the preceding decade exploring myths and mysteries from popular culture, in the quest to promote public understanding of science and the tenets of scientific skepticism. They include (in alphabetical order): Rachael Dunlop, Mark Edward, Emery Emery, Pamela Gay, Susan Gerbic, Ryan Johnson, Karl Kruszelnicki, Michael Mann, Joe Nickell, Steven Novella and company, Ben Radford, James Randi, Natalia Reagan, John Rennie, Tamara Robertson, Lee Sanders, Kirsten Sanford, Richard Saunders, Eugenie Scott, Michael Shermer, Blake Smith, Joe Uscinski, and Reichart Von Wolfsheild.

Contents

Contents

Introduction

Did you know that the Earth is flat? That the world is run by a shadowy cabal of reptilian beings who wear human disguises to avoid detection? That Finland doesn't really exist, but aliens (who are kept hidden by the government) do? That powerful navies across the globe trained dolphins to act as weapons of war? Welcome to the world of conspiracy theories—where members of the powerful elite fight for control of your mind, your money, and even your health.

If you're nervous about entering this world of conspiracies alone, don't worry. I'll be here to walk you through it, every step of the way. As a professional science writer, I've been hosting and producing the weekly podcast *Skeptoid®* (https://skeptoid.com) for more than a decade, revealing the true science and real history behind conspiracy theories. My job has been to do the research and separate the fact from the fiction. I've found the most success by examining each conspiratorial belief purely upon its actual merits and how well it fits with the proven historical record.

So here in *Conspiracies Declassified* we'll take a look at fifty of the most notorious (and well-known) conspiracy theories of all time. To qualify for inclusion in this book, each must satisfy two criteria:

1. *They must be specific enough to be falsifiable.* Too often, proposed conspiracy theories are so uselessly vague that they are always going to be true. The government is up to something secret. Well, of course they are, nobody doubts that. There are still unknown details about Lee Harvey Oswald. Of course there are, probably unimportant ones that weren't published. Claims such as these are

always going to be true. They don't prove you've uncovered a conspiracy theory.

2. *They must be known by the conspiracy theorist before being revealed by the media or law enforcement.* Many times, conspiracy theorists will look back on historical conspiracies and claim they are examples of conspiracy theories proven true. But in so many cases, the story never existed as a conspiracy theory; history shows that it remained unknown and unsuspected until it was revealed to the world by investigators or whistle-blowers.

For each entry that meets these criteria, you'll learn the who, what, when, where, and why of the theory; you'll discover how each theory was formed, why it exists, and the historical or sociological context that allowed it to thrive; and you'll see each and every theory either debunked or proven.

Debunked or *proven*? Yes, it's true that most of the conspiracy theories in this book, and most conspiracy theories in general, are just that: theories. This is what you'll see when we investigate various conspiracies having to do with suspicious deaths, government oppression, suppressed science, and more throughout the book. But the conspiracy theories that we'll investigate in the final section of the book? Well, some of these have elements of truth that are tough to deny. And, as frightening as it may be to examine these theories, it's worth it to know just what those in power are *really* up to.

So lock your doors, make sure your phone's not tapped, and let's take a look at these conspiracy theories that are now declassified.

PART 1
Those Who Run the World

The ultimate conspiracy theory is that the illuminati run the world, and that all governments and corporations are willingly subservient to the secret powers that be. It is the conspiracy theory that best satisfies our most primal need to believe that everything happens for some reason, according to some plan; that there is a method to every apparent madness; and that we ourselves are the ultimate targets of this simmering malevolence.

The conspiratorial mind-set compels us to look everywhere for *them*. *They* who run the world. *They* who know the secrets. What *they* don't want us to know. Wherever *their* secret headquarters is, it must be a busy place, for just about every group you can think of has been charged by someone somewhere to be secretly running things from it.

What the conspiracy theorist's special insight does not ever seem to reveal to him, though, is why? Why would nations and corporations give up their sovereignty? For money they already have? Wouldn't they rather control their own destinies than become powerless pawns of this shadowy global cabal? This is a pretty large and glaring question, and it's one for which the conspiracy theorists don't seem to have a very persuasive answer.

The big question is: Who are these illuminati? In this part, we'll look at some of the candidates most often proposed for who really runs the world.

The Knights Templar

Date: 1119–Present
Location: All Christian nations
The Conspirators: The Knights Templar
The Victims: Christians worldwide

The Theory

According to conspiracy theorists, a legendary Catholic order called the Knights Templar has been involved in just about every major power shift of the past thousand years. Although the popular story says that the Templars were all simultaneously executed in 1307, and the official story says they were formally dissolved in 1312, conspiracy theorists believe that the order of Templars survived and operate today as a secret society whose unidentified members include many of the world's elite, who use the order's vast hoard to finance wars and manipulate global events.

The Truth

The Templars did have a colorful (and powerful) history, but they were disbanded by the church after the Crusades. Since they no longer exist, they have no influence.

The Backstory

The Knights Templar was one of many monastic orders created under the authority of the Catholic Church following the success of the First Crusade. During the Crusade, which was started to reassert the control of the fracturing church, the land that now makes up modern Turkey, Syria, Lebanon, Israel, and Jordan was conquered. To try to maintain control of this enormous empire, the pope ordered this land subdivided into four new "Crusader states"—Edessa, Antioch, Tripoli, and Jerusalem—which the Crusaders would now have to protect.

Jerusalem proved the most troublesome to defend, and Christian pilgrims who traveled to the Holy Land were under constant threat of attack from Muslims, from Eastern Orthodox Christians who did not recognize the authority of the Catholic Church, and even from ordinary highwaymen. Crusader knights petitioned the pope to create a monastic order that would protect these pilgrims. Once approved, the order chose Temple Mount in Jerusalem, the traditional location of Solomon's Temple, as their headquarters and took inspiration from the location for their name: the Knights Templar.

Skeptoid® Says...

There were already a number of other monastic orders created for similar purposes. The Knights Hospitaller, the Order of the Holy Sepulchre, and the Order of Saint Lazarus were orders that were already headquartered in Jerusalem. The most famous and successful was the Teutonic Order, founded just to the north, and it soon controlled and defended much of what is now Transylvania and the Baltics.

The Knights Templar operated like a charity, and as a charity it sought wealthy donors and sponsors. Gradually the order's holdings, and thus its influence, increased. For nearly 200 years, the Knights Templar was one of the most powerful institutions in the world. Economists have noted that they appear to have been the world's first true multinational corporation. Eventually they were able to self-fund through investment and lending. Unfortunately, this very success is what led to their very public downfall.

As the story goes, deeply in debt to them, France's King Philip IV ordered all the Templars, wherever they were, to be simultaneously executed. He sent hundreds of bailiffs all over France with sealed orders, and on Friday the 13th, the orders were carried out...supposedly. However, stories persist that say the Templars simply vanished, taking the secrets of their vast treasures with them, and surviving even today to wield the influence granted them by their unfathomable resources. Books and TV shows have characterized the Templars as shadowy overlords somehow involved in nearly every urban legend: pirate treasures, international finance conspiracies, Freemason mythology, the tomb of Jesus, the Holy Grail, the Nazis, even 9/11 and the assassination of JFK.

Today there is no headquarters, no publicly identified Templars, and no traceable bank accounts. So whatever these Templars are up to, it is done well out of the public eye.

The Explanation

The truth about the end of the Templars is more complicated than what you see in movies and TV shows. To start, all of these monastic orders had to compete against one another to secure the wealthiest patrons. Sponsorship was usually granted to the order that presented itself as the most exclusive and offered the best perks. The stories that connect the Templars to important historical events and artifacts like Jesus' tomb and the Holy Grail were essentially stories invented by Templars to impress patrons.

Now, it's true that King Philip IV was deeply in debt to the Templars. Not only that, many of his French officials were Templars who were more loyal to the pope than to him. He wanted very much to see the Knights Templar disappear. In addition, for some time Pope Clement V had been attempting to merge the Knights Templar and the Knights Hospitaller to reduce the number of orders he had to contend with, and in 1307 he happened to have the heads of both orders in France for talks. Philip seized the opportunity. Using made-up charges such as heresy and corruption, Philip sent bailiffs out with secret orders for a simultaneous morning arrest of all Templars. However, his orders were to arrest the Templars, not kill them, and since Philip was the king of France, not of the whole world, his orders only applied to Templars who were located in France. Probably about 625 Templars were arrested. None were immediately executed.

The majority of the Templars confessed to heresy, since doing so allowed them to be released, retain their property, and either retire or join the Hospitallers. A month later, under pressure from Philip, Clement did make a papal order for the Templars located everywhere else to be arrested, but by then they had all had plenty of warning, and nearly all had either retired or joined another order.

So what about the Templars' wealth and influence? History records no sudden disappearance of vast fortunes and treasures, but it did keep track of a well-accounted merging of the assets of the Templars and the Hospitallers. In fact, in 1312 the church formally merged these assets (although it had already long since been done), and the Knights Templar were formally dissolved.

So do the Templars control the world today? It would seem unlikely, since they have no authority to exist, no money, and certainly no influence.

Skeptoid® Says...

A few dozen Templars were eventually executed for recanting their earlier confessions. Most famously, the head of the Knights Templar, Grand Master Jacques de Molay, together with the Preceptor of Normandy Geoffroi de Charny, were burned at the stake in 1314 after seven long years of imprisonment.

The Rothschild Family

Date: ca. 1800–Present
Location: Worldwide
The Conspirators: The Rothschild family
The Victims: Everyone anywhere who hopes to save money

The Theory

Long the subjects of conspiracy theory, the infamous Rothschild family is said to have been making international loans to finance wars in Europe since the 1700s. Believers claim that each time the family financed a war, the debts they held effectively gave them control over the governments on both sides—giving them nearly unlimited influence on every major nation in the world by the late 1800s. The Jewish Rothschild family is claimed to have financed both Nazi Germany and the creation of the state of Israel, profiting massively each time. Today they are described by some to be the single most powerful entity on the planet.

The Truth

Prior to the World Wars, Rothschild family banks were indeed quite large and powerful, but the family has since diversified and slid into relative insignificance.

The Backstory

Mayer Amschel Rothschild was born in 1744 in a Jewish slum of Frankfurt. As a teen he began working in the coin trade, assisting clients with buying and selling rare coins. He wisely sought out the wealthiest clients he could, and diversified the investment opportunities he offered them as much as he was able. Rothschild's big break came at about the age of forty when his best client, Landgrave Wilhelm I, Elector of Hesse, inherited his father's vast wealth and began looking to make some large international transactions.

By then, Rothschild had five sons, all of whom he brought into the family business. He sent his five sons out to be his agents in the five biggest financial centers of Europe: Frankfurt, Vienna, London, Naples, and Paris. When four of these sons had sons of their own, Mayer ordered that the trend continue, and most of his grandsons joined the business and opened offices of their own. Mayer even encouraged the intermarriage of first cousins to keep the family locked down tight against outsiders.

The Rothschild family business hit its height around the turn of the twentieth century. With agents in every major financial center, Rothschild banks did, indeed, as the conspiracy theorists say, finance both sides of European wars. They won no matter what. But most important, the Rothschilds filled a crucial role in international finance, one held today by the International Monetary Fund. Their investments greatly stabilized various currencies by facilitating international trade and credit. When a nation faced a crisis, the Rothschilds were always there to help—for a price. However, very soon the needs of nations exceeded what any one institution could provide.

The First and Second World Wars spelled the beginning of the end for the Rothschild dynasty. World War I was so great in scope that nearly every financial institution in the world had to pitch in to finance the massive buildups on all sides, which greatly leveled the playing field on which the Rothschilds competed. And as bad as World War I was for their dominant position, World War II was even worse. The Rothschilds were European Jews, with deep roots in the countries held by Nazi Germany. The family members escaped to the United States but it cost many of them nearly everything to do so: their fortunes were seized and their dozens of fantastic mansions were destroyed or given away.

Skeptoid® Says...

Conspiracy theorists often cite certain early Rothschild transactions as important moments when they "took over" England or "took over" Europe. Generally, the versions of these stories told are grossly misrepresented or outright fabrications. The Rothschilds made savvy investments and profited from the losses of others. That's business; it doesn't require a secret cabal of evil.

The Explanation

Although the Rothschilds did have a formidable start in the world of finance, the exaggerated stories today are more the result of bigotry than a reflection of true history. The spread of malicious stories about the Rothschilds is a manifestation of anti-Semitism in the conspiracy theory community. Throughout much of the past millennia, institutionalized anti-Semitism throughout Europe had consequences such as prohibitions against Jewish people owning property. Such policies often forced people of Jewish heritage to seek expertise in business or finance, where assets could be kept liquid and easily transferred or hidden; at any rate, this was the reputation they were eventually given. Thus, conspiracy theories involving Jewish wealth are nothing new.

Today, wealth held in public funds is intermixed, at some level, with every other fund in the world. So saying that a Rothschild family member owns some of every company in the world is true, but only true in the sense that you do too if you have any kind of interest-bearing account. The money in your checking account is invested by your bank in various securities (such as stocks, bonds, and mutual funds), each of which invests their own holdings in the same way. With some creativity, it's possible to trace a line of ownership between any person in the world with a bank account and any publicly held company in the world, and vice versa.

Claims that the Rothschild family has $500 trillion in assets are even more problematic. Prior to World War I, the Rothschild family did indeed control a disproportionate amount of wealth. But in the century since, the family has diversified and diluted substantially. Many family members work in unrelated industries. Many have divested whatever they inherited. There is no longer a single, central "House of Rothschild." The closest thing is a Swiss company called Rothschilds Continuation Holdings AG, which manages interests in many Rothschild-founded companies, as well as other businesses. There are no Rothschild family members on its board, and only eight Rothschilds are known to hold any shares in the company; most of it is owned by non-Rothschild financial institutions. Its annual revenues are about $500 million (compare this to the world's largest company, Walmart, with revenues of $500 *billion*). Rothschilds Continuation Holdings AG has billions in assets, but this is small potatoes compared to the many banks with trillions in assets, such as Deutsche Bank, Mitsubishi UFJ Financial Group, HSBC Holdings, and others.

The idea of a single family owning a controlling portion of the world's wealth, while romantic, is simply absurd. The rest of the world caught up with and surpassed them generations ago.

Skeptoid Says...

The world's wealthiest Rothschild, Benjamin de Rothschild, appears way down at #1,376 on *Forbes*'s list of the world's billionaires with an estimated net worth of $1.5 billion. There are so many others ahead of him on the list that they even include a Rothschild with no relation to the famous family: Jeff Rothschild, a founding engineer at Facebook, at #896.

The Bohemian Club

Date: 1872–Present
Location: San Francisco and Sonoma County, California
The Conspirators: The Bohemians
The Victims: Innocent civilians worldwide

The Theory

Once a year, the Sonoma County Airport fills with a staggering collection of private jets, and the 2,700-acre Bohemian Grove fills with military members, former US presidents, and other members of the powerful elite. Welcome to the sixteen-day annual retreat of the Bohemian Club, held under tight security. Here, conspiracy theorists say, bizarre activities take place in the redwoods—everything from occult ceremonies to drag shows to skinny-dipping. But they believe that the world's most powerful men (no women are allowed) aren't just here to have a good time. They say the Manhattan Project to create the world's first atomic bomb was planned in the Grove, and wars, corporate takeovers, military plots, and overall global domination are strategized inside. Some theorists say that the bohemians (sometimes called bohos) represent the most dangerous gathering of power brokers on the planet.

The Truth

The bohemians are patrons of the arts and enjoy hobnobbing with well-connected associates who have similar interests. They get drunk in the woods, but aren't planning to take over the world.

The Backstory

In the early days of the nineteenth century, San Francisco was home to a burgeoning theatrical arts community. It was also home to men who had made fortunes off the exploding West Coast economy. It was a match made in heaven. Artists are always looking for patrons, and patrons are always looking for more patrons to share the expense of supporting an active arts community. So a group of the social elite, including both leading artists and leading patrons, formed the Bohemian Club as a place where the two groups could mingle, and where the wealthy could buy a unique opportunity to hobnob with legendary musicians and artists. It quickly attained an exclusive reputation, exactly as its founders hoped, and it successfully cemented not only support for the arts community in San Francisco, but also personal relationships between its wealthy members.

The conspiracy theorists, on the other hand, say that it is also much more than a place to mingle. Why? Well, a sizable portion of San Francisco's wealthiest industrialists in the late 1800s also happened to represent much of government and finance. That never changed. The bohemians have always strived to recruit the biggest names they could—including US presidents. But not all potential recruits are impressed. Richard Nixon came away from a Bohemian Grove retreat with some incredibly disparaging language directed at the boho arts community, many of whom were gay. But you don't need to express Nixon-level homophobia to find some of the Grove activities odd. There are, indeed, other off-the-wall performances. Most famous is the ceremony held every year on the first day, a live fifty-minute dramatic play featuring a full orchestra and a six-figure budget. At its climax, cloaked figures perform a human sacrifice by burning a man in a coffin on an altar at the feet of the pagan god Moloch, a giant 30-feet-tall stone owl. An artificial lake and the world's second-largest outdoor pipe organ are part of the show. Misinterpretation of the play's imagery is what has led many critics to describe it as "occult."

Skeptoid® Says...

This group of artists and wealthy patrons called themselves the Bohemian Club in reference to the then-popular bohemian arts movement, in which it was fashionable to be offbeat, nonconforming, or free-spirited. Mark Twain and Jack London identified as bohemian writers, and both were elected as honorary members of the club. London became an active member, while it seems Twain never took the club up on its invite.

Whenever the rich, the powerful, or world leaders gather, a natural reaction among the more paranoid is that they're up to something malevolent. Accordingly, given the impressive roster of Bohemian Grove attendees—and especially given the appearance of US presidents and the connection to the Manhattan Project—charges of planning world domination have always been leveled at the gatherings.

The Explanation

Although US presidents would sometimes visit, by itself that's not quite enough to force us to conclude that the bohos are running the world. Each of the claims about the retreat falls apart under even modest scrutiny. For example, the "occult ceremony" is hardly as it's popularly described. The play, called *The Cremation of Care*, is about letting go of the troubles of the daily grind in order to achieve freedom. The antagonist, named Dull Care (from a 1919 Oliver Hardy short film), is the one in the coffin, his death symbolizing freedom from monotonous daily tasks. The pagan god depicted by the owl represents knowledge and has always been the club's mascot.

Skeptoid® Says...

If the CEO of a *Fortune* 100 company ever wanted to star in his own Broadway musical, well, the Bohemian Grove would be his chance. Each retreat closes with an original play, produced to the highest standards, called the *High Jinks*. However, there are also lesser productions performed throughout the two weeks called the *Low Jinks*, and these are the goofy drag shows and whatever stuff members want to throw together for fun. And yes, they often live down to their name.

Although conspiracy theorists such as far-right radio personality Alex Jones have long charged that world leaders meet at the Grove to hold confidential talks and plan global domination, little evidence supports this. Members do present informal "Lakeside Talks" on various public policy issues throughout the retreat, but nothing confidential or surprising has ever been said. Contrary to the claims of Jones and others, security during the retreat is actually quite lax. Many reporters have found that they've been able to walk in and out and come and go without ever being stopped or questioned, and the goings-on inside the Grove have been extensively reported. Although we can't prove a negative, the fact that no undercover reporter has ever caught a whiff of global domination being planned is telling.

What about the theory that the Manhattan Project was planned at Bohemian Grove? Well, the Grove is vacant most of the year, and members are allowed to rent it for private events. At the time the project was discussed, member Edward Teller (known as the "father of the hydrogen bomb") had privately rented out the facility. The meeting was then run by J. Robert Oppenheimer and Ernest Lawrence, who went on to head national laboratories working on the Manhattan Project. Other than Teller, no Bohemian Club members were present or allowed. Nevertheless, this one 1942 closed meeting is as close as the Bohemian Club ever came to "planning world domination."

Now, you may be tempted to ask, if power brokers are going off to the woods, wouldn't they be doing it for some reason more important than merely acting like drunken frat boys from the drama club? The Department of Sociology at UC Davis wrote a paper analyzing the Bohemian Grove encampment, and found that what happens there is essentially the same as team-building exercises popular in the corporate world. In essence, groups are more cohesive when they see themselves as high in status and when they interact in a relaxed and cooperative environment. Team building is an effective way for groups to learn to deal with problems more easily. So, in short, these men in positions of authority or status work better together in the outside world when they've developed camaraderie at the Bohemian Grove.

And this, it turns out, was one of the group's founding principles: not to bring any business into the club itself. The club motto is "Weaving spiders come not here." Leave the work outside. Become better friends inside.

The Bilderbergers

Date: 1954–Present
Location: Europe and North America
The Conspirators: Bilderberg conference attendees
The Victims: Innocent citizens worldwide

The Theory

Once a year, according to conspiracy theorists anyway, scores of the world's most powerful leaders in business, finance, militaries, and arts meet at a different luxury hotel. Although members of this Bilderberg Group—named for the hotel where they held their very first meeting—claim that they meet merely to exchange ideas and discuss solutions to problems faced by many nations, conspiracy theorists charge that they are actually the secret world government. The belief is that the power brokers hold these highly-secure, closed meetings to decide all the national foreign and domestic policies that all attending nations must abide by. Attendees then return to their home countries with their new orders in hand, and their governments then carry these orders out—no matter how nefarious they may be.

Have we all been duped? Are the conspiracy theorists correct, and this is how the real policies of the world's nations are decided? Are elections just fictions, and world leaders just pawns of the Bilderbergers?

The Truth

The Bilderberg Group offers plenty of evidence that they meet for exactly the reasons they say: the free exchange of ideas and solutions to mutual world issues. There is nothing secret about their meetings, no orders are given to nations or heads of state, and they have no plans to take over the world.

The Backstory

The Bilderberg Group is indeed real, and they do indeed meet about once a year at a luxury hotel somewhere in Europe or the United

States. This annual conference arose from the tensions of what would become the Cold War.

In 1954, the Socialist states of Central and Eastern Europe began rising after World War II as the Communist Bloc. Many leaders in the West wanted to join forces to resist the rise of Communism, but post-war Europe was fractured and there was substantial anti-American sentiment spreading across the Continent. Clearly, if the Western nations couldn't learn to get along, it would be increasingly difficult to mount a credible defense against the Communist Bloc. These international tensions were characterized by fear of the United States' rising economic status that led to mistrust throughout Europe. It seemed that if progress were to be made, it must be handled through unofficial channels.

Józef Retinger, a Polish politician, was among the first to see this, and was the first to act. He spoke with Prince Bernhard of the Netherlands and Belgian prime minister Paul van Zeeland about the need to create an unofficial working group of world leaders, with one liberal and one conservative representative from each nation. They agreed, and in turn, they spoke with other leaders from Europe and the United States. Their whole idea was to find common ground and ways for Europe and the United States to work together to counter the rising Communist threat. However, world leaders are often bound by the restrictions of their office, so leaders from business and economics, who were often more free to meet than military or government leaders, were included as well.

Skeptoid® Says...

The Bilderbergers hold their meetings under the Chatham House Rule, a set of protocols intended to encourage free and open discussion by maintaining confidentiality. Participants are free to use the information gleaned from the meeting, but the identity and affiliation of each speaker is not recorded, guaranteeing anonymity. In addition, there is no detailed agenda, no resolutions are proposed, no votes are taken, and no policy statements are issued.

Retinger's idea came to life and sixty prominent representatives, including politicians, industrialists, academics, and editors, met for three days at the Bilderberg Hotel in the Netherlands in May of 1954.

Their stated agenda was to discuss the Soviet Union, European attitudes toward Communism, relevant economic policies, and European defense. The meeting was a great success. Two more meetings followed in 1955, and there's been about one a year ever since. A steering committee invites participants to each meeting. Each year brings largely a different group of attendees, making the discussions as broad as possible, and most attendees are only invited to one or two conferences.

The Explanation

The Bilderberg meetings continued on as scheduled for many years, but in 2006 public awareness of the group increased when conspiracy theorist and author Daniel Estulin published *The True Story of the Bilderberg Group*. This book claims that the group secretly plans global domination and, each year, sends its attendees home with orders to follow. Who picked up this book? Fidel Castro, longtime dictator of Cuba, which was part of the Communist Bloc that the Bilderbergers were formed to protect the world against. Castro read the book voraciously and believed every word of it. His official endorsement has given the theorists their best fodder.

Hungry for more news about the Bilderbergers, the media sought out former meeting attendees to interview. In 2010, a Dutch radio program found Willy Claes, the secretary-general of NATO during the 1994 Bilderberg meeting. Claes told the program that each session is run by a rapporteur who speaks for ten minutes, laying out a particular problem faced by the West. This is followed by a group discussion, during which the rapporteur takes notes and attempts to find a consensus from the group. The group's conclusions are then provided to attendees. During his interview, Claes said:

> and everybody is supposed to use those conclusions in his circle of influence.

Taken out of context, this sentence has been trumpeted by conspiracy theorists as proof that orders are given to nations at the Bilderberg meetings, and attendees are required to take those orders back to their home nations. However, in context, it's clear that Claes also said there is no voting, no resolutions made, and the purpose of the exchange is to accommodate different—and even contradictory—opinions. One must make a deliberate misinterpretation of Claes's one sentence in order to find anything suspicious or ominous in the interview.

Another central claim made by the conspiracy theorists is that the meetings are held in secret. Although the meetings are private, they are definitely not secret. The Bilderberg Group puts out press releases for each meeting, the list of attendees and the agenda of topics to be discussed is always public, and a press corps is present at each meeting. It is only due to the necessary restrictions of the Chatham House Rule—which is what makes the meetings both possible and useful—that the actual minutes are not published.

Skeptoid® Says...

Check out www.bilderbergmeetings.org. Here you'll find info about each of the Bilderberg meetings since the group's inception in 1954. The transparency is impressive; they freely discuss how the meetings are financed, how the invitations work, and the names and affiliations of the dozens of steering committee members (mostly bigwigs from companies you know). One thing missing from the website, unfortunately, is an outline of their plans for taking over the world.

Now, let's talk about the idea that the Bilderberg meetings are held to allow a select group of power brokers to plan global domination. To start, the meeting is alleged to be some sort of obedience pact, presumably threat-driven, but it is made up of a completely different group of people each year. What if an attendee is given orders that he doesn't like or refuses to carry out? The theorists say that, when a first-time attendee walks in the door—like Bill Gates did in 2010— he is told that he will be required to carry out whatever orders he is given, or else face some consequences. If that were true, it would mean that all of the thousands of attendees over the decades were okay with this arrangement, having no idea what such orders might entail. While people in positions of influence and responsibility do have real reasons for wanting to come together in an open forum to discuss problems and find mutually beneficial solutions, it's unlikely that such people would be willing to throw away their autonomy and voluntarily enter into threat-driven obedience pacts with foreigners who may have radically different agendas.

In all probability, the Bilderbergers are no more and no less than what their website openly proclaims them to be: "an annual forum for informal discussions, designed to foster dialogue between Europe and North America." And there is no better evidence of this than the extraordinary diversity of the meeting's many attendees and their broad satisfaction with the tools the meetings provide.

The North American Union

Date: Imminent
Location: North America
The Conspirators: The governments of the United States, Canada, and Mexico
The Victims: The citizens of the United States, Canada, and Mexico

The Theory

Conspiracy theorists believe Canada, Mexico, and the United States are actively planning to merge into a single police megastate called the North American Union, or NAU. Why? Maximum profits for those in control (exactly who those might be is a little vague), with a half a billion laborers being forced into a Socialist dystopia to benefit those at the top. Under Socialist martial law, the dollar would disappear, and the new currency would be called the Amero. These theorists regard trade agreements such as NAFTA (North American Free Trade Agreement, 1994) and the SPP (Security and Prosperity Partnership of North America, 2005) as first steps to this imminent merging. Nothing like this has ever been presented to the legislative bodies or voters in any of the three countries, nor will it, claim the believers—it will simply be thrust upon everyone by force.

The Truth

The idea that the United States, Canada, and Mexico are planning to merge into a single, giant police state isn't true. And, in fact, very few people would want this to happen—including those whom the conspiracy theorists claim would benefit.

The Backstory

Rumblings of a North American Union have always existed in the conspiracy theory community, mainly based on the existence of the Soviet Union, which was formed when a number of Eastern European states merged in 1922 and became a powerful Communist megastate. Then in 1992 the European Union was formed and theorists, who saw this as a precedent to a similar North American Union, began to talk about the idea as something that could actually happen. After all, if the Euro currency could happen over there, the Amero currency could certainly happen here.

Then, in 1994, NAFTA went into effect, which was seen by many of the more paranoid thinkers as a first step toward larger unification. Many American tradespeople found NAFTA distasteful; they believed that it benefited larger corporations at the expense of the American worker. In the aftermath of NAFTA, some academics published works that argued in favor of an Amero currency. Chief among these was a paper from a Canadian think tank called "The Case for the Amero." Here economist Herb Grubel made a compelling case, but also pointed out that the benefits were probably outweighed by the importance to the governments of Canada and the United States of maintaining control over their own currencies.

Now, the vision of an NAU that the conspiracy theorists had in mind involved a violent takeover. There would be city-sized prison camps, forced labor, mass executions. By themselves, NAFTA and a few fringe papers just didn't quite have this flavor...but then, on September 11, 2001, the world changed. Conspiracy theorists who took 9/11 as a false flag attack by the government upon its own people became convinced that martial law was imminent, and believers in the NAU took it as a sign that a violent takeover was underway. Over the years other destructive events, like the 2010 explosion of the oil rig Deepwater Horizon and various hurricanes (which some believe the government creates using some unspecified technology) were also seen as deliberate attacks upon the people by some emerging shadow cabal to weaken local economies and make the populace more susceptible to takeover.

Throughout it all, images of Amero currency have appeared regularly on the Internet. All are hoaxes, yet every image of a piece of Amero currency has its share of believers who fully accept that minting has begun, and that the takeover might happen as early as tomorrow.

The Explanation

A principal benefit of an economic union, such as the European Union, is that it makes commerce between many small, neighboring nations simpler. When everyone uses different currencies, transactions are a lot more complicated, and it's hard to keep on top of pricing when different currencies are always fluctuating. A shared currency makes many of those problems go away.

That said, it is not without cost. When nations share a currency, they lose control over their own inflation and interest rates. The currencies of small economies are stabilized at the expense of the larger economies who can no longer control what happens to their rates. For this reason, economic unions are usually favored by smaller, more volatile economies and avoided by larger, more stable economies. Thus, when certain politicians or economists have called for a North American economic union using an Amero currency, they've usually been from Mexico and also from Quebec, which has always sought to be less tied economically to the rest of Canada and to be able to trade more freely with the United States. There has been little or no support for an Amero by any economists in the United States.

So, with this in mind, if an NAU is created it would be a huge net loss for the United States. This largest of the three economies would have to take on the duty of supporting the much smaller Mexican economy, draining resources away from where they are currently enjoyed. Very few American members of the alleged conspiracy would support this.

Furthermore, according to conspiracy theorists, the NAU would be far more than just an economic union. Rather, it would be a full political unification into a single state, more like the Soviet Union than the European Union. But in making this comparison, the conspiracy theorists are radically misunderstanding what took place when the Soviet Union was created. Far from being the surprise imposition of martial law upon an unsuspecting population or a secret takeover by hidden illuminati intent on deceiving the masses, which is what the conspiracy theorists think will happen when the NAU is created, the Russian Revolution of 1917 was a popular uprising by the people, led by a majority party, the Bolsheviks, against the autocratic tsars. The Bolsheviks had a lot to gain through creating a union, but this isn't true for the United States. In fact, such a move would require the United States, a major world superpower, to give away its sovereignty. This would be unprecedented in geopolitical history, for obvious reasons. What leading nation would ever want to hand over the keys to its own destiny to someone else?

Neither Canada nor Mexico, let alone the United States, has expressed any burning desire to give away its sovereignty. None of their political or social situations resemble Russia in 1917. There are no official proposals to form a North American Union, no evidence that anyone plans to create such a union by force, and no specific individuals known to be interested in such a thing. This particular conspiracy theory is one you probably don't need to worry about all that much.

The Denver Airport Conspiracy

Date: 1995–Present
Location: Denver, Colorado
The Conspirators: The New World Order
The Victims: Unsuspecting innocents worldwide

The Theory

Conspiracy theorists claim that the New World Order—a mysterious and poorly defined shadow cabal of illuminati—built the Denver International Airport to act as both a headquarters from which the world's elite would launch global genocide and a vast prison camp made to contain those who resist.

When the airport opened in 1995 to replace Stapleton International Airport, questions began to emerge almost immediately from the fringe. Why was it even needed, since Stapleton appeared to be perfectly good? Why is so much of it hidden underground? Why does it appear to be built like a giant prison camp, with tall razor wire fences canted inward as if to keep people in, not out? And above all, what's with all the weird symbolism in its bizarre artwork? According to the conspiracy theorists, just about everything about the airport is another piece of proof that the takeover by the New World Order is about to begin.

The Truth

Denver International Airport is an international airport in Denver. There are no reliable reports of anything contradicting that.

The Backstory

In 1990, construction started on the Denver International Airport and the project ended up as a topic of conversation right away. For starters, why was the airport even being built at all? Many people felt that the old Stapleton International Airport was just fine. And why was it being built so far outside of the city?

Then something odd happened. Large concrete bunker-like buildings were constructed in excavated pits and then buried. While an unsuspicious observer might think nothing of underground spaces being built, some online communities took this very seriously. To this day they insist that the builders explained this away by saying the buildings had been "built wrong" and were therefore buried—an odd explanation for an odd event.

Soon bizarre nonsense phrases like "DZIT DIT GAII" were found inlaid in the airport's floors. Some have interpreted these as alien languages, perhaps foretelling who shall assist the New World Order when it comes time to exterminate humankind. How will this be accomplished? Another inlay, "Au Ag," has been interpreted to refer to Australia antigen, a powerful toxin, possibly the weapon of choice.

The Denver International Airport's art collection is said by conspiracy theorists to be proof of the New World Order headquarters. Two such pieces are the two diptychs (two-part murals) created by artist Leo Tanguma. One part of the first diptych depicts a frightening Nazi-style soldier wreaking havoc; in the second part the soldier lies dead, vanquished by the children of the world who have now reforged his weapons into plows. In the other diptych, a future Earth is shown laid to waste, with the only remaining animals being exhibits behind museum glass; the second part shows children tending a rejuvenated Earth. Both murals have been interpreted as depicting the New World Order's plans to destroy the planet and all those on it, only to then rebuild it with a Utopian society of their own design.

Particularly chilling was the 2007 breakage of a large number of aircraft windshields, said to have been caused by an electromagnetic pulse weapon, possibly a test of some defensive weapon to protect the New World Order headquarters. But perhaps most suspicious of all is a massive object labeled as a time capsule: a granite capstone with a mysterious control keypad inscribed with unintelligible symbols, and a brass plaque proclaiming the "New World Airport Commission." This keypad holds what conspiracy theorists believe to be the buttons that the New World Order will press to initiate global genocide.

The Explanation

While it's easy to take a look at the theories and think something may be going on, there are rational explanations for every issue theorists bring up about the Denver International Airport. The razor wire fences said to make it look like a prison are the most commonly cited piece of evidence. However, a drive to the airport reveals that this is not the case at all. The runways are protected by fencing, like runways at all airports, but stockades consisting of inward-canted razor wire simply don't exist there.

They say a new airport wasn't needed and this was just an excuse to build a New World headquarters. Well, it turns out that a new airport was desperately needed, and no conspiracy was necessary to explain its construction. Stapleton was a major noise nuisance inside Denver, its runways were too short to accommodate modern jets, and there were too few runways to accommodate all the international flights. A new airport was absolutely needed, one located comfortably far away where neither noise nor space were a problem.

And those underground buildings? Simply a new state-of-the-art automated baggage handling system. Unfortunately, it never worked well and was eventually abandoned, but its underground spaces are still used for conventional baggage handling. No discernible mystery exists down there.

The flooring? Well, "Au Ag" are simply the chemical symbols for silver and gold, a nod to Colorado's mining history, as the mining carts and other objects inlaid in the floor indicate (strange that the conspiracy theorists missed those). It doesn't represent Australia antigen, because that's abbreviated as HBsAg. Regardless, it isn't a toxin; it's the surface protein of hepatitis B, which is treatable and rarely fatal. Therefore it's unlikely that those who use the words "DZIT DIT GAII" are going to kill us all with it. And who are these people who use those words? The Navajo. Those words in that "alien language" are actually the Navajo names for sacred mountains in Colorado.

The same goes for the two murals. Denver International Airport hosts an extensive permanent art collection and numerous temporary exhibitions, all of which explore many different themes. Why the conspiracy theorists have selected these two in particular, and attributed nefarious symbolism to them while ignoring the many others, is singularly bizarre.

Skeptoid® Says...

One of the pieces in the airport's art collection is a giant blue sculpture of a rearing horse with glowing eyes. While it's true that during its construction a piece of it did fall and fatally injure its creator, Luis Jiménez, there is no clear reason to interpret the sculpture, which is nicknamed Blucifer, as a prelude to global genocide.

In addition, those 2007 windshield breakages were neither unusual nor unexplained. Colorado often has high winds, and an investigation by the National Transportation Safety Board (NTSB) confirmed that these were all caused by wind-thrown debris. It happens at windy airports everywhere. And sufficient proof that no electromagnetic pulse weapon was involved lies in the fact that glass is not affected by electromagnetic pulses.

So what about the "New World Airport Commission"? Well, far from being the illuminati, this was simply an association of local civic and business leaders who sponsored the celebratory events at the airport's opening, which is easy enough to find by anyone willing to look up newspaper articles from 1995. And that alleged control pad with strange buttons? It's just the braille translation of the words inscribed on the time capsule's brass plaque. The time capsule's capstone, by the way, bears the symbol of the Freemasons, an organization that has played no small part in sparking the imagination of the conspiracy theorists. It's there simply because the time capsule was placed by the local Freemason lodge, as is the case with a large percentage of such capsules around the country.

Generally, successful conspiracies are those that are never discovered. When theorists discover what they believe to be evidence of conspiracy broadly and publicly trumpeted all over a giant public space, chances are they've probably misinterpreted it. And let's be honest: evil plans are not typically publicized with artwork. Did Nixon order that a mural showing GOP spies breaking into a hotel room be installed in the lobby of the Watergate Hotel? No, and neither should you expect some mythical New World Order to announce their genocidal plans in this way.

The Reptoids

Date: The Present
Location: Worldwide
The Conspirators: An unknown alien reptilian culture
The Victims: Citizens of Earth

The Theory

Have you ever paused an old video of almost any world leader or business executive and caught a strange-looking frame of the person's face? While most people would casually dismiss this as just a video glitch (the technical term is a compression artifact, or simply noise in the signal), conspiracy theorists believe that these distortions are not in the video itself, but in the electronic holographic disguise worn by the world leader. They believe he, along with many other prominent people, is a reptilian being.

The theory asserts that many prominent people—including political leaders, business and religious leaders, and even famous actors and sports personalities—are actually these disguised reptilian beings called reptoids. They are reptilian in appearance like alligators, but humanoid in their upright posture. At some point in the past, theorists believe, important people worldwide began to be replaced and impersonated by reptilians. Little by little, they believe, we are being replaced—and the reptoids' origin and purpose remain unknown.

The Truth

There is no such thing as reptilian beings wearing electronic disguises and replacing world leaders.

The Backstory

Today's believers in the reptoids can pause video to see the evidence they seek, but that wasn't always the case. This conspiracy theory is an old one, and while only the video version of the theory shows up today, the story's origins stretch back to the early days of the American West.

Back in 1934, a mining engineer named G. Warren Shufelt was searching for gold in southern California. Using a device he called a radio X-ray, he discovered a series of tunnels underneath the city of Los Angeles. By taking readings all over the city, he eventually put together a detailed map. It was a complex labyrinth, many rooms connected by tunnels, some wet and some dry. Shufelt's device detected the presence of large quantities of gold scattered along the tunnels and stacked in some of the rooms. It was a treasure beyond accounting.

Seeking investors to fund the mining that would be needed to reach the treasure, Shufelt went to the newspapers. The *Los Angeles Times* published an account of his findings along with a reproduction of his map, and investors stepped forward to fund enough of Shufelt's project to bore a shaft down to 250 feet. Unfortunately, it promptly filled with water. The mine was never able to get ahead of the water problem, and Shufelt's dream of extracting gold from beneath Los Angeles soon ended.

Bolstering Shufelt's story of buried gold was the testimony of a man named L. Macklin, who went by the name Little Chief Greenleaf and identified as a Native American from the Hopi tribe. Macklin corroborated Shufelt's claimed caverns with what he said was an old Hopi legend of an underground city built some 5,000 years ago by a race known as the Lizard People.

Macklin's testimony catapulted the story of the underground Lizard People into popular culture—and the community of people who believed the tale was just getting started. A growing community also believes that Lizard People live in caverns inside Mount Shasta, a peak in California. Mount Shasta is frequently referenced in New Age mythology, and in addition to Lizard People, some New Age practitioners believe it's also populated by an ancient race called the Lemurians. Creatures such as Bigfoot and small dwarflike beings called Guardians are also believed to live inside Mount Shasta, in a grand multilevel city called Telos.

Based on little more than these mythological foundations—the Hopi legend and the ancient Lemurians—belief in a race of reptoid beings is actually not all that rare. Today, the leading proponent of the reptoids is David Icke, a British conspiracy theorist best known for his book *The Biggest Secret*, in which he laid out his "discoveries" about many world leaders being reptoids in electronic disguises. (Icke has also argued that the Moon is a hologram projected from Saturn.) For many theorists—bolstered by the legitimacy of an ancient Hopi legend—the video evidence of glitchy electronic disguises constitutes a solid case that many world leaders are actually reptilian beings.

Skeptoid® Says...

According to conspiracy theorist David Icke, and the many who follow his beliefs, the reptoids are not necessarily enemies of the human race. A separate conspiracy theory concerns an alleged secret base outside Dulce, New Mexico, where there is a deep, multilevel city that houses as many as 18,000 gray aliens, who are there as a result of some sort of deal with the US government. Here the aliens perform experiments on human subjects. Icke and his followers believe the reptoids are actually the sworn enemies of the grays. However, the claims about who is allied with whom don't really seem to be all that consistent.

The Explanation

In recent years, there has been less repetition of the conspiracy theorists' claims when it comes to the video evidence of the reptoids. The reason for this decline is likely the advent of high-definition video. Today when we pause a video, there is much less compression artifacting. In fact, most of the time you can't see any at all. But when David Icke first began promoting this idea, pausing video meant pausing a VHS tape. If you remember seeing this, you'll recall that, when paused, the picture would jitter and flash and sometimes flicker between two frames, and that every edge was shattered into interlacing lines. It was easy in those days to pause a video and see just about anything you wanted to see. And in the early days of *YouTube* with low-resolution, highly compressed videos, the situation was only marginally better.

Now let's talk about the foundations of the reptoid legend. First, let's make it clear that there was never anything to G. Warren Shufelt's alleged city underneath Los Angeles. He showed his "radio X-ray" device to a *Los Angeles Times* reporter, and it had nothing to do with either radio or X-rays. It was a dowsing pendulum, the same trinket used in "water witching," where a practitioner swings a small pendulum, believing that its movements guide the way toward water or some other valuable discovery. Shufelt's dowsing pendulum was suspended from a tripod with an elaborate (and hollow) glass and metal case he'd constructed. It actually had no capabilities of any kind. Shufelt's claim that he took detailed photographs of the caverns with it strains credibility.

The other problem is that the interpretation of the Hopi legends that emerged was deeply flawed. No known Hopi legend ever referred to people who were half lizard. Searching through modern volumes of collected Hopi legends, one finds numerous references to clans who took their names from animals: the spider clan, the bear clan, the lizard clan. But these were not to be interpreted as half-human hybrid creatures. In addition, nothing in the Hopi literature references underground cities, gold, or anything else in the tales told by Macklin to Shufelt.

Why? Well, it's unlikely Macklin had any actual knowledge of Hopi legends. Hopi birth and death records are available online through the website of the Navajo Nation, and no person with the names of Macklin or Greenleaf (or any reasonable variation of these names) was recorded during the period when these men lived. Given common practices in the mining days, the persona of Little Chief Greenleaf was almost certainly an invention intended to excite potential investors with promising tales of buried gold.

But what not even Shufelt could have foreseen was the unusually long legs his story would prove to have, and the extraordinary nature of its eventual mutations—no matter how far out they all are.

PART 2
Government Oppression

Do you wish you were wealthier? Healthier? More successful? Whose fault is it? The oppressive government's, of course. The government overtaxes you to keep you at the poverty level. The government keeps you sick by providing inadequate healthcare, covering up miracle treatments, and perhaps even spreading germ agents. The government suppresses technologies and discoveries that could help you. It's all done in the name of power.

Notice how much fiction has been written about the concept of an overreaching government: *Brave New World, Fahrenheit 451, 1984, Atlas Shrugged, The Handmaid's Tale, The Hunger Games*... These books and other fiction found online feature governments that have grown so powerful that they control people's everyday lives. It is a theme that is deeply attractive to us at a gut level. Why? Well, this fiction satisfies our idea of something called agency detection, the evolved trait that favors a certain amount of natural paranoia to help protect us from threats. Overgrown government control is the ultimate validation of our native paranoia.

What does all of this mean? It means it's natural for all of us to believe that the powers that be have a hidden agenda to persecute us...but conspiracy theorists take this idea and run with it. They assign the ideas undue importance and alter their lives to avoid these perceived threats, which gives us some interesting theories about the various ways the government is supposedly out to get us. Let's take a look and debunk some of these extreme theories.

Vaccines

Date: 1809–Present
Location: Worldwide
The Conspirators: Governments
The Victims: Innocent civilians

The Theory

Today, vaccine conspiracy theories are everywhere and could easily make up an entire book of their own. Most take the general form of governments secretly knowing that vaccines do more harm than good, but forcing vaccines onto the public anyway to give the government more power. Other theories promote the Big Pharma version of this, which puts forth the idea that Big Pharma makes huge profits from vaccines by having the government force people to buy them. Some also push a connection between vaccines and autism, claiming that the government conspires with Big Pharma to force vaccinations in order to give as many people autism as possible, in order to then profit from people seeking autism treatments.

The Truth

Vaccines are the single most important and successful public health initiative. They are responsible for saving more lives than any other medical intervention in history.

The Backstory

By 1800, smallpox was responsible for about half a million deaths annually, but scientists knew that inoculating a person with material from a cowpox lesion could cut the chances of contracting smallpox by about 95 percent. This has been widely recognized as the first major medical advance in history.

It was so effective that in 1809 the Commonwealth of Massachusetts enacted the first compulsory vaccination law that required all citizens to receive the smallpox vaccine. Opposition—and conspiracy theories—took hold right from the start. Many felt that it was a forced intrusion of government into people's private lives—which, of course, it is. Mistrustful and ignorant of the science, some people concluded that there must be an unknown dark purpose behind the government's forced medication initiative, and vocal opposition was mounted. Although embattled, the law stood, and other localities also began mandatory vaccinations.

Skeptoid® Says...

In 1905, nearly a century after the Massachusetts law went into effect, the United States Supreme Court declared that public health justified compulsory vaccination. This decision remains the primary ruling on the subject even today.

Throughout the twentieth century, schools began requiring vaccinations before students would be allowed to attend. Because children are the most vulnerable to disease, and schools are where children are most likely to infect one another, this policy is actually one of the most important public health initiatives on the books.

Skeptoid® Says...

The early American statesman and scientist Benjamin Franklin deferred the smallpox inoculation for his son Francis because the boy was sickly, so Franklin feared he might be too weak to tolerate the vaccine. It was a decision Franklin soon regretted. In his autobiography, he wrote:

In 1736 I lost one of my sons, a fine boy of four years old, by the smallpox, taken in the common way. I long regretted bitterly, and still regret that I had not given it to him by inoculation. This I mention for the sake of parents who omit that operation, on the supposition that they should never forgive themselves if a child died under it; my example showing that the regret may be the same either way, and therefore that the safer should be chosen.

Unfortunately, toward the end of the twentieth century when the worst diseases were all but eradicated, an amazing new phenomenon occurred: parents began seeking exemptions from compulsory vaccinations for their children, usually citing religious or ideological reasons. Ever since, the rates of some vaccine-preventable diseases such as whooping cough have been growing steadily. It's as if parents have been saying, "We know it's been proven that this vaccine will save lives, but we want our child excluded, which will put them at risk as well as other children around them."

Why? Conspiratorial thinking.

The Explanation

According to UNICEF, vaccines save about nine million lives per year. They work, and they work amazingly well. They also do not cause harm—at least not to 99 percent of people who receive them. (For most vaccines, about 1 percent have some adverse reaction. Serious reactions, depending on the vaccine, range from about 1 in 100,000 to 1 in 1,000,000. Pretty darn safe.) And, the smallpox vaccine alone has been saving lives since the 1700s, probably totaling close to one billion lives. Vaccination is science's greatest achievement in the fight against disease. No other public health measure comes close.

Should vaccines be discarded because they are a Big Pharma conspiracy? Well, to analyze this claim, let's be clear about one thing. Pharmaceutical companies who manufacture vaccines do get paid for it. But not nearly as much as you might think. It turns out that vaccines are among the least profitable products that pharmaceutical companies make. Prices are often capped by the public agencies that buy most of them. Most vaccines go to developing nations, where money is scarce and it's hard to cover costs. Financial incentives to manufacture vaccines became so low that companies started dropping out of the business entirely, in favor of selling more profitable drugs instead. In 1967 there were twenty-six pharmaceutical companies manufacturing vaccines; that number dropped to about half by the 1980s.

Today the number is rising again as more manufacturers get back into the business, driven by major public health initiatives to sell hundreds of millions of annual doses in poor countries, as well as newer vaccines such as hepatitis B and HPV that can be sold at a profit in wealthier countries. In 2014 Merck sold $1.7 billion in HPV vaccines, while the entire rest of their vaccine product line treating measles, mumps, rubella, and chicken pox brought in only $1.4 billion.

However, the short answer to the Big Pharma version of the vaccine conspiracy theory: at only about 2.5 percent of the global pharmaceutical market, vaccines are hardly the place where Big Pharma makes its money. So if Big Pharma were going to pay off the government to conspire to make their product required for all citizens, wouldn't they be likely to choose a more profitable one?

And what about the conspiracy theory that vaccines—particularly the MMR (measles/mumps/rubella) vaccine—cause autism? Is it true that autism is more common now than it used to be? No. Or, more accurately, there is no evidence of that. It is true that far more cases are being *diagnosed* today than used to be. There are two reasons for this. First is that the definition of autism spectrum disorders keeps getting broadened as we recognize more and more cases to be connected. Second is that the stigma of being autistic is going away, and parents are more likely to allow their children to be tested and diagnosed than they used to be. So while we do indeed have more *diagnoses* being reported, there is no reason to suspect that the actual prevalence of autism is higher today than ever before.

In response, science advocates have pointed out that the rise of autism more closely correlates with the rising popularity of organic food; shown on a graph, the lines match up astonishingly well. Although this is obviously a joke directed at the fact that the people who reject vaccine science are often the same people who reject food science, it is a perfectly serious lesson in the dangers of confusing correlation with causation. We can say that these trends correlate with the rise in autism diagnoses, but it's clearly incorrect to say that they *cause* autism.

Each iteration of the vaccine conspiracy theory falls apart on its own under the slightest scrutiny. They simply make no sense. Vaccinate yourself, and vaccinate your children to keep them (and their schoolmates) healthy.

Water Fluoridation

Date: 1931–Present
Location: Worldwide
The Conspirators: Governments and municipal water suppliers
The Victims: Innocent civilians

The Theory

Claims that the government adds fluoride to our water to harm us are everywhere you look. Some say fluoride is a dangerous neurotoxin and the government wants to give us all brain damage so we can be easily controlled. Some say fluoride is a poison and the government wants to kill us as part of some mass eugenics or population control scheme. Others believe the government just wants to make us generally sick so that we will have to purchase more pharmaceutical drugs. About the only thing they agree on is their belief that the government's official story about adding fluoride to prevent tooth decay is just a cover-up. As final evidence that fluoridation is a nefarious project of the US government, activists point out that many European nations choose not to fluoridate their water at all.

The Truth

Fluoride is added to America's drinking water supplies at a rate of 0.7 parts per million (ppm), which is high enough to reduce tooth decay, and low enough to avoid tooth discoloration. The government wants to harm cavity-causing dental plaque, not you.

The Backstory

The idea that fluoridation is an evil government plot received its most public exposure in the 1964 movie *Dr. Strangelove*, in which the antagonist, General Ripper, says:

> Do you realize that fluoridation is the most monstrously conceived and dangerous Communist plot we have ever had to

face?...Do you realize that in addition to fluoridating water, why, there are studies underway to fluoridate salt, flour, fruit juices, soup, sugar, milk, ice cream?...It's incredibly obvious, isn't it? A foreign substance is introduced into our precious bodily fluids without the knowledge of the individual. Certainly without any choice. That's the way your hardcore commie works.

But the actual genesis of fluoridation has a much more down-to-earth cause. In 1901 a Colorado dentist named Dr. Frederick McKay noted that a lot of his patients seemed to have brownish teeth, and that those patients had better dental health than those with white teeth—with only about a third as many cavities! He called it Colorado Brown Stain. Dr. McKay subsequently spent thirty years collecting data on tooth discoloration and tooth decay. He even visited parts of Texas where brown teeth were so common that they were simply called Texas Teeth. The data were clear: the browner the teeth, the less likely they were to decay.

Then, in 1931, scientists working with Dr. McKay discovered that high natural fluoride levels in the drinking water were responsible for both the dental discoloration *and* the resistance to decay. High levels of fluoride in drinking water create dental fluorosis, or harmless discoloration. This very same fluoride confers a hardness to the tooth enamel that make it resistant to decay. If you wanted healthy teeth, it seemed you had to take the bad with the good.

But many years of study eventually taught us that we could reduce the fluoride levels just enough to avoid the ugly dental fluorosis, but still protect against tooth decay. This level has been adjusted a few times, but the best data we have now shows that a level of 0.7 parts per million is ideal. When the city of Grand Rapids began a fifteen-year test of fluoridated municipal water in 1945, cavities dropped by 60 percent, making tooth decay a preventable disease for the first time in history.

So how did we get from an important public health measure to a 1964 movie talking about it as a Communist plot? During the Red Scare of the 1950s—a period of hysterical fear of Communist influence within the United States—many patriotic Americans began taking a dim view of anything they perceived to be Communist or Socialist in nature. For some, public measures such as vaccination and welfare were regarded as the leading edge of Communism forcing its way into American society. Fortunately, this was still a fringe view that most people didn't take very seriously, and by the time *Dr. Strangelove* was produced, irrational fear of fluoridation was seen by most as a comically silly viewpoint, so the filmmakers gave it to their character who had a mental illness. Although it was merely a Hollywood black comedy, *Dr. Strangelove* did have the effect of making fluoride conspiracy-mongering more mainstream.

But then the 1970s came along with its hippie and New Age movements, where anything technological was out, and anything natural was in. As this perspective has become more and more popular in the decades since, concerns about fluoride in the water have grown increasingly common. In fact, for the first time in the history of modern medicine, we are actually seeing a public health measure beginning to fail as a growing number of cities and towns are deciding to take fluoride out of their water supply.

The Explanation

Whether conspiracy theorists like it or not fluoride is the thirteenth most common element in the Earth's crust, so it's naturally occurring in groundwater and is there to stay. It is not some evil man-made poison. Now, just because a compound is natural does not mean that it's safe, but the toxicity level of every compound is determined by the dose. Just as oxygen is toxic at a high enough concentration, so is fluoride safe at a low enough concentration.

Most anti-fluoride theorists seem to miss the idea that the term *fluoridation* often means *reducing* a high fluoride level. The goal is to bring the fluoride level to 0.7 parts per million; sometimes that means adding fluoride, and sometimes it means taking it out. Removing it is much more difficult and expensive, so some municipalities with naturally high fluoride levels don't do anything about it. Now, the concentrations of fluoride found in natural groundwater are usually quite low, but are sometimes as high as 20 parts per million. Let's take a look at the effects:

- Below 0.7 ppm, your teeth are at increased risk of cavities.

- Between 1 ppm and 4 ppm, your teeth are at risk of discoloration from fluorosis, which is totally harmless, just unattractive.

- Above 4 ppm, you are at increased risk of skeletal fluorosis, which is usually without symptoms, but in extreme cases can cause pain in major joints. When Dr. McKay discovered Texas Teeth, the regions where he found it had naturally occurring fluoride levels of between 2 and 12 ppm.

This is why regulators try to keep the levels below 4 ppm in all cases, and right at 0.7 ppm ideally.

It is true that many countries outside of the United States do not fluoridate water, especially in Europe. Although the activists attempt to portray this as enlightened European recognition that all fluoride is poisonous, that's not true. In these nations, they typically fluoridate salt instead of municipal water. The reason has to do with their infrastructure being different from that of the nations that fluoridate water. It is simply easier and cheaper for them to deliver the ideal concentration by adding it to the salt.

Skeptoid® Says...

Hemlock, bubonic plague bacterium, plutonium, box jellyfish neurotoxin, asbestos, arsenic, mercury, anthrax, radiation, and rattlesnake venom are all 100 percent natural, and yet none are harmless. The same goes for fluoride.

It's important to note that the Internet is full of sites that provide incredibly bad misinformation about fluoride, much of which is untrue. These claims are so numerous that it is impossible to disprove all of them here. The bottom line is that if you have a question about the safety of fluoridation of water, don't go to an Internet site that sells magical water filters or supplement products or superfoods they claim will remove fluoride. Instead, simply ask your dentist, who probably knows better.

Plum Island

Date: 1954–Present
Location: Plum Island, New York
The Conspirators: US Department of Agriculture, US Department of Homeland Security, other government agencies
The Victims: Unsuspecting innocent civilians

The Theory

According to conspiracy theorists, Plum Island, New York, is home to a secret government laboratory. It's been blamed for everything from creating bizarre hybrid creatures to creating diseases in order to wipe out large segments of the American population. Most notably, it has been blamed for creating Lyme disease and releasing it onto the public. Conspiracy theorists charge that Plum Island's primary duty is the creation of germ warfare agents, which it regularly tests on the local population.

The Truth

The Plum Island Animal Disease Center works primarily to keep foot-and-mouth disease at bay to protect the American agriculture industry.

The Backstory

Plum Island is a real place, and has long been associated with the American government. The island is strategically located right in the middle of the narrow entrance to Long Island Sound, where most of New York's busiest and most important harbors are located. Ever since the days of the American Revolutionary War, it has been under government control.

In 1897 a defensive fort called Fort Terry was built on the island, but after World War II, the fort became obsolete. In 1952 the US Army Chemical Corps took a look at the island and planned to build a chemical weapons factory on it. However, the new buildings were taken over by the Department of Agriculture in 1954 before any chemical weapons work was started.

It turned out that the Department of Agriculture was strategically more important to the United States than chemical weapons. Foot-and-mouth disease (FMD), a rapid-spreading viral infection, was turning out to be a clear and present danger to Americans, specifically via the livestock industries. FMD rarely kills the livestock it infects, but it makes them unsuitable for milk or meat production. Just think of the ripple effects throughout the economy and food security if a nation the size of the United States suddenly lost all its livestock industries: cattle, pigs, sheep. The Plum Island Animal Disease Center (PIADC) was established to work on treatments for FMD but also for all other threats to livestock: swine fever, vesicular stomatitis, rinderpest. The Department of Agriculture saw the same benefits as the Army did with the Plum Island location. It's far out from shore, and so it is effectively isolated from the vulnerable population, yet it's close to cities all around so workers could get there easily.

On Plum Island the livestock are kept indoors, and the entire facility is negatively pressurized so that air only flows in, not out. The deeper inside you go to the higher security levels, the lower the pressure. Yet, at least twice animals have been found to be infected where they weren't supposed to be, but all such accidents have, apparently, been contained within the facility. News reports of such accidents began to drive increased suspicion of the facility—suspicion that, at least at certain times in its history, was not entirely unjustified.

Skeptoid® Says...

Plum Island's history is not completely innocent. There is evidence that PIADC research was used in the planning of potential animal disease attacks against enemy nations in the 1960s. However, in 1972, the United States signed the Geneva Protocol and Biological Weapons Convention, banning all biological warfare. President Nixon did order all such research to cease, and from all that's known from the PIADC records, it did.

The main source of the conspiracy theories about PIADC was a 2004 book called *Lab 257: The Disturbing Story of the Government's Secret Plum Island Germ Laboratory.* Conspiracy theorist author Michael Carroll made many imaginative claims about the island, including one that said Plum Island created Lyme disease. Carroll also pointed to pretty much every animal disease outbreak on the continental United States that he could find and made speculative charges that Plum Island was somehow responsible. Carroll planted the seeds of conspiracy, and they've only grown—like a viral outbreak. For example, Plum Island was notably featured in a 2010 episode of the TV show *Conspiracy Theory with Jesse Ventura,* where he approached the island by boat and was refused permission to land, thus proving (according to the show) that the darkest of the theories about it must all be true.

The Explanation

Because FMD continues to be a serious concern, it is essential to continue to research treatment and prevention. So PIADC has their hands full with real work, that's thoroughly proven to exist, and would scarcely have time or staff available for fanciful projects like creating hybrid monsters or unleashing disease outbreaks on American civilians for their own amusement. And when it comes to Michael Carroll and his claims of Lyme and other diseases? Lyme disease predates written human history; its bacterium was even discovered in Ötzi (also known as the Iceman), the ice mummy who died in the Alps 5,300 years ago. Carroll's claims are clearly at variance with the known histories of these diseases.

And when it comes right down to it, there is little secrecy at PIADC. The facility is well known, listed in the telephone directory, and shown on public map databases. The microbiologists and other scientists who work there are listed on their website, and they publish the research in scientific journals. A lot of them are from Yale University and the University of Connecticut. Many of them discuss their current projects on their pages at the PIADC website. Want to know what really goes on at PIADC? Email and ask any of the scientists who work there, using their contact links. You could choose to decide that they're lying, but since their publications verify their work, you'd have a hard time proving it to anyone.

But just because there's not a lot of secrecy about the island, that doesn't mean it's easy to get there. To maximize the containment of diseases and minimize any risk of anything getting out, access to the island is strictly controlled and visitors are seldom permitted. This is why Jesse Ventura and his camera crew were not allowed to simply roll up to the island and go blustering about, not because the scientists are secretly breeding hybrid monkey soldiers, or whatever it is that Ventura suspected.

In addition, the events of 9/11 drew increased attention to the security at PIADC. It's possible that some terrorists could break in, steal a disease agent, and wreak havoc on the American economy by spreading FMD or another disease. There was even a highly publicized strike by maintenance workers on the island in 2002, and since security can't be maintained without maintenance, the striking workers were immediately fired and replaced—which highlighted another security problem: vulnerability to work stoppages. Security has been tightened since 9/11, while at the same time, containment technology has been improving to the point that the isolated location on an island really isn't needed anymore. So it appears that the future of the PIADC will be to move to a new, modernized location in Kansas where the additional physical space and improved access will allow construction of a BSL-4 (biosafety level 4) facility. Level 4 is the highest level of safety, which simply wasn't possible at Plum Island's small and aging facilities.

Skeptoid® Says...

The Montauk Monster was a dead animal found washed ashore on a beach in Montauk, New York, in 2008. It was unlike anything anyone had seen, so it was popularly believed to have been a horrific government-created hybrid beast that must have escaped from Plum Island. (Or a weird alien if you were watching History Channel's *Ancient Aliens*.) Turns out it was simply a dead raccoon, which had decomposed so much in the ocean that it was tough for most people to recognize.

FEMA Prison Camps

Date: ca. 1982–Present
Location: United States
The Conspirators: FEMA, the US military, other government agencies
The Victims: American citizens

The Theory

For as long as the United States has existed, the Constitution has allowed the government to deploy the military domestically during certain emergencies. These government powers are further defined by a number of statutes in addition to the Constitution, which describe the conditions under which they can be used, the scope of the deployment, who would have the authority to order this, and under what conditions.

In reaction to the existence of these government powers, a community of conspiracy theorists exists that believes FEMA (the Federal Emergency Management Agency) maintains a nationwide network of prison camps intended for the incarceration, and possibly the execution, of millions of law-abiding American citizens. If the government has the power to use the military against its own citizens, they reason, huge numbers of citizens would be arrested and the military would need to have someplace to put them. Why? Well, so the government can impose martial law, and perhaps reduce the population to a more manageable size…or something like that. It is not often made very clear. Over the years, these theorists have named some 800 sites that they believe are the locations of these FEMA camps.

The Truth

FEMA does not have any prison camps being maintained in a state of readiness to incarcerate and execute law-abiding US citizens.

The Backstory

Article I of the US Constitution states (in part):

> Congress shall have power...to provide for calling forth the Militia to execute the Laws of the Union, suppress Insurrections, and repel Invasions.

The president doesn't even need Congress to do the same thing: Title 10 of the US Codes allows the president to call up the military in support of civilian law enforcement agencies to suppress such things as insurrections, rebellions, and domestic violence—basically, riots.

There has always been a bit of a back-and-forth struggle in efforts to limit these powers. The US Congress passed the Insurrection Act of 1807, which limited the president somewhat in his ability to do these things on his own authority, and the Posse Comitatus Act of 1878 limited the president's powers even more. But then, especially since the 9/11 terrorist acts, legislators have tried to roll *back* these limits a number of times, returning more power to the president, recognizing that in a national emergency the president can act more swiftly on his own.

History gives us at least one such case when the president employed these powers to avoid congressional delays. In February 1942, President Franklin D. Roosevelt signed the infamous Executive Order 9066. Fearful of domestic Japanese espionage and sabotage during World War II, Roosevelt ordered 110,000 law-abiding Japanese-American citizens rounded up and held without recourse in internment camps. Most lost whatever property they had owned, in addition to their liberty.

All this, say the conspiracy theorists, is evidence that broad usage of the military against the citizenry is imminent. The first time this became a widely held claim was in 1982, when federal agencies held training exercises called Rex 82 (Readiness Exercise 1982) Proud Saber, in which they practiced dealing with a large-scale civilian emergency such as a major strike, an unlawful assembly, or a mass looting. They practiced martial law, arresting and holding potentially large numbers of people, and mass relocations. The exercise was well publicized, and the alternative media exploded with reports that what was happening was real and that FEMA was building camps all around the country to imprison civilians. Rex 82 was followed by a similar exercise, Rex 84 Night Train, bolstering the conspiracy theorists' beliefs.

Skeptoid® Says...

One of the most frequently seen manifestations of this conspiracy theory first appeared in the 1994 film *America Under Siege* by conspiracy theorist Linda Thompson. She went to an Amtrak repair facility in Beech Grove, Indiana, and asserted that it was actually a FEMA camp intended to hold massive numbers of civilian prisoners, and pointed her camera at the barbed wire atop its fences as evidence. (She apparently had not considered the possibility that Amtrak installed the fencing simply because it didn't want to have its stuff stolen.)

Many theorists feel that their beliefs were confirmed when then-Congresswoman Cynthia McKinney (most famous for punching a US Capitol Police officer when she refused to show required credentials for bypassing Capitol metal detectors) gave every indication that she fully believed these stories. After Hurricane Katrina devastated New Orleans in 2005, McKinney announced to a press conference that 5,000 young men had been illegally arrested by the National Guard, wrongfully imprisoned, and then executed:

> [The] charge by the Department of Defense was to process 5,000 bodies that had received a single bullet wound to the head, and these were mostly males....The data about these individuals was entered into a Pentagon computer. And then reportedly the bodies were dumped in the swamp in Louisiana....I have verification from insiders, who wish to remain anonymous, at the Red Cross, that this is true.

Why McKinney felt the Red Cross would be involved in such an operation was not convincingly argued.

In 2005, a Halliburton subsidiary won a $385 million construction contract that required them to be ready to construct temporary facilities for disaster evacuees or large numbers of immigrants following an emergency. Conspiracy theorist Peter Dale Scott wrote that these "detention centers could be used to detain American citizens if the Bush administration were to declare martial law." In addition, there are many online "patriot" and "militia" websites that list the FEMA prison camps that have been identified so far. Any Internet search for "FEMA prison camp locations" returns a treasure trove of locations inside the United States. Every former World War II POW and Japanese-American internment camp is described as being "renovated," as is every former military base. A site in Colorado is claimed to be staffed and ready to hold 400,000 people; 20,000 at Fort Chaffee in Arkansas; 15,000 in Oakdale, California; and 35,000 at Fort Dix in New Jersey. Some 800 entries are claimed by nearly all such lists. (Not a single photograph or piece of evidence is ever provided, however.)

The Explanation

The fact that law-abiding Japanese Americans were rounded up and interned during World War II, combined with the existence of actual laws permitting the government to do such a thing again, gives the FEMA prison camps conspiracy theory a unique hint of plausibility. However, it seems improbable. The Civil Liberties Act of 1988, which authorized reparations to the Japanese survivors, recognized and certified that such internment was unjustified. Times change. We should not expect something like that to recur any more than we should expect slavery to be reintroduced. In addition, the internment of Japanese Americans was not done under any of the laws cited by conspiracy theorists as justification for the alleged FEMA plans, but by a special wartime executive order. It took an active world war to persuade President Roosevelt to depart so far from civil liberties.

Strictly speaking, the president and Congress have the same powers today that allowed the Japanese-American internments, and have the same powers that allowed the National Guard to intervene in major historical riots. But that's a far cry from supposing that every Halliburton contract means the illuminati are out to get you.

And what about all those locations that conspiracy theorists have identified as FEMA camps? Each, at least that anyone has been interested in looking at, has been child's play to debunk. For example, one location in Alaska is said to have a capacity of two million people, but Alaska's entire population is only about a third of that. Another supposed location described by theorists as a "fully staffed full gassing/cremating death camp with airstrip, dedicated to the termination of all on FEMA's red/blue list under martial law" that was recently inspected by "high-level Illuminati Luciferians" (whatever those are) is just a long-abandoned and overgrown airstrip in the middle of nowhere in the Mojave Desert. And most of these "camps" are just empty spots on the map, home to nothing more than someone's Internet-fueled delusion.

FEMA, by the way, can only react to a disaster when a governor declares a state of emergency. Assuming that most state governors do not wish for their citizens to be rounded up into federal extermination camps, it seems that FEMA may not have been the most logical choice for the conspiracy theorists to dream up.

Skeptoid® Says...

The US government has domestically called in the military to quell rebellions before. Four thousand National Guardsmen were called in to help suppress the 1965 Watts riots in Los Angeles, and 3,000 for the 1967 Newark riots. Nearly 13,000 military were needed to quell the 1967 Detroit riots, which included the 82nd and 101st Airborne Divisions. The Los Angeles riots of 1992 involved 3,500 soldiers of the 7th Infantry and 1st Marine Division in addition to 10,000 National Guardsmen.

The Branch Davidian Assault

Date: 1993
Location: Waco, Texas
The Conspirators: US Attorney General Janet Reno, President Bill Clinton, FBI, ATF, and the Texas and Alabama National Guards
The Victims: Seventy-six Branch Davidian cult members

The Theory

On April 19, 1993, troops assaulted the Branch Davidian cult compound in Waco, Texas, that had been refusing to surrender to arrest warrants for two months. All inside died, mostly by fire. Conspiracy theorists claim that during the assault, the FBI intentionally started the fire in order to destroy the compound and kill everyone—including the children. Some other theories put forth in a series of low-budget documentary films and books include claims that the fire was started either by flame-throwing armored vehicles or by incendiary grenades fired into the flimsy wooden buildings. Many of those inside were found to have died by gunfire, so the conspiracy theory states that the FBI and National Guard fired into the burning buildings to make sure everyone died.

The Truth

Evidence proves the Branch Davidians had rigged their entire complex with firebombs, which they set off themselves when the assault began, in the belief that purification by fire would transcend them to heaven.

The Backstory

The history of how the Branch Davidian complex came to be is an interesting and colorful one, but it ended with cult leader David Koresh barricaded inside the sprawling compound of wooden buildings with about a hundred followers, including men, women, and children. Some had lived at the compound for three generations. The men had all turned their wives and daughters over to Koresh, and he was "married" to many of them. His wives were as young as twelve.

Koresh and other cult members had a large arsenal and numerous firearms violations, so the ATF (the Bureau of Alcohol, Tobacco, Firearms and Explosives) executed a search warrant in February of 1993 to seize illegal automatic weapons. A gunfight ensued in which four ATF agents and six Davidians died. The FBI took over and, together with the Texas and Alabama National Guards, surrounded the complex in a stalemate that was to last for two months.

US Attorney General Janet Reno and President Bill Clinton favored waiting out the Davidians, as they believed this was the best strategy to avoid loss of life. But upon receiving a report that children inside were being beaten, they ordered the compound assaulted with tear gas on April 19, in hopes of ending the siege with non-lethal weapons.

The combat engineer vehicles (CEVs) broke down the walls as soldiers fired tear gas. Simultaneously, fires broke out throughout the compound, and it quickly became an inferno. Automatic gunfire was heard from inside the compound. When all was said and done, some seventy-six people who remained inside were all dead, including Koresh and twenty-five children. Most of the children had been shot or stabbed to death, as had some of the other Davidians.

Many in the public were outraged, and the belief that the FBI had started the fire began to spread. Conspiracy theorist Linda Thompson made a video called *Waco: The Big Lie*, which made specific claims that the government started the fire using a combination of incendiary grenades and flamethrowers mounted to the CEVs. Other films followed. A few years after the assault, surveys found that 61 percent of Americans believed that the FBI started the fires, either accidentally or deliberately.

The Explanation

Under intense public pressure from a population who increasingly believed the FBI deliberately executed the Davidians, Janet Reno ordered a full investigation. The findings are known as the Danforth Report, and it was published in 2000.

A crucial finding of the report was that the Branch Davidians' religious beliefs compelled them all to die. This information came from the cult members themselves, a few of whom ran from the fire and were captured or were arrested in town. The Davidians were going to kill themselves one way or another, preferably by fire, to purify themselves and transcend to heaven. They had even planned a mass murder at a local McDonald's in order to all be killed by responding police officers. These people had violent death on their minds, and they were absolutely committed to it. There is virtually nothing that the government could have done differently that would have saved them; they never wanted to be saved.

Accordingly, the FBI found that the Davidians had rigged the entire complex with firebombs consisting of hay and camping fuel. When the FBI sent in food in the weeks before the assault, it included milk cartons that were bugged, so they had hours of tape recordings of the Davidians placing and charging the firebombs.

Thompson's claims of a "flame-throwing tank" were also investigated. There was never any such thing. The only weapon used by the CEVs was a Mark V liquid insertion system, which is a CO_2-powered squirt gun capable of shooting tear gas about 50 feet. No fire broke out in the areas where the CEVs were. But not only did the report prove that there weren't flamethrowers attached to the CEVs, it also provided an explanation for why this was even claimed in the first place:

> The FBI FLIR tapes showed rapid "flashes" on and around the complex and the vehicles. These flashes were solar reflections off of certain types of debris, including glass, that was strewn around the complex.

The report also found a total lack of evidence that incendiary grenades were used, or that any National Guardsmen or FBI agents fired any sort of weapons into the compound. The evidence was unanimous that the Davidians started all the fires and killed themselves and each other.

All of this said, the government is not blameless for the events at Waco. The report that said children inside the complex were being beaten was found to be false, as no evidence of beatings was ever discovered. No one was prosecuted for the false report, because no one was found who could be proven to be at fault.

The Danforth Report also found that for six years, the FBI failed to report that three XM651E1 pyrotechnic tear gas rounds had been fired. Although these rounds were fired at a concrete structure far removed from the wooden buildings, and despite the fact that these rounds have been proven to not start fires, the FBI probably covered up their use to avoid charges that they had started the fire. This cover-up can easily be considered criminal withholding of evidence.

Finally, the government unfairly pinned blame on two scapegoats, the ATF agents in charge of the initial raid in February. They were fired with the explanation that they should have been aware that the Davidians were prepared to violently repel the raid. The excuse is thin, because from everything that was learned about the Davidians, they all planned to die inside the complex no matter what. There is little the ATF agents could have done that would have saved the lives of the Davidians who died in the raid.

At its core, the government's actions at Waco were an effort to rescue children whose lives were under immediate threat. The FBI had ample information that the Branch Davidians all intended to die for religious reasons, and that turned the siege into a rescue effort. In the weeks before the final assault on the compound, the FBI even went so far as to "purchase" children from Koresh by giving him time on the radio to preach. Ultimately, twenty-one children were saved in this manner. The only government conspiracy on that day was one of desperation to rescue children from the darkest depths of delusional extremism.

Skeptoid® Says...

In the crowd of onlookers who watched the Branch Davidian complex burn to the ground was a young man named Timothy McVeigh, who, exactly two years to the day later, became a mass murderer himself when he blew up the Oklahoma City Federal Building.

Part 2: Government Oppression

Chemtrails

Date: 1996–Present
Location: Worldwide, but primarily the United States
The Conspirators: Airlines, unknown government agencies
The Victims: Unsuspecting citizens

The Theory

When you look up in the sky and see an airliner leaving a condensation trail—commonly called a contrail—you're probably not alarmed and recognize it as a normal phenomenon. But if you're a conspiracy theorist you may take a different view, supposing the trail to be explainable only as some poisonous or otherwise harmful gas or drug being sprayed by the airplane in order to hurt the people below. They call it a chemtrail, a combination of the words *chemical* and *contrail*.

Some believers insist that the chemtrail is made up of a psychoactive drug meant to damage the intelligence of the population to keep them more susceptible to government abuses. Others believe it is an ongoing weather modification scheme, perhaps to combat global warming, that is done without any regard to its impact on people's health or the environment.

The Truth

The contrails you see behind airliners are normal and unavoidable condensation created by the plane burning hydrocarbon fuel in certain high-altitude conditions. No chemtrails are needed to explain them.

The Backstory

Although contrails have been familiar since the 1930s when planes first started going high enough, conspiracy theorists had never paid much attention to them until 1996, when a panel of US Air Force officers presented a paper entitled "Weather As a Force Modifier: Owning the Weather in 2025." Without going into how it might be accomplished, this report muses on how a hypothetical ability to control the weather could be useful in battle situations. Storms, floods, or droughts could be sent to the enemy. Favorable conditions could be orchestrated for our own troops. Space weather—conditions in the Earth's magnetosphere that can impact radio transmissions and electronics—could be used to interfere with enemy communications. Fog could be created or removed on either side for a tactical advantage. And so on, and so on. Although the paper was speculative and did not presume the existence of any such technologies, conspiracy theorists took it to mean that the US government is absolutely able to do all of these things. The precise genesis of the legend isn't clear, but somehow the idea got started that this weaponization of weather was to be accomplished using chemicals sprayed from innocent-looking airliners.

Global warming was also coming into the public's attention about that time, and the Internet chemtrail community quickly made the connection. As CO_2 emissions continue to saturate the atmosphere, and the resulting greenhouse effect continues to add heat to the Earth's climate systems, governments are growing increasingly concerned about strategic effects from sea-level change, sea ice, and other impacts. Conspiracy theorists have thus (rightly) assumed that governments would like very much to do something about it, and (wrongly) assumed that whenever they see a contrail from a jet, it's likely to be some secret effort to somehow reduce global warming—perhaps an aircraft spraying something to alter the atmosphere's chemistry.

Eventually, the Internet chemtrail community broadened its scope to include drugging of the population. They believe that if the people can be dumbed down, they can be more easily controlled. Internet trolls began writing elaborate stories, claiming to be airline executives or maintenance engineers coming forward to reveal secret modifications to airliners, including vast chemical tanks hidden on board. Photographs have been attached to the stories appearing to show airliners with gutted interiors, their seats replaced with rows of tanks to hold liquids.

This conspiracy theory was significantly reinforced when the Space Preservation Act of 2001, which banned weapons in space, was presented to the US House of Representatives. The bill included a long list of speculative future "exotic weapons systems," and on this list was chemtrails. It also listed other ideas, purely science fiction, such as plasma weapons and tectonic weapons—basically, anything and everything these particular senators speculated might eventually exist, based on whatever Star Trek episodes they'd seen. Nevertheless, conspiracy theorists took it as proof that these systems all exist today.

Skeptoid® Says...

Additional chemtrail conspiracy theories were discussed in a 2014 paper from *The Geographical Journal*, which took a look at the contents of twenty popular websites that promote the chemtrail conspiracy theory. These theories were mostly profit motivated, including that weather modification could alter agriculture and other industries and allow futures markets to be manipulated; warming polar regions could allow improved access for Big Oil; crop poisons were being sprayed by the prominent agricultural company Monsanto to kill all crop varieties grown from seeds sold by any other producer; engineered disease organisms were being introduced worldwide to create new outbreaks in order to generate massive profits for Big Pharma; and population control for just about any nefarious purpose you want to think up.

The Explanation

The main problem with all the chemtrail beliefs is that, under common conditions, airplanes are always going to produce contrails. Burning hydrocarbon fuels, such as jet fuel, produces water at about the same volume as fuel burned. Thus, an airplane is always spraying water into the atmosphere as it flies. At altitudes above 25,000 feet and temperatures below −40° (both Celsius and Fahrenheit, as −40° is where the scales happen to intersect), the saturation point is exceeded, and the water condenses into a visible cloud, which we call a contrail. This is a fact of simple physics, and there is no need to introduce the spraying of a mysterious chemical to explain it.

Similar problems plague other claims made by chemtrail believers, such as the idea that the government is spraying mind-control drugs. There are a number of factual problems with the idea of drugging a population by spraying the compound from airlines. The main problem is that airliners fly way too high. The jet streams would carry the drug far away from the areas it was sprayed over, and the majority of it would rain down into the oceans. Note that when crop dusters spray fields, it's done at an altitude of only around 500 to 1,000 feet, not thousands of feet. The chemicals are expensive, and we usually want them to go where we intend.

Another problem is the concentration. Any drug released from a plane wouldn't be concentrated enough to have an effect—even if by some miracle it floated directly down rather than being carried away by the jet streams. Think about it this way, when a dentist gives nitrous oxide, it's given at a concentration of about 30 percent. But stratospheric delivery at airliner fuel tank volumes, by any reasonable calculation, would result in a concentration measured in parts per trillion. There really aren't any medical gases that produce a pharmacological effect in such trace quantities.

We encounter similar problems if we take the alternate theory that the idea is to address global warming instead of drugging the populace. Again, the altitude at which planes fly is the culprit. If airliners were trying to spray something into the troposphere where they fly, it would soon rain right back down to Earth. If you wanted it to stay up there, you would need to put it well up into the stratosphere instead.

Such geoengineering has actually been studied, and may indeed be enacted. This theorized technique is called SAI (stratospheric aerosol injection) and it involves the act of depositing certain compounds into the stratosphere, resulting in a screen of sulfate aerosols to reflect a tiny percentage of sunlight back into space. Airliners fly at a maximum of 45,000 feet, but the sulfate aerosol gases work best to reflect sunlight at an altitude about twice that high. In addition, it would be impossible to get enough of the compound even up as high as only 45,000 feet without making an unreasonably huge number of flights, up to a million a year! Fighter-type aircraft could be used, but balloons or rockets would be better choices, both for cost and payload. So if SAI was indeed happening clandestinely, visible aircraft chemtrails would likely not be correlated with it, as planes fly too low, would be too expensive, and can't carry enough payload.

But does the 1996 Air Force report "Weather As a Force Multiplier" prove that we are indeed using chemtrails to change weather?

Not if you read it carefully. Not only does the report say that "artificial weather technologies do not currently exist," but it actually proclaims clearly on its second page, "This report contains fictional representations of future situations/scenarios."

The chemtrail theory also suffers from a total lack of evidence. If airliners around the world truly all had been retrofitted with huge chemical tanks and spraying equipment, airport maintenance workers would know about it. No one has ever produced any photographs or other evidence. The pictures online of airplane interiors filled with large tanks and pipes turn out to simply be ballast tanks used in testing of airliners.

Contrails are 100 percent reproducible and are often visible when you look up into the sky. When we compare a known, proven phenomenon to a purely speculative, implausible, and scientifically impossible phenomenon, it doesn't take much computation to determine which is the real explanation.

PART 3
Suspicious Deaths

Whenever some person of prominence dies, there's almost always somebody whose agenda is accidentally satisfied. This, of course, makes it really easy to paint anyone who's benefited from the death as a murder suspect. This is the basic genesis of every conspiracy theory surrounding the mysterious death of someone famous. And when a theory starts, you know you're looking at that rare occasion where the death is somehow unusual, and the person is well enough known that the public wonders about them.

The deaths of the famous people that you'll find in this part are among those that provoked the strongest responses in conspiratorial thinking. No way, the theorists think, could these deaths have been accidents, or carried out in the way the "official story" claims. Our need to see patterns in randomness means that these deaths, tragic and thoroughly resolved as they are, will always remain suspicious in the eyes of many. Let's take a look.

Amelia Earhart

Date: 1937
Location: Pacific Ocean
The Conspirators: The Japanese military
The Victims: Amelia Earhart and Fred Noonan

The Theory

History tells us that pioneering aviator Amelia Earhart perished at sea along with her navigator Fred Noonan when attempting to be the first female pilot to fly around the world in 1937. Some conspiracy theorists, however, reject this fact, and embrace one of several alternate fates for Earhart. Among the most popular alternate beliefs is that she was captured by the Japanese and held prisoner for espionage. Most theorists do not claim to know Earhart's ultimate fate, but usually believe that she was eventually killed by her captors. Others cling to a different history in which Earhart flew to a remote island where she crashed safely and lived for a time as a castaway.

The Truth

Amelia Earhart ran out of fuel in the immediate vicinity of her intended refueling stop while flying a search pattern.

The Backstory

At the time of her disappearance, Amelia Earhart was one of the most famous people in the world, and arguably the single most famous woman. Her round-the-world flight caused a media circus at every stop. So when it ended prematurely in tragedy, wild stories were proposed almost immediately.

Earhart and Noonan were on the third-to-last leg of their round-the-world flight in 1937. They were flying from Lae in Papua New Guinea to an island called Howland, a small, bleak atoll with nothing on it but an airstrip, which was used by the United States as a refueling point. From there they planned to go to Honolulu, refuel

Part 3: Suspicious Deaths

again, then complete their trip by flying to Oakland, California. A US Coast Guard cutter, the *Itasca*, regularly serviced the airstrip at Howland Island and would stand by to provide a radio direction-finding beam to incoming planes, including the one piloted by Earhart and Noonan. As history shows, Earhart and Noonan failed to reach Howland, disappearing somewhere in the immediate vicinity. And that's when all the conspiracy theories and alternate histories began to appear.

Many ships were involved in the search for Earhart, not only US Navy ships, but also ships of the Japanese navy and fishing boats as well. Earhart's fame was such that anyone in the area with a boat sped to the region to help. Some conspiracy theorists believe that one of the Japanese boats, either civilian or military, found Earhart and Noonan at sea and rescued them. But rather than turn them over to the Americans, they were taken prisoner, perhaps charged with espionage, and brought to the Japanese island of Saipan where they were held prisoner. There are many stories from Saipan about her captivity there, including from people who claim to have seen her. Some in Saipan promote this story to draw tourism; there is even a plan to erect a statue of Earhart there.

Skeptoid® Says...

Amelia Earhart was thirty-nine years old when she died. She served as a nurse during World War I; was awarded the Distinguished Flying Cross; and held numerous speed, solo, and nonstop flight records.

There are other theories too. National Geographic and the Discovery Channel have taken sides with a group called TIGHAR (The International Group for Historic Aircraft Recovery) who claim that Earhart and Noonan, hopelessly lost and out of fuel, decided to abandon their search for Howland and fly 400 nautical miles directly out to sea in hopes of reaching an island called Nikumaroro. TIGHAR has cited an old discovery of a partial skeleton plus a number of pieces of litter that they claim have no reasonable explanation other than Earhart having survived on the island for a time as a castaway.

The Explanation

It seems that just about everyone with an idea for a sensationalized TV show or book has come up with some radical false history for Earhart's final flight and disappearance. The "captured by the Japanese" theory is one that Japanese historians find deeply offensive, as there were no hostilities between the nations at the time, and no known reason why the Japanese would have done such a thing. Indeed, Earhart's fame was such that she was well known in Japan as well, and they eagerly participated in the search for her.

If, as some theorists claim, the Japanese took her captive to use as propaganda against the United States, then keeping her captivity a secret would have defeated the whole purpose. Also, all of the evidence that Earhart was brought to Saipan is anecdotal. The History Channel explores the possibility that it might be true in the documentary *Amelia Earhart: The Lost Evidence*, citing a single photograph many claim is Earhart seen from behind in the distance, sitting on a dock at a port called Jaluit, presumably being allowed ashore to stretch her legs on the way to Saipan. The photo also appears in a 1935 picture book published in Japan, so it clearly cannot be relevant. And if it's not relevant, that whole part of the theory goes up in smoke.

When it comes to the theory of Earhart and Noonan reaching the island of Nikumaroro, that's easily debunked as well. The pair had no reliable navigation vector and no remaining fuel. TIGHAR claims that this strategy was successful since they found a few scraps of bones and litter. However, Nikumaroro had been inhabited by hundreds of littering people for a century both before and after the time of Earhart's flight, so their claims that these bits of trash could only be explained by Earhart's life as a castaway are unlikely.

Earhart's disappearance is often characterized as an "unsolved mystery," but the final fate of Earhart and Noonan is actually known beyond any reasonable doubt. The first thing to understand is that aviation in the Pacific Ocean was not nearly as primitive as many theorists seem to believe. At the time of her flight, Pan Am Clipper flying boats were already making scheduled passenger flights across the ocean. US Navy aircraft carriers had been flying in the area for years, and naval aviators had flown just about everywhere. The island Earhart was targeting, Howland, was a heavily used refueling stop for airplanes. In context of the state of aviation over the Pacific in the late 1930s, there was really nothing unusual or especially risky about Earhart's flight.

In addition, the *Itasca* was highly experienced at guiding planes into Howland and refueling them. In fact, the *Itasca* had to temporarily leave the search for Earhart to return to Howland to refuel another plane that was coming in from Hawaii. Also, the *Itasca's* radio operators kept meticulous logs of what transmissions were received, and Earhart and Noonan told them their direction and their signal strength (indicating the distance) over the radio. The pair had properly navigated to the island, relying both on the *Itasca's* direction-finding beam, and on Noonan's expertise with the E6B flight computer. The problem was that they arrived slightly ahead of schedule, and passed over Howland (or nearby) just at sunrise with the sun's glare directly in their eyes, which caused them to miss seeing the island. Once the error was discovered, they advised the *Itasca* that they were in the immediate vicinity and were flying a search pattern. They kept the *Itasca* advised of their diminishing fuel levels, and continued with the search pattern until they ran out and ditched at sea. As we know, the search was unsuccessful.

That is tragic but unsurprising, given the vast size of the search area. The boundaries of the area where the plane went down were determined by the *Itasca's* radio technicians and verified by other Navy and Coast Guard experts. It was a pie slice north-northeast of Howland with its sides at 337° and 45°, its minimum distance at 40 nautical miles, and its maximum distance at 200 nautical miles. This area covers 30,000 square miles, which made the search close to hopeless. All of this information, and its supporting data, is freely available from the National Archives in the Navy's ninety-six-page report.

JFK

Date: 1963
Location: Dallas, Texas
The Conspirators: Almost everyone in the world, apparently, except Lee Harvey Oswald
The Victim: President John F. Kennedy

The Theory

President John F. Kennedy was assassinated on November 22, 1963, in Dallas, Texas, while on an official visit. Soon police arrested Lee Harvey Oswald, an ex-marine who had lived for a time in the Soviet Union. Many conspiracy theorists believe that Oswald was a scapegoat who had nothing to do with the killing whatsoever. Kennedy was killed by a conspiracy, they claim, and the government pinned the blame on Oswald to cover it up. Variations on this theory are seemingly countless.

The Truth

All available evidence shows that JFK was assassinated by a lone gunman whose psychological profile matches very closely with similar killers today. No evidence suggests otherwise.

Skeptoid® Says...

There is a conspiracy theory that claims the CIA invented the term *conspiracy theory* in the 1960s to discredit those who doubted the finding that John F. Kennedy was killed by a lone gunman. It's not true, of course. The term can be found in the literature as early as 1870, and quite often throughout the twentieth century. But it demonstrates that the very term *conspiracy theory* has developed a derogatory meaning. Conspiracy theorists don't care to have the term applied to them, and so they came up with a story to dismiss it.

The Backstory

Lee Harvey Oswald was a former US Marine living in Dallas. He had a wife and two children, but that's where his similarity to the "all-American boy" ends. For he was also a self-described Marxist who had lived for two years in the Soviet Union, and his wife was Russian. Oswald was angry at the anti-Communist attitude of the United States, and at President John F. Kennedy's actions against Cuba, such as the near military outbreaks of the Bay of Pigs and the Cuban Missile Crisis. So when Oswald learned that JFK would be coming to town—and would be driving right past the place where Oswald worked—he brought a little something extra to the office that day: a 6.5 mm Carcano model 91/38 scoped rifle.

From a sixth-floor window of the Texas School Book Depository building where he worked, Oswald killed Kennedy with three shots from his rifle. But he'd been seen, and a description went out over police radio. Forty-five minutes later, a police officer stopped a young man on the street who matched the description. The man pulled out a pistol and shot the officer dead, then ran into a movie theater, pursued by citizens and other police officers. Oswald was captured and arrested, just as his clumsily hidden rifle was being found.

But he was never tried. Two days later, as Oswald was being led through a crowd of reporters at the police station, local nightclub owner Jack Ruby ran up and shot him at point-blank range, killing him. Ruby was said to have had mob connections, suggesting a Mafia connection to JFK's slaying, and thus was born a barrage of conspiracy theories the likes of which the world has never seen before or since.

Surveys indicate that today more than half of Americans do not believe that Oswald acted alone. Claims by conspiracy theorists include the idea that Lyndon B. Johnson had JFK killed so he could ascend to the presidency; the Mafia had JFK killed to retaliate for his actions against organized crime; the CIA had him killed for one reason or another, including that he wasn't tough enough on Castro; the Soviets or Cubans had him killed for his stance against Communism; the Ku Klux Klan killed him because of his support for civil rights; and so on, and so on. If it can be imagined, some conspiracy theorist has proposed it, and probably takes it very, very seriously.

The Explanation

Following Kennedy's death, newly instated President Lyndon B. Johnson ordered the chief justice of the Supreme Court to chair a commission, later called the Warren Commission, to investigate what happened and who was responsible for JFK's assassination. The 889-page Warren Commission Report took nearly a year to produce and the investigation didn't find any evidence whatsoever of anyone acting in concert with Lee Harvey Oswald. According to all they could uncover, he (and also Jack Ruby) had acted completely alone.

The rational way to investigate the JFK assassination—or any other mystery—is to start by looking at the solid, testable evidence, and then following it to see where it leads. Every time this has been done, it has led to Lee Harvey Oswald. However, conspiracy theorists have come to their conclusions by working backward and beginning with the idea that the Warren Commission Report is a lie and everything in it is uselessly unreliable. Thus freed of any and all evidence, the conspiracy theorist can land on whatever conjecture he prefers. This is what all the theories have in common: they differ from the government's official story.

Now, to accept the version of events laid out in the Warren Commission Report, you don't have to get rid of the background info brought up in the conspiracy theories. Kennedy *had* taken actions against organized crime, and probably *was* disliked by that community. He *had* taken actions against Cuba, and Communists probably *did* resent him. There *were* probably elements in the CIA who were frustrated with Kennedy's lack of progress against Castro. He *was* a civil rights leader and the Ku Klux Klan probably *did* dislike him. When he was vice president, Lyndon Johnson probably *would* have liked to take over as president. However, every president makes decisions that ruffle some feathers. It is not possible for any US president to be universally liked. These facts are not proof of assassination conspiracies.

Skeptoid® Says...

Today, Lee Harvey Oswald would have been even easier to convict than he would have in 1963 had he survived to be tried. One reason is that our psychological profiles of killers are much more refined. Psychologically, Oswald fits right in with other ideology-driven murderers such as the Oklahoma City bombers, the Columbine High killers, the guy who shot Ronald Reagan to impress Jodie Foster, and so many others. Oswald was an angst-ridden loner, frustrated and angry with the system, his grip on reality overshadowed by an imaginary official campaign to repress him. The reason we've been able to develop this profile is that, tragically, sometimes such individuals do act out.

Paul McCartney

Date: 1966
Location: London, England
The Conspirators: The Beatles
The Victims: Beatles fans

The Theory

A community of staunch conspiracy theorists believe that Beatle Paul McCartney left the Abbey Road studios one night and died in a car accident. The Beatles then found a look-alike who has lived and performed as Paul McCartney ever since. These theorists point to what they believe are clues on the record jackets and in the music, which they claim the surviving Beatles planted to spread the message that Paul had been killed.

The Truth

Paul McCartney's fatal car crash never happened, he did not die, and he was not replaced with a look-alike.

The Backstory

The Beatles formed in 1960 in Liverpool, and within just a few years were the most popular rock band in the world. Inevitably, stories and rumors began to spring up around them. One of these was a story among the Beatles' UK fans that stated Paul McCartney had been killed in a car crash on January 7, 1967, on the M1 motorway. This rumor was repeated to the point that the Beatles' fan club had to refute it in the February issue of *The Beatles Book Monthly*:

> But, of course, there was absolutely no truth in it at all, as the Beatles' Press Officer found when he telephoned Paul's St. John's Wood home and was answered by Paul himself who had been at home all day with his black Mini Cooper safely locked up in the garage.

But this story got its biggest boost almost three years later, all the way across the Atlantic Ocean, in the United States. During those intervening years, some of the Beatles' most famous albums came out, in 1967, 1968, and 1969, including *Sgt. Pepper's Lonely Hearts Club Band*, *Magical Mystery Tour*, *The Beatles* (better known as the White Album), *Yellow Submarine*, and *Abbey Road*. And it is in this collection that fans started to notice certain details that they perceived as oddities, details that seemed related to the old story about Paul being killed in a car crash. One of these fans was Tom Zarski, a student at Eastern Michigan University, who called into a radio program hosted by disc jockey Russ Gibb in October 1969.

This was the first time Gibb had ever heard the story, and at first he was skeptical, given that all famous people had stories made up about them, sometimes even deliberately by public relations companies. But Zarski told him, on the air, to play the Beatles' song "Revolution 9" backward. Gibb did so, on the radio. He later said:

> A very pronounced English accent says, "Number 9, Number 9," and it very clearly said, "Turn me on, dead man. Turn me on, dead man. Turn me on, dead man."
>
> Well, that floored me. That absolutely floored me.

From that moment, the story reached a level that can only be described as hysteria. Kids from all over the United States began calling in with clues they had either heard in the music or seen on the album covers.

It just so happened that Gibb was good friends with guitarist Eric Clapton, who often worked closely with the Beatles in the UK and knew them well. On air, Gibb called Clapton and told him of the rumor that Paul had been killed and replaced:

> And he said, "No, what are you talking about? What, Paul McCartney is dead?"
>
> I said, "Yeah, they've got it in a record, and they've got it on so forth..."
>
> He said, "No, that's not—" and then he said, "Wait a minute," he said, "You know, come to think of it, I haven't seen Paul in about a month and a half."
>
> And that did it. After he said that, all hell broke loose.

Fred LaBour, a student reporter at the University of Michigan, heard the radio broadcast, and got to work at his typewriter. Two days later his article appeared in *The Michigan Daily*: "McCartney Dead: New Evidence Brought to Light." It began:

> Paul McCartney was killed in an automobile accident in early November 1966 after leaving EMI recording studios tired, sad, and dejected. The Beatles had been preparing their forthcoming album, tentatively entitled *Smile,* when progress bogged down in intragroup hassles and bickering. Paul climbed into his Aston Martin, sped away into the rainy, chill night, and was found four hours later pinned under his car in a culvert with the top of his head sheared off.

LaBour's article went viral and was quoted in newspapers all across the United States. The story was even picked up by both of the two most popular national magazines, *Time* and *Life*. LaBour's article did not give a source for any of the facts of the car accident, but he did point out some twenty clues found in Beatles music and art. These included details like Paul being barefoot and out of step with the other Beatles in the famous Abbey Road crosswalk photo; his back being turned in one photo; wearing a black flower when the others were wearing red; and certain images of text believed to symbolize dates or ages if reversed or turned upside down. Such claims go on and on.

Details matching the crash story can be found in the lyrics of many Beatles songs. "She's Leaving Home" includes the line "Wednesday morning at five o'clock as the day begins," which is when the crash happened; "Lovely Rita" is about the attractive meter maid who caught Paul's eye and distracted him as he drove (though it's not clear how anyone would have known this); "Good Morning Good Morning" says "Watching the skirts you start to flirt, now you're in gear"; and the song "A Day in the Life" continues with his car crash from distraction with "He blew his mind out in a car / He didn't notice that the lights had changed." Some of the songs, played backward, include phrases such as "Turn me on, dead man, turn me on" (from "Revolution 9"); "Paul is dead now, miss him, miss him, miss him" (from "I'm

So Tired"); and "Paul is dead, ha ha" (from "I Am the Walrus"). There are others as well.

The Explanation

Although there was plenty of discussion from conspiracy theorists that Paul was dead, there wasn't any evidence that a car crash had happened, nor any signs from Paul McCartney or his family or friends that anything had happened to him. No police, medical, or news reports mentioned the death in public of one of the world's most famous people.

While it's true that fans found all of these details in the Beatles' records, and one did call in to Russ Gibb's radio show to talk about them, what's not true is a single word that Fred LaBour put into his *Michigan Daily* article that really started the furor. He made the whole thing up, inspired solely by the radio interview and his own stack of records. He even made up the 1966 date of the car crash, which is why it differed from the 1967 date the Beatles' magazine debunked. LaBour has always openly declared that it was fake, and that he never meant for it to get so out of hand.

Nevertheless, the facts never get in the way of a good story. Even today, hoaxed "new evidence" is always being produced, including a 100 percent fabricated "deathbed confession" by George Harrison. A documentary film has even promoted the made-up claim that British MI5 intelligence agents were behind covering up the death and planting the look-alike. What the history of urban legends tells us is that as long as the Beatles' music continues to live (which will probably be forever), so will the hoax of Paul McCartney's death.

Skeptoid® Says...

Decades after the breakup of the Beatles, Paul McCartney released a solo album titled *Paul Is Live*, which contained a number of tongue-in-cheek references to the old conspiracy theory that he died and was replaced. Its album cover was an altered version of the iconic Abbey Road crosswalk photo. The original 1969 cover featured a VW Bug with license plate LMW28IF, which theorists interpreted to mean he'd be 28 IF he had lived; the 1993 *Paul Is Live* album had this altered to LMW51IS, meaning that he IS 51 now. A clever chap, that Paul.

Elvis Presley

Date: 1977
Location: Memphis, Tennessee
The Conspirators: Elvis Presley, the FBI, possibly other unknown individuals
The Victims: Elvis fans everywhere

The Theory

Arguably the world's biggest superstar of the late 1950s, Elvis Presley was the personification of rock and roll. After a successful career in both music and Hollywood, history records that Elvis died young at forty-two of a drug overdose. As wildly famous as this heartthrob was, there were bound to be people who just refused to believe he was dead. Enter the conspiracy theories!

Some say that Elvis faked his own death in order to escape the pressures of fame and live out his life as an ordinary anonymous citizen. Others claim that he was heroically assisting government agents fighting either organized crime or the drug trade, and is living in the Witness Protection Program. There are even claims that he is on Mars. Suffice it to say that the theories certainly cover a wide range.

The Truth

Elvis died at his Graceland estate in Memphis on August 16, 1977.

The Backstory

Especially during the last decade of his life, Elvis enjoyed a fast-moving celebrity lifestyle that was far over the top, and included chronic drug abuse. One night at his Graceland estate in Memphis in 1977, he had a heart attack and died while sitting on his toilet. His body was discovered in his bathroom by his girlfriend, Ginger Alden. He was transported to a hospital where he was pronounced dead. The body was autopsied with multiple doctors present. The cause of death was a combination of prescription drug overdose (he had fourteen drugs in his system) and cardiac arrest, possibly brought on by a Valsalva maneuver (straining on the toilet, leading to heart stoppage; constipation is common among drug abusers). An open-casket service was held at Graceland and the body was viewed by thousands of fans. A cousin of Elvis accepted an $18,000 bribe to allow a *National Enquirer* photographer to take a picture of Elvis's corpse, which ran on the front page. Bolstered by a vast amount of evidence, the truth is that Elvis died that night in 1977.

Fans all over the world were incredibly distraught. One of these was Gail Brewer-Giorgio. Immediately after Elvis's death, she wrote a novel blatantly based on Elvis's life called *Orion: The Living Superstar of Song*. The book was about a rock star, Orion, who has humble Southern origins. But the fame is too much for him, so he fakes his own death, buries a wax dummy, and lives in freedom with a false identity. It was, perhaps, her own projection of what she wished the truth could have been for Elvis.

In 1979, Sun Records signed an artist named Jimmy Ellis to their label. And Ellis just happened to have a speaking and singing voice that was virtually identical to Elvis's. Sun Records was looking to see if they could do anything with their soundalike recording artist and decided to try to capitalize on Brewer-Giorgio's book. So they released Ellis's debut album *Reborn*, which featured a photo of Ellis dressed and groomed exactly like Elvis, wearing a Lone Ranger–style mask. They gave him the pseudonym Orion Eckley Darnell, which was directly lifted from Brewer-Giorgio's book. For a few years, Ellis and Sun Records enjoyed the boost by having half their fans believe that Ellis was an incredibly talented Elvis impersonator, and the other half believing that he actually was Elvis, hiding in plain sight as an impersonator of himself. And so began decades of claims that Elvis was still alive, including conspiracy theories more varied than you can imagine. And, of course, the never-ending "Elvis sightings."

Over the years Brewer-Giorgio has remained the public face of this conspiracy theory. She wrote two books expanding on her theories, *Is Elvis Alive?* (1988) and *The Elvis Files: Was His Death Faked?* (1990). Then she wrote and was featured in two TV documentaries hosted by Bill Bixby (of *The Incredible Hulk* fame): *The Elvis Files* (1991) and *The Elvis Conspiracy* (1992). Call-in votes following the second program revealed that 79 percent of callers believed Elvis was still alive. By this time, Elvis sightings had become commonplace, and the Bill Bixby programs featured a number of people who claimed to have either seen or spoken to Elvis.

As time went on, Brewer-Giorgio's claims evolved and deepened in both scope and complexity. In her latest book, *Elvis Undercover: Is He Alive and Coming Back?*, she claims that Elvis had once sold an airplane to an organized crime family she called The Fraternity, and the FBI had approached him to work for them to infiltrate the group. But he was discovered, and the FBI whisked him out of danger and placed him into the Witness Protection Program. His death was faked as a cover story, and from then on, Elvis lived an anonymous life somewhere.

But this was just a drop in the bucket full of Elvis books that came out in 1999, and the cause was an unexpected one: 1999 was an important year for many, due to religious beliefs that the Messiah would return in the year 2000. One of these was *The Elvis–Jesus Mystery: The Shocking Scriptural and Scientific Evidence That Elvis Presley Could Be the Messiah Anticipated Throughout History* by Cinda Godfrey, which posits that Egypt's Great Pyramid is actually a temple to Elvis Presley (built in anticipation of his Coming thousands of years later), and that the most blessed of people have an image of Elvis's face hidden in their fingerprints. Another was from self-described psychic Jay Gould, who claimed to be Elvis's personal psychic during the last year of his life. In 1999, Gould published *Elvis 2000: The King Returns!*, which purports to be a series of psychic communications Elvis made to him in the decade after his death. By Gould's account, Elvis said he'd been living with Martians but would return, like Jesus, in the year 2000 to make a series of startling revelations, perform new music with a band consisting of angels, and would personally redeem the poor and the suffering.

Skeptoid® Says...

One of the most popular pieces of evidence offered for Elvis's faked death is that the middle name given to him by his family, Aron, is misspelled on his gravestone as Aaron. Various explanations have been floated for this, including the possibility that Elvis himself may have simply preferred the *Aaron* spelling. Nevertheless, how this is supposed to prove he's not actually dead has yet to be determined.

The Explanation

In order to best understand the conspiracy theories surrounding Elvis, we need to understand the people who promoted them and their reasons for doing so. Gail Brewer-Giorgio was no ordinary fan of Elvis. She was obsessed. And when her book *Orion* sold poorly, she interpreted this to mean that some conspiracy was afoot, which of course meant that *Orion* must have accidentally told the truth about how Elvis actually did fake his own death, and some cabal wanted it covered up. However, in the same book, she also asserted an alternate claim: that Elvis was secretly a drug enforcement agent and was placed into the Witness Protection Program.

Brewer-Giorgio makes a similar claim in *Elvis Undercover*, where she claims Elvis is in the Witness Protection Program because he was working with the FBI to infiltrate the mob group named The Fraternity. But on the FBI's website of information that's been made public via Freedom of Information Act requests, known as the Vault, there are all 760 pages of FBI information pertaining to Elvis. Most of it has to do with several actual extortion attempts made against him. There is no mention of him ever working for the FBI, or of any group called The Fraternity.

Cinda Godfrey's interest in Elvis was similarly unhealthy. As a born-again Christian, Godfrey wrote that she had been having trouble reconciling her religious views with her fixation on Elvis. But when she watched Brewer-Giorgio describe her conspiracy theories about Elvis on *The Oprah Winfrey Show* in 1988, she claimed to have had a revelation that tied everything together. Adam, Jesus, and Elvis were the Trinity, who walked on Earth in the person of Orion. As a result of her epiphany, she wrote the book *The Elvis–Jesus Mystery*. As for how her friends and family regarded her obsession with Elvis as a mystical, religious figure, she wrote:

> I...could think of no one who supported me or encouraged me throughout this endeavour. In fact, my family ran like rats on a sinking ship and my passion for the subject of my manuscript actually estranged me from those I love.

Regarding the psychic Gould's claim that he communes with Elvis from Mars, we can offer only author Christopher Hitchens's famous Hitchens's Razor: "That which can be asserted without evidence, can be dismissed without evidence." We look forward to Gould's presentation of proof, or at least an explanation of what went wrong with Elvis's 2000 concert with angels that we were supposed to get.

The more you take a look at the various origins of the Elvis conspiracy theories, the easier it is to understand why there is no evidence for them at all. They turn out to be, at their core, fairly disturbing noise from infatuated fans that says more about them than about The King.

Tupac Shakur and The Notorious B.I.G.

Date: 1996–1997
Location: Las Vegas, Nevada, and Los Angeles, California
The Conspirators: Various
The Victims: Tupac and Biggie and anyone who loved their music

The Theory

Rappers Tupac Shakur and The Notorious B.I.G. were at the top of their games when they were murdered six months apart in drive-by shootings. And their fame was such that their deaths drew conspiracy theories from all sorts of fans desperate to find a rationalization. Some theorists blamed the police, some blamed the rappers' own associates, and some even claim they are still alive.

The Truth

Although both their killings remain officially unsolved, authorities have little doubt that both Tupac and Biggie died as the result of gang retaliations, no conspiracy theories needed.

The Backstory

The mid-1990s saw the beginning of the infamous East Coast vs. West Coast hip-hop feud—if you believe the newspapers. Today's popular version of the story says that rapper Tupac Shakur "represented" the West Coast, and his rival Chris "Notorious B.I.G." Wallace, aka Biggie, "represented" the East Coast. The alleged feud began when East Coast artists were said to be resentful that West Coast labels wouldn't publish their music, and so began putting insults directed at the Los Angeles scene into their music. L.A. artists fired right back, and there were plenty of petty disputes and gang rivalries to go around.

The rivalry became firmly established as a violent one in 1994 when Tupac—who was in New York City on trial for sexual assault—was shot five times by three assailants in a recording studio, and was robbed of the $45,000 worth of jewelry he was wearing. Tupac survived, and made no secret that he blamed Biggie and his associate Sean Combs (later known as Puff Daddy) of being behind it.

Tupac then served his prison sentence for the sexual assault. Once he got out in late 1995, he contracted with Suge Knight, owner of Death Row Records, and the two became friends. Knight blamed Combs for the murder of a friend. There was no love lost between the pairs of Tupac and Knight, and Biggie and Combs.

Then, in 1996, Tupac was in Las Vegas with Knight for a Mike Tyson boxing match. Later that night, Tupac and Knight were driving on the strip when their car was sprayed with bullets, mortally wounding Tupac, who died a few days later.

Six months later, Biggie and Combs were in Los Angeles—Tupac and Knight's turf—for an event, when a car pulled alongside Biggie's and opened fire, killing him. Combs, following in the car behind, was uninjured.

Now, the two biggest names in the East Coast vs. West Coast hip-hop feud were both dead...and it didn't take long for the conspiracy theories to arise.

Some have claimed that it was Suge Knight himself who contracted for Tupac to be killed, believing that Tupac wanted out of his contract to start a rival label. And Knight himself has been the primary promoter of two contradictory claims. One says Tupac was accidentally murdered by a conspiracy between Knight's ex-wife Sharitha Golden and Death Row employee Reggie Wright Jr. They say Tupac simply got caught in the cross fire in a failed attempt to kill Knight himself. Another theory says that Tupac is actually still alive.

Skeptoid® Says...

Suge Knight is not the only one who suspects Tupac might still be alive. Tupac's album *The Don Killuminati* and its cover art of Tupac crucified has led some to suspect that Tupac faked his death, and will make a second coming one day, like Jesus.

Part 3: Suspicious Deaths

When it comes to theories surrounding Biggie's death, his mother is responsible for most of them. Biggie's mother filed a wrongful death lawsuit against the LAPD in 2002 claiming that rogue police officers were the ones who murdered her son. The case turned out to be one of the longest and most expensive in the history of Los Angeles. This theory was publicized in the book *LAbyrinth*, which claimed that the LAPD did not investigate this lead out of fear that it would draw attention to corruption in their anti-gang unit. The lawsuit was ultimately dismissed—with Biggie's estate claiming the reason was that the investigation against the LAPD was "reinvigorated," and the LAPD claiming the dismissal was initiated by Biggie's estate. The court does not give its reason, and so the mystery continues to fuel the conspiracy theories.

The Explanation

Conspiracy theories notwithstanding, the Los Angeles Police Department has always generally known what happened; it just doesn't have specific names and faces to bring to trial. The deaths of Tupac and Biggie were simple gang retaliations. You see, Suge Knight was a close associate of a violent L.A. gang called Mob Piru. Knight also wanted to publish Tupac's next albums. So when Tupac had his legal troubles in New York, Knight offered to pay Tupac's legal fees in exchange for Tupac letting him publish his next few albums. Tupac agreed, but when he took Knight's money, he automatically made himself a target of Mob Piru's enemies.

These enemies notably included the Compton Crips, another violent L.A. gang. While in Las Vegas, Tupac, Knight, and others of their entourage violently attacked Compton Crips member Orlando Anderson inside the casino. A few hours later Tupac was shot in the drive-by shooting. Investigators had little doubt that it was other Compton Crips who were responsible, retaliating for Anderson's beating. They believe both Tupac and Knight knew who the killers were, but it's not the kind of information gangs freely share with the authorities. When police asked the dying Tupac who pulled the trigger, he spoke his final words: "F--- you." His murder remains unsolved.

As for the theory that Knight himself contracted the shooting? Well, Knight was seated in the car next to Tupac and was struck in the head by shrapnel. If he were going to contract a hit, you'd think he'd make sure it happened when he was out of the line of fire.

Regarding Knight's assertion that it was his ex-wife trying to murder him that resulted in the accidental death of Tupac, it's just another claim that is backed up by no evidence. Police investigators never found any reason to suspect her. Her own response to Knight's charge was fairly pointed:

If I wanted to kill Suge, believe me, his ass would be dead.

Now, when it comes to Biggie's gang ties, whenever Biggie and Combs were in Los Angeles, they hired the Compton Crips as personal security. So just by being in town, Biggie was an irritant to Mob Piru, many of whom blamed him and/or Combs for Tupac's murder, which makes it pretty likely that any Mob Piru gang member could have killed him. Some evidence has also suggested that Biggie may have been killed by one of the Compton Crips—his own security— with whom he had a financial dispute.

After Biggie was killed, Combs, who was a witness, would not cooperate with police—much like Tupac. Almost certainly, it was another case of gangsters preferring to handle their own retaliation, rather than be snitches for the police.

A Mob Piru gang member named Poochie, aka Wardell Fouse, aka Darnell Bolton, has often been implicated in Biggie's murder. One retired LAPD detective has claimed that confidential informants verified that Knight's girlfriend paid Poochie $13,000 to kill Biggie to get revenge for Tupac, but the detective was pulled off the case before he could prove it.

Further tipping the scales toward both murders having been no more than gang retaliations is that immediately following Tupac's murder, violence broke out in Los Angeles between the Compton Crips and Mob Piru. At least two gang members were killed.

When all is said and done, conspiracy theories that claim that the deaths of Tupac Shakur and The Notorious B.I.G. were part of an East Coast/West Coast hip-hop rivalry are just not true. These theories are not only inconsistent with the structure of the gang tensions that are known to have existed; they also don't really explain either murder since both Tupac and Biggie were born and raised in New York. Instead, these theories appear to be the invention of the media, eager to link the two deaths by attaching a romantic pop culture angle to them.

Skeptoid® Says...

Tupac's parents had, in their younger years, been associated with the Black Panthers, labeled a subversive group by the FBI in those early J. Edgar Hoover days. In line with Hoover's war on anything he considered subversive, a book came out in 2008 called *The FBI War on Tupac Shakur and Black Leaders*, which claimed that the government assassinated Tupac as part of the FBI project COINTELPRO (see the section in Part 8) to discredit leftist groups.

Princess Diana

Date: 1997
Location: Paris, France
The Conspirators: British MI6 Intelligence
The Victims: Princess Diana, Dodi Al-Fayed, Henri Paul, Trevor Rees-Jones

The Theory

The British royal family is an institution, centuries old, that represents stability and ideals. But to some who take this to an extreme, a significant component of this stability is that the royal family has always consisted of only white Christians. When Princess Diana—who had divorced from Prince Charles the previous year—became secretly engaged to Dodi Al-Fayed, a Muslim of Egyptian descent, and was said to be carrying his child, some conspiracy theorists suspected that this diversity might be too much for the British government to bear. Therefore, they believe, she was murdered by a secret conspiracy cooked up by the intelligence agency MI6 to protect the purity of the royal family.

According to the theorists, while traveling by car from the Hôtel Ritz Paris to an apartment across town, Diana and Dodi were pursued by paparazzi. To prep for the murders, security cameras in the vicinity were disabled, Diana's security forces were mysteriously not present, and a white Fiat Uno was dispatched by MI6 to run them off the road. Sure enough, as their Mercedes entered an underpass tunnel at high speed, it hit the Fiat and struck a pillar. The accident killed three of the four occupants in the car, including Diana and Dodi. The Fiat was never found.

When the government arrested several of the paparazzi who were on the scene, the conspiracy theorists claim that the government was using them as scapegoats to cover up their own involvement.

The Truth

The deaths of Princess Diana and the others in the car with her were caused by a lack of seat belts and a drunk driver going too fast and losing control. She was not murdered by British intelligence agents.

Part 3: Suspicious Deaths

The Backstory

Although Prince Charles and Princess Diana separated in 1992, they did not formally divorce until 1996. But by then it was clear they were both pursuing separate lives. Charles had been seeing Camilla Parker Bowles, with whom he had an on-again/off-again relationship both before and during his marriage to Diana. And Diana had been seeing Dodi Al-Fayed, son of the billionaire Mohamed Al-Fayed.

About a year after the divorce, Diana and Dodi spent nine days aboard the Al-Fayed family's yacht, the *Jonikal*, off the French and Italian Rivieras. They then went to the family's hotel in Paris, the Hôtel Ritz Paris. They dined late and then decided to head to a family-owned apartment across town.

Diana and Dodi were in the back seat of the Mercedes S-Class sedan, which was driven by Henri Paul, deputy head of hotel security. Riding shotgun was Trevor Rees-Jones, a former paratrooper and personal bodyguard to Dodi. Diana had no security of her own. None of them were wearing seat belts, and the driver, Paul, was drunk.

The relationship between the British royals and paparazzi photographers has often been a contentious one. The paparazzi's reputation has often been to intrusively pursue the royals almost to the point of harassment, and the usual response from the royals has been to try and get out of their eye. On this night, Paul drove faster and faster to get away from the paparazzi that were chasing them. Going down a ramp to enter an underpass tunnel at approximately 60 mph, Paul swerved to avoid a slower white Fiat Uno, but grazed it. As a result of the hit the Mercedes began to fishtail and Paul lost control. The car hit a concrete support pillar head-on, nearly splitting in half. It spun and slammed to a stop against a wall.

Dodi and Paul were killed outright. Rees-Jones (who had put on a seat belt a few moments before the crash) was unconscious with severe facial and head injuries. Diana lay fatally injured on the floor in the back. Most of the paparazzi stopped. Although some took photos, others rendered what aid they could. When authorities arrived minutes later, seven of the paparazzi were arrested. Diana was conscious, but she died three and a half hours later. Unusually, the hospital embalmed Diana's body that same day.

Very soon after the deaths, Dodi's bereaved and outraged father revealed that the couple had been just about to announce their engagement and were expecting a baby (a claim that the embalming made impossible to verify). He began asking questions and leveling charges against the government. Why were there no security videos of what happened? Why was her body embalmed, if not to hide her pregnancy by a Muslim man? Where were Diana's private security personnel? And why had the government not found this mysterious white Fiat?

The Explanation

By 2004 Mohamed Al-Fayed had made so many claims of a murder conspiracy that the Metropolitan Police were compelled to form Operation Paget, a special investigation unit, to look into the matter. Their report ran 832 pages divided into sixteen chapters. It investigated 175 separate charges made by Mohamed, and each was found to be without any evidence. Let's take a look.

Skeptoid® Says...

The Operation Paget report was made freely available online by the BBC (British Broadcasting Corporation), and you can find it by searching for *The Operation Paget Inquiry Report Into the Allegation of Conspiracy to Murder* online. Proponents of Mohamed's conspiracy charges tend to dismiss it as government propaganda meant to discredit Mohamed, but you can read it and judge its contents for yourself.

For starters, Diana had no security personnel of her own by choice. She disliked them and, once she divorced Prince Charles, she wasn't required to have them. The Al-Fayed family had their own private security team and that was enough for her. On the evening of her death, Henri Paul and Trevor Rees-Jones were the security. So she had exactly as much security as she wanted.

The lack of security camera video of the crash turned out to be unfortunate but not mysterious. There were a good number of private security cameras along the route, and police looked at all of them, but they showed mainly building entrances, not the streets the Mercedes took. There was, however, a single video camera mounted above the entrance to the tunnel, and this camera should have been able to capture the actual moment when the Mercedes and the Fiat came together. Unfortunately, this camera only monitored live traffic and didn't record the feed. The accident would have been witnessed live by somebody in the traffic office, but the office had closed more than an hour before the accident, so there was nobody to see whatever may have been visible on the screen.

The embalming of Diana's body was, indeed, improper for the hospital to have done because she should have had a postmortem examination, and embalming made that impossible. If Diana's death had been caused by anything suspicious, the embalming procedure almost certainly would have erased any traces, so Mohamed was well justified in questioning this. However, the French police ordered the hospital to do it because they knew French president Jacques Chirac would be viewing the body. Although the embalming could possibly have erased evidence, it doesn't prove that any such evidence ever existed in the first place.

And what about that mysterious white Fiat Uno that was never found? Authorities only knew that it had existed at all because of reports from the witnessing paparazzi and from the paint that it left on the Mercedes wreck. The paint was a commercial white paint called Bianco Corfu, numbered either 210 or 224, which had only been used on Fiat Uno cars manufactured between 1983 and 1987. A massive dragnet by French police examined roughly 2,000 cars with this paint, but none of them were a match. Every so often a new claim about a white Fiat Uno comes out in the news, but the car involved in the crash has never been found. Certainly MI6 had the resources to permanently disappear a Fiat, but there's no evidence they did so.

Also, even if MI6 had indeed chosen to kill Diana, using a Fiat Uno as the murder weapon was a horrible plan. Having a compact, lightweight Fiat bump a much heavier Mercedes S-Class (one of the safest cars in the world) is pretty far away from being a sure-thing assassination.

When all is said and done, Diana's was a tragic death, but an accidental one, according to all the evidence. Henri Paul was drunk and driving too fast, which is precisely what the Operation Paget report found. Any other wild claims are just false conspiracy theories.

PART 4
The World at War

War and other large-scale conflicts result in death and destruction that are not imaginary—unlike many of the other things that inspire conspiracy theories. And it is common to believe that every military engaged in war has some secret interest that is hidden from the public view (and with good reason, for they often do). But sometimes conspiracy theorists take this belief a little too far and believe that we're being manipulated more than we know.

In this part we'll deconstruct conspiracy theories that claim the United States allowed the Japanese to bomb Pearl Harbor as an excuse to enter the war; that the United States waged war against its own citizens on 9/11; and that the Holocaust was a myth perpetuated by colluding governments. Why would governments do such things? Or a better question might be, why do conspiracy theorists try so hard to hang unimaginable crimes on their own governments?

One potential answer lies in the uber-popular belief that the Nazi regime was driven by occult mysticism. Books and documentaries abound claiming that the Nazi Party was secretly obsessed with the occult. It's completely fictional, of course, and yet it's wildly popular. It satisfies our desire for there to have been some unearthly evil driving the regime. The cruel deeds of the Nazis have been matched very few times in history; our brains try to rationalize them by assigning a motivation that's equally bizarre. We'll find similar themes throughout this section.

Nazi Wunderwaffen

Date: ca. 1930–1945
Location: Germany
The Conspirators: The Nazis
The Victims: World War II Allied Forces

The Theory

The Nazis were well known for having the world's most advanced technology during World War II, but less well known are some of their Wunderwaffen (wonder weapons) that were kept secret and destroyed so the Allies couldn't get their hands on them.

The fact that these wonder weapons did actually exist has led to a whole subculture of conspiracy theorists who credit the Nazis with technologies that were not just too advanced for 1945, but almost impossible even by today's standards. The most impressive one is a flying saucer called Die Glocke (the Bell), which was powered by antigravity technology—a substance known as Vril—that even today, theorists say, remains unknown to top scientists in the West. Vril is said to be a source of unlimited power that was known even to the residents of Atlantis. These theorists claim that pictures of the Nazi saucer can even be found online.

The Truth

The technology developed by the Nazis at the end of World War II was indeed cutting edge, but they didn't make any flying saucers, or anything else quite so extraordinary. Fairly complete records and all their design facilities were captured and analyzed at the end of the war, and nothing they actually *did* create remains unknown today.

The Backstory

It's 100 percent true that Nazi scientists were ahead of Allied scientists in many ways, or at the very least at the same level. This is especially true when it comes to their aeronautical engineers. They had

Part 4: The World at War

a high-altitude reconnaissance aircraft called the DFS 228 that later inspired the designers of the U-2 spy plane. They had a single-seat jet fighter prototype under construction called the Messerschmitt P.1101 with a variable geometry swing wing similar to that on the American F-14 Tomcat fighter plane developed in the 1970s. Its captured prototype was actually studied by the engineers who designed the Bell X-5 test aircraft of the 1950s. The Nazis had even completed glide tests on a delta-winged ramjet-powered fighter, the Lippisch P.13a, believed to be capable of going Mach 2.2—a concept the Allies were still only dreaming about.

Skeptoid® Says...

Considering how close the Germans were to the Allies with their own development of an atomic bomb, and their clearly superior ability to deliver it via their infamous V-2 guided ballistic missiles, the real "wonder" of their Wunderwaffen is that the Allies won the war. Germany's Uranium Club was their analogue to the American Manhattan Project to develop an atomic bomb. Even though the Allies had a clear advantage in conventional forces, if the war had lasted only a little longer, the Nazis' advanced technology might well have proven more than the Allies could have handled.

When World War II ended, Nazi scientists generally destroyed their records and even their prototypes, so there is some unknown amount of technical knowledge that died alongside their war effort. But today we have no public record of anything like Die Glocke being recovered at the end of the war. With each passing decade of records declassification and research through old archives, it is increasingly unlikely that anything like it actually existed. And, certainly, any substance with properties as amazing as those attributed to Vril would either be well known and incorporated into daily life, or would be the highest of all government secrets.

So how does anyone know about Die Glocke? Well, we know about Vril because, in 1960, two French authors published an account of the occult underpinnings of Nazi society in their wide-ranging book *The Morning of the Magicians*. According to them, the very deepest core of the Nazi Party was the Vril Society, an inner circle among inner circles. *The Morning of the Magicians* was key to popularizing the belief that the Nazis practiced the occult, and this discussion of a Vril Society is what supercharged the belief in the reality of Die Glocke.

Nearly everything known about Die Glocke comes from a book written as recently as 2000 by a Polish military historian named Igor Witkowski called *The Truth about the Wunderwaffe*. In it, he recounted his examination of the classified transcript from an interrogation of captured Nazi SS officer, Jakob Sporrenberg. According to Witkowski, Sporrenberg said Die Glocke was powered by a pair of rotating drums containing a mysterious iridescent purple fluid, which later authors have presumed to be Vril. This gave Die Glocke antigravity powers and permitted it to fly at fantastic speeds.

The Explanation

Okay, so when it comes to Die Glocke and Vril, all we have in the way of evidence is a third-hand anecdotal account of something that's desperately implausible, backed up by neither evidence nor even a corroborating account. So once again we call to mind Hitchens's Razor: "That which can be asserted without evidence, can be dismissed without evidence."

That said, we can still follow the threads of the tale backward to see if its origins are sound. Was the interrogation transcript Witkowski claimed to have read reliable? Unfortunately, he said he was allowed only to read it, not to copy it, and didn't even say where or when this reading took place. This means that Witkowski's story leaves us with nothing to verify.

We can, however, track down the SS officer who was being interrogated. Jakob Sporrenberg was a real SS officer. However, he was a field officer, not a researcher or scientist. Sporrenberg fought resistance fighters in Belarus, and served as police chief of occupied Poland. He was executed as a war criminal in 1952 for the murders of some 43,000 Jewish civilians in Poland. According to his official military record, he never had any connection to anything involving engineering or aviation, and there's no reason that he might have been privy to the details of a top secret project entirely unrelated to his duties. What does this mean? Well, it means that even if we choose to believe

Witkowski (which is a stretch), there's not much of a reason to believe Sporrenberg.

Now, if Die Glocke and Vril didn't exist, how did they enter the narrative enough to become a major conspiracy theory? Vril was first introduced in 1871 in the science fiction novel *The Coming Race* by Edward Bulwer-Lytton. In this story, Vril was the power source and life elixir employed by the people of Atlantis to escape when the mythical island sank. No researchers have yet found a primary nonfiction reference to Vril.

Vril entered the German popular consciousness during the years between World War I and World War II. This was a time when esotericism, an emphasis on the metaphysical rather than the physical, became something of a fad in Germany. Modern authors have since tried to exaggerate this fad into a fictional Nazi obsession with occultism (the so-called esoteric Nazism movement). Willy Ley, a German rocket scientist and author who emigrated to the United States in 1935, wrote of this period in a 1947 essay for *Astounding Science Fiction* called "Pseudoscience in Naziland":

> That group which I think called itself Wahrheitsgesellschaft—Society for Truth—and which was more or less localized in Berlin, devoted its spare time looking for Vril. Yes, their convictions were founded upon Bulwer-Lytton's *The Coming Race*.

Even though Ley was clear that this group's interest in Vril was based purely in fiction, his one brief comment here became the main reference from which the French authors drew their "Vril Society" for *The Morning of the Magicians*. The French book, so often referenced as a trusted source describing interwar Germany's fascination with the occult, is in fact quite an imaginative and speculative work. It also discussed ancient astronauts, a race of giants who once ruled the Earth, prophecies, alchemy, and the paranormal. Much of *The Morning of the Magicians* appears to have been inspired by the fiction of imaginative horror author H.P. Lovecraft. Even in the book itself, the authors wrote "There will be a lot of silliness in our book." Thus, the stories of Die Glocke and Vril turn out to have no historical basis at all—outside of esoteric fiction.

Holocaust Denial

Date: 1933-1945
Location: Europe
The Conspirators: Zionists
The Victims: Students of history

The Theory

Although history proves that Nazi Germany murdered millions of Jewish people during World War II, some believe that this is a story made up by Zionists (Jewish patriots who advocate for a strong Israel). Believers in this conspiracy theory sometimes say that all Germany did was relocate a large number of the Jewish population. They say that probably a few hundred thousand people were resettled, and they've just been missed in subsequent population counts. The ultimate goal of the Zionists who created the myth, according to the theorists, is to garner worldwide sympathy to help advance the political goals of Israel.

The Truth

Some six million Jewish people were murdered by the Nazis in the Holocaust. No serious evidence suggests otherwise.

The Backstory

When the Nazis came to power in Germany in 1933, more than nine million Jewish people lived in Europe. Over the next twelve years, two-thirds of them were murdered by the Nazi regime, in what the Nazis called their Final Solution. Today we refer to it as the Holocaust, which is Greek for "sacrifice by fire." In addition to the nearly six million Jews, some 200,000 Roma (or Gypsies) were killed, as were some 200,000 mentally and physically disabled Germans.

But from the very beginning, some anti-Semites and other Nazi sympathizers have denied that this took place. The campaign to deny or soften what was happening in Europe was successful enough that it wasn't until the war's end, when Allied troops physically walked into the concentration camps and saw the death with their own eyes, that its scope became fully understood.

This community of Holocaust deniers remains strong even today, two generations later. Most of them characterize the Holocaust stories as Zionist propaganda. Here are some of the most common claims:

- There is no record of any specific order by Hitler to exterminate Jews.
- Many of the most famous "death camps" (Belzec, Chelmno, Sobibor, Treblinka) do not exist.
- There is no evidence of mass graves.
- The Zyklon-B gas the Nazis bought huge quantities of was used for delousing, not killing.
- Gassing someone with diesel engine exhaust wouldn't be lethal.
- Wartime aerial reconnaissance photos of Auschwitz do not show mass graves or cremations.
- The death toll of six million has no evidentiary basis.

These would all sound pretty compelling—if any of them were true. Let's take a look.

Skeptoid® Says...

Holocaust denial is actually illegal in some countries (Germany and Israel being two obvious ones), which is a notable exception to most country's free-speech laws. While this law is justified by the staggering toll of the Holocaust, this exception to free speech is called out as an example of the suppression of the truth by many Holocaust deniers.

The Explanation

Anti-Semitism is, sadly, a cornerstone of many conspiracy theories. Some political scientists trace the reasons for this all the way back to the Bible story of Caiaphas and Judas who conspired to betray Jesus to the Romans. Ever since those times, many people have been mistrust-ful of Jewish people and some have held much harsher views, so we often find Jewish people to be the villains in modern conspiracy the-ories. The historical hatred toward Jewish people that drives today's Holocaust deniers is the very same thing that made it easy for the Nazis to condemn them as the cause of their nation's problems and launch the Holocaust.

Holocaust denial is often done by citing vast stores of trivial minu-tiae: factoids or extrapolations that are so many and varied as to give the impression of comprising an impregnable vault of proof. In their book *Denying History: Who Says the Holocaust Never Happened and Why Do They Say It?* authors Michael Shermer and Alex Grobman discuss this strategy:

> Most Holocaust deniers are very knowledgeable about very spe-cific aspects of the Holocaust—a gas chamber door that cannot lock, the temperature at which Zyklon-B evaporates, or the lack of a metal grid over the peephole on a gas chamber door—so that anyone who is not versed in these specifics cannot properly question and answer their claims.

However, information to disprove the claims noted earlier is easy to come by. The only reason a researcher would look past that infor-mation is a desire to find only information that supports a desired viewpoint. What would drive such a desire? The only driver com-mon to all Holocaust-denying authors is anti-Semitism. Here's what a search intended to learn the true facts would reveal about each of the claims laid out in the Backstory section:

- It is true that there is no single order of the form "I order all Jews exterminated, signed Adolf Hitler." But just because the order didn't fit onto a single Post-it note doesn't mean it didn't exist. The evidence that the Holocaust was a fundamental of the Third Reich's strategy is so manifold and vast that to claim otherwise is just plain absurd.

- The "missing death camps" in Poland that can't be found on any maps were razed for a good reason, and that reason is not that they never existed. In 1943 as the Soviets advanced and pushed the Germans out of Poland, the Germans aggressively destroyed the evidence of their concentration camps. By the time the Russians arrived nothing remained but bulldozed fields, and by the end of the war, they looked just like more forest. Immense quantities of records exist for the camps, however, beyond the obvious eyewitness testimony.

- The claim that no evidence exists for mass graves is preposterous. Auschwitz alone employed 900 full-time *Sonderkommandos*, Jewish prisoners tasked with disposing of the dead. Many survived the war and their jobs became guiding the international excavation efforts, which lasted more than a decade.

- Zyklon B consisted of an adsorbent (basically kitty litter) infused with hydrogen cyanide and a warning irritant. It was indeed used widely for delousing clothing and fumigating buildings. Deniers claim it was not efficient for killing people, but mountains of evidence dispute this. It was widely used, primarily at Auschwitz, in the gas chambers.

- Gassing was also done with diesel trucks. By simply piping the truck's exhaust into the cargo compartment, Jewish prisoners could be transported to a disposal camp and be dead upon arrival. The claim made by some deniers that this would not be lethal is easily disproven.

- The claim that aerial photographs of Auschwitz don't show any evidence of mass burials or cremations can be disproven with a single *Google* image search. Just go online and try it.

- For the war crimes trials in Nuremberg, the bulk of the evidence presented proved that nearly 6 million Jewish civilians were murdered during the war (the actual number ranges between 5.5 and 5.9 million), and this number cannot be accounted for by "relocation." For one thing, population censuses taken before and after the Holocaust showed that many Jewish civilians no longer existed. Anywhere. The rest of the evidence—which included documentation for all the points made earlier—consisted (in part) of 3,000 tons of documents seized from the Nazis: *3,000 tons!* That's a lot for even the most convinced conspiracy theorist to deny...

Skeptoid Says...

During the liberation of Europe, General Dwight D. Eisenhower toured the concentration camp at Ohrdruf and wrote:

> I made the visit deliberately, in order to be in a position to give first-hand evidence of these things if ever, in the future, there develops a tendency to change these allegations merely to "propaganda."

He also ordered every Allied soldier in the area to tour the camp, so as many men as possible could bear witness to the Holocaust.

Attack on Pearl Harbor

Date: 1941
Location: Pearl Harbor, Hawaii
The Conspirators: US Navy
The Victims: Servicemen and civilians stationed at Pearl Harbor

The Theory

When the Japanese executed their successful sneak attack against the US Navy at Pearl Harbor on December 7, 1941, 2,459 servicemen and civilians were killed and another 1,282 were injured. Four battleships and two destroyers were sunk and another eleven ships were heavily damaged. Three hundred and forty-three American aircraft were destroyed or damaged.

Could all of this carnage been avoided? Did the Navy have advance knowledge of the attack, but allowed it to happen because they wanted to declare war on the Japanese? Yes, that's exactly what the conspiracy theorists believe.

The Truth

The attack on Pearl Harbor happened because the Japanese put together a solid plan for a sneak attack and executed it perfectly.

The Backstory

The conspiracy theories surrounding Pearl Harbor were inevitable, given the enormous loss of life, and, indeed, a number of things that happened on the morning of December 7, 1941, do look suspicious. For starters, Admiral Husband Kimmel, the commander in chief of the Pacific Fleet who was based in Pearl Harbor, had written to Washington repeatedly throughout 1941 to advise them of his concerns of a Japanese sneak attack. So why wasn't anyone prepared?

One reason that conspiracy theories have risen around the Pearl Harbor attack is that it does indeed appear that the Americans made a lot of mistakes before and during the attack—mistakes that, some feel, were so boneheaded that they must have been deliberate. Here are some of the most prominent:

- Aircraft were gathered in groups way out in the open, where they were most vulnerable to machine-gun fire from attacking planes.

- Ships in the harbor were similarly gathered, making them easy targets for torpedoes.

- Americans had broken the Japanese code called *Purple* and should have known everything about any planned attacks.

- A destroyer, the USS *Ward*, sunk a Japanese midget submarine outside the harbor early in the morning on the day of the attack, but no alarm was raised.

- The mobile radar station at Opana Point (the place closest to where the Japanese planes flew in from) did detect the incoming strike force, but instead of raising the alarm, the commander, Lt. Kermit Tyler, ordered everyone out of the station to go get breakfast.

- And of course, the big one: the three missing aircraft carriers, at least one of which was always supposed to be guarding Pearl Harbor.

It certainly does appear that the US Navy deliberately allowed themselves to be attacked, but the evidence proves otherwise.

The Explanation

So many mistakes appear to have been made by the Americans; can there be some other explanation besides a conspiracy to allow the attack? In 1944, the secretary of war ordered a lawyer in the US judge advocate's office to conduct an independent investigation and find out how the Navy could have been caught with its pants down. This lawyer was Henry Clausen, and he followed every imaginable lead to find out what went wrong. He began by looking at the political situation between the United States and Japan.

Relations between the two countries had been growing increasingly strained throughout the 1930s. Japan wanted to expand its empire in East Asia, threatening the United States' trade relations with China. The US tried to put the brakes on Japan by stopping all sales of war materials to them, mostly steel and oil. But as high as the tensions were by 1941, the Americans still had no specific knowledge of any imminent Japanese attack against them. And even if they had, the war hadn't yet started, which means the US Navy had no experience in how best to respond to such threats. President Roosevelt knew as much as anyone about what the Japanese might do, and the preparations he ordered were generally poorly interpreted and poorly handled by people trying their best with insufficient knowledge and experience.

Kimmel's warnings to Washington were not ignored, contrary to what's in the conspiracy theory books; Roosevelt took them very seriously. Unfortunately, everyone believed that Kimmel was wrong, that an air strike was unlikely, and that espionage and sabotage were what they needed to be worried about. And, when sabotage was expected against an air base, the best defense was to take all the planes out of their hangars and group them together out in the open. This makes it hard to approach the planes without being seen, and it makes them easy to guard. So this is exactly what was done.

The same was done with the battleships in the harbor. It is easier to guard one cluster of ships than ships scattered around the harbor. So while grouping the ships may have deterred saboteurs, it just made them sitting ducks when the torpedo bombers came in.

Now, one of the biggest efforts to combat Japanese espionage was to crack their codes. Although the code *Purple* had indeed been broken, it was a diplomatic code, not used by the Japanese military, and intelligence gained from it provided no warning of the Pearl Harbor attack. The code that the Japanese military *did* use was called *JN-25*.

The Americans had made some progress against *JN-25*, but they'd only been able to decipher about 4 percent of the phrases and numerals that came in—not very useful yet. If they *could* have cracked it, they might well have known of the planned attack.

Skeptoid® Says...

The Japanese happened to have replaced the codebook for *JN-25* on December 4, three days before the Pearl Harbor attack, rendering all the progress that the Americans had made to date absolutely useless. This put the American codebreakers almost all the way back at square one.

The *Ward*'s sinking of the midget submarine on the morning of the attack is not well known, perhaps because it was (obviously) overshadowed by the later events of the day. It should be understood that the defense forces were jumpy, and while a Japanese sub or some other threat was reported every day, most of these reports were false alarms. It's no small task to send a ship out, so reports had to be analyzed to determine which threats were worth acting on. The *Ward* got its first report of a submarine at 3:42 a.m. It went out, but found nothing. It found a sub at 6:37 a.m. and sunk it by dropping explosive depth charges (its wreckage was found in 2002).

The *Ward*'s report reached the watch officer at 7:15, and it was relayed to Kimmel and Rear Admiral Claude Bloch at 7:30. For twenty minutes they discussed the report and then reluctantly ordered another ship to go out and verify the story, doubting that whatever the *Ward* had fired upon was a real Japanese submarine. Five minutes after this order was given, the first Japanese aircraft screamed overhead and explosions began rocking the harbor.

That's when the radar operators from Opana Point dropped their forks in the restaurant and ran back to the radar station. Opana Point was still under construction and none of the guys who worked there had been trained yet. Fifty-three minutes earlier, the serviceman at the scope, who had never even used the equipment before, saw the incoming Japanese aircraft and pointed it out to Lt. Tyler. Tyler hadn't been trained yet either, but he did know that a flight of American B-17 bombers was on its way in. Since it was time for breakfast and there didn't seem to be any cause for alarm over the expected B-17s, Tyler did, in fact, take his whole crew away to breakfast. A 1942 court of inquiry cleared him of any wrongdoing.

This leaves the theory about the "intentionally" absent aircraft carriers. With the threat of war looming, Kimmel knew he needed to bolster the defenses at Midway and Wake Islands, which lay between Hawaii and Japan. The carrier USS *Saratoga* was in over-haul in San Diego, leaving only USS *Lexington* and USS *Enterprise* on duty. Kimmel had them deliver aircraft to reinforce Midway and Wake on staggered schedules so that at least one was always there to defend Pearl Harbor. But just as *Lexington* left and *Enterprise* was supposed to get back, *Enterprise* struck bad weather and was kept at sea a full two days longer than planned. Unfortunately, that second day was December 7. It was a vulnerability that nobody could have foreseen.

One area of agreement between historians and conspiracy theorists is that Admiral Kimmel was unfairly made a scapegoat. It is widely agreed today that he acted properly with the information he had, but he was reduced in rank and replaced by Rear Admiral Chester Nimitz, an experienced naval commander who had been serving as chief of the Bureau of Navigation.

Skeptoid® Says...

The tragic events of the attack on Pearl Harbor are commemorated at the World War II Valor in the Pacific National Monument, which includes the famous USS *Arizona* Memorial—the mighty battleship sunk during the attack, with 1,177 lives lost—as well as sites in Alaska and California that also figured prominently in the war in the Pacific.

The Philadelphia Experiment

Date: 1943
Location: Philadelphia Naval Shipyard
The Conspirators: US Navy scientists
The Victims: US Navy sailors

The Theory

According to conspiracy theorists, in October 1943 the US Navy conducted a daring experiment at the Philadelphia Naval Shipyard. They attempted to create a force field around an entire ship, a Cannon-class destroyer escort called the USS *Eldridge*, number DE-173. This field was supposed to make the ship not only invisible to the naked eye, but to radar as well. They say that hundreds, possibly thousands, of Navy sailors witnessed the experiment from other ships that were also at the shipyard at the time.

The results of the experiment, claim the theorists, were pretty awful. They say that some crewmen actually dematerialized during the event, and when it was over, they were founded melded in with the ship's metal. Others were rendered psychotic and had to be permanently institutionalized. At least one crewman reappeared turned inside out, and quickly died. Others were simply never seen again. Even the lucky people who made it through uninjured have reported "phasing" in and out of existence: they will fade out to near invisibility, and then fade back in, greatly fatigued. This is claimed to have happened to a few sailors when they were carousing ashore in a bar where it was witnessed by many other patrons.

The conspiracy theory says that at least two of these tests were run, and perhaps as many as 144. In the first, the ship did disappear almost entirely, with witnesses aboard a nearby merchant marine ship, the SS *Andrew Furuseth*, reporting that a green fog took its place until it reappeared. In the second test the *Eldridge* completely disappeared and then reappeared some 200 miles away, where it remained for some minutes. The *Eldridge* then returned to its original location in Philadelphia, having traveled backward in time about ten minutes. That's the theory, anyway.

The Truth

The Philadelphia Experiment is a work of pure fiction, conceived by an imaginative loner.

The Backstory

The story of the Philadelphia Experiment didn't actually begin in 1943 when it is claimed to have taken place. In fact, the story didn't exist at all until thirteen years later in early 1956 when the US Navy's Office of Naval Research (ONR) received a copy of Morris Jessup's 1955 book *The Case for the UFO* in the mail. The book was full of strange annotations that outlined the basic facts of the Philadelphia Experiment. Hoping others might be able to help shed some light on whether this meant anything of interest to the US Navy, the ONR made 100 copies and distributed them to other departments. Some of the copies eventually made it out into the wild.

In 1979 authors Charles Berlitz (creator of the Bermuda Triangle mythology) and William Moore (longtime UFO researcher and author) got ahold of one of the copies and published a book called *The Philadelphia Experiment: Project Invisibility*, which they presented as a factual account. They also gave information outlining supposedly real research that they felt justified the effects seen in the experiment.

In 1984 their book was turned into a Hollywood movie, *The Philadelphia Experiment*. It's been followed by at least four sequels and remakes. Inevitably, any number of men have come forward over the years claiming to have been part of the experiment—but only after it became a popular legend based on the 1984 movie. So far, none of their backstories has held up to scrutiny.

The Explanation

The true story of the Philadelphia Experiment began shortly after Morris Jessup published *The Case for the UFO*. Jessup received a series of letters from a man calling himself Carlos Allende. In the letters, Allende said that he'd been one of the men aboard the *Furuseth* and witnessed the *Eldridge*. Albert Einstein, on hand to run the experiments, observed Allende stick his hand into the invisibility field, decided he was a man of rare scientific talent, and spent two weeks tutoring Allende on the science of invisibility. Allende wrote Jessup several times to advise him that Jessup's thoughts on UFO propulsion had stumbled onto the same technology. Allende's letters were full of strange wording, crazy sentence structure, and an apparently random use of capitalization. Jessup, believing Allende to be a crank, did not reply.

Soon thereafter, the ONR received their annotated copy of *The Case for the UFO* in the mail. The annotations were very unusual. Three people appeared to talk among themselves in the dense margin annotations: Jemi, Mr. A., and Mr. B. They wrote in three different colors of ink, but as the handwriting was all the same, it seemed clear that one person had done the writing of all three people. Their conversation revealed the basic facts of the Philadelphia Experiment, and how Jessup's UFO technology ideas were probably related. It also stated that the ONR had run these experiments.

Now, it so happened that the ONR was always on the lookout for ways to make their ships less visible to radar, so they did not immediately dismiss this strangely marked book, at least not without a cursory inquiry into whether these people actually knew something that might be of value to the Navy. So they met with Jessup, showed him the annotations, and asked if he had any idea who might have written them. Jessup knew who it was right away. The annotations were almost certainly written by Allende, since they contained the same weird capitalization and sentence structure.

The ONR easily determined that neither the *Eldridge* nor the *Furuseth* had been anywhere near the locations assigned to them by the story, that nobody aboard either ship had ever heard of such a thing, and that both ships had in fact been very busy with their convoy duties in the Atlantic during the time the 1943 experiment had supposedly taken place. And why would a badly needed destroyer escort be taken from service and used for an experiment that could have easily been done with any old hulk? The ONR also knew that their own office, which was supposedly responsible for the experiment, had no record of it, hadn't even existed until three years after the experiment was supposed to have taken place, and had never worked with Einstein. Officially, the matter was dropped, but in pop culture, copies of the annotated book were circulated and published, and the story is now a popular conspiracy theory and urban legend.

Skeptoid® Says...

In 1968 independent paranormal researcher Robert Goerman recognized Allende's return address while reviewing published copies of Allende's letters to Jessup. They were from the Allen home, family friends of his, right there in his town of New Kensington, Pennsylvania. Carlos Allende was actually Carl Allen, the family's dark-horse son, who spent nearly all his time reading and annotating everything he could get his hands on. When Allen was at sea during World War II, he mailed whole volumes of more annotated stuff back home, all of it nonsensical. Allen remained a recluse and eventually moved to Greeley, Colorado, where he died in 1994, after a lifetime of staunchly defending his story.

Nuclear War and Nuclear Winter

Date: 1983
Location: United States
The Conspirators: The TTAPS authors: Richard Turco, Owen Toon, Thomas Ackerman, James Pollack, and Carl Sagan
The Victims: US policymakers

The Theory

In 1983 a paper titled "Nuclear Winter: Global Consequences of Multiple Nuclear Explosions" was published in *Science*, the most prestigious of all the scientific journals. It was written by Richard Turco, Owen Toon, Thomas Ackerman, James Pollack, and Carl Sagan and, using the first letter of each of these authors' last names, has come to be known as the TTAPS paper.

TTAPS reported on the results of computer simulations that showed what the effects would be if enormous amounts of smoke were added to the atmosphere, which is what would happen during a nuclear war. The nukes would light entire cities on fire and when the atmosphere became sufficiently filled with smoke particulates, it would block out enough of the sun that a "nuclear winter" would result, cooling the planet to the point of destroying all agriculture and killing billions of people—an outcome far worse than even the nuclear war itself.

Scientists soon disputed the paper's findings, and its doomsday scenario was thoroughly discredited, but that's not the end of the story.

Noting that the TTAPS nuclear winter was likely to influence political policymaking when it came to the use of nuclear weapons, conspiracy theorists have charged that the TTAPS authors deliberately published a false paper in order to promote their antinuke agenda.

The Truth

The TTAPS findings were largely overstated, as some of the authors themselves have since admitted. The true impacts of atmospheric smoke following a nuclear war cannot easily be predicted, and cannot be authoritatively claimed to be as high as TTAPS said.

The Backstory

TTAPS was indeed influential; it raised awareness of a consequence of nuclear war that few policymakers had considered. And its authors, like most people, were opposed to nuclear war, just like the conspiracy theory claims.

TTAPS was published during the Reagan administration, a critical time in the Cold War when both the United States and the Soviet Union were rattling their nuclear sabers. President Ronald Reagan was keen on the SDI (the Strategic Defense Initiative space-based missile defense system nicknamed Star Wars). Dr. Edward Teller, the "father of the hydrogen bomb," was a passionate advocate for building a stronger deterrent against the Soviets. In this pro-escalation environment, a caution against the perils of nuclear war had more of an appearance of anti-defense political propaganda than it did of sound science. Teller and other conservative scientists branded the TTAPS authors as peaceniks who conspired to publish faulty science to promote their antinuclear agenda.

But TTAPS also came under fire from mainstream science. The first serious rebuttal to TTAPS came three years after its publication from Joyce Penner at the Lawrence Livermore National Laboratory. Penner looked at the TTAPS analysis and found that the result of nuclear winter was tied almost entirely to a single variable in the equation: exactly how much smoke would be produced by the fires triggered by each nuclear bomb. Penner found that this question was virtually impossible to answer, because every instance would be different. And, from the historical data available, the level of smoke would almost certainly be far lower than the value TTAPS gave it to arrive at the nuclear winter scenario.

But perhaps the most influential rebuttal was a paper titled "Nuclear Winter Reappraised," which was published the same year as Penner's paper. However, this rebuttal wasn't published in a scientific journal, but in the political journal *Foreign Affairs*. Its two environmental scientist authors Starley Thompson and Stephen Schneider found that TTAPS was indeed exaggerated, but not nearly as much as Penner had characterized it. They used the term *nuclear autumn*, which is probably considered the most accurate description today.

In 1991 the TTAPS theory was put to the test when, pursued by the Coalition Forces in the Persian Gulf War, Iraqi forces retreated from Kuwait. In a literal scorched-earth policy, the Iraqis set fire to some 700 oil wells throughout January and February, which took most of the year to put out. These fires produced about a million tons of smoke, and the TTAPS team predicted global climate consequences, which ultimately never happened. Analysis revealed that although the quantity of smoke was enough to justify the TTAPS prediction, that smoke failed to get into the upper atmosphere, and so was unable to form the long-lasting screen that was predicted. Thus, the climate consequences were negligible.

The second test came in June of 1991, when Mount Pinatubo in the Philippines erupted, forcing roughly 17 million tons of smoke into the air. This time, the TTAPS theory held up. Global temperatures dropped by nearly a full degree and sunlight was reduced by 10 percent. It took nearly three years for things to get back to normal. However, global agriculture was not significantly impacted.

Skeptoid® Says...

In 1995 Carl Sagan, the most famous of the five TTAPS authors, published his famous book *The Demon-Haunted World: Science as a Candle in the Dark*. In a chapter discussing how the scientific method works, he discussed in detail how and why the TTAPS team had been wrong with its predictions.

The Explanation

Although some regard TTAPS as a conspiracy—a case of ideology-driven scientists bending reality to promote some political agenda—there is no evidence of this. What there is evidence of, however, is that the TTAPS paper and its subsequent corrections are exactly how the scientific method works. Any scientist knows that science is a continually self-correcting process. In good science, all conclusions are provisional, and they are always subject to change if new information turns up.

Prior to the TTAPS paper, there had actually been two atomic (though not nuclear) bombs detonated in the cities of Hiroshima and Nagasaki, in 1945. Had those events produced smoke sufficient to cause a nuclear winter? No, but there are clear reasons for this.

First is that a modern nuclear war, a worst-case scenario such as that discussed in the TTAPS paper, would involve many more than just two weapons—about 150, according to strategic thought of the day. Second, thermonuclear weapons today are far larger than the atomic bombs of World War II and would destroy and/or influence a much larger area.

The bomb in Hiroshima did trigger a large number of fires. In fact, it created a firestorm, where a central upward-flowing draft of heat draws in wind from the circumference. It took about six hours for everything combustible within a 1.5-kilometer radius of ground zero to be completely consumed, leaving a total of about 8 square kilometers completely burned. Hundreds of smaller fires were scattered over a larger area, but nearly all had been put out by the next day. Thus, when we look at photographs of Hiroshima after the bomb, we do not see large volumes of smoke.

Nagasaki was a simpler case. The landscape there was hilly, which kept that bomb's effects much more contained. The fires that burned after the Nagasaki bomb burned longer because they were more geographically scattered, but they were also much smaller and fewer in number than the ones in Hiroshima. Photos of Nagasaki also show clear skies above; the smaller fires simply didn't produce enough smoke to have any real effect.

Charges of a conspiracy by TTAPS to influence politics simply do not hold up. Its methods were valid; however, it erred in choosing an absolute worst-case scenario for it principle variable. Far more likely is the less destructive nuclear autumn, where some cooling and loss of agriculture would probably be easily survivable. It was easy for most reasonable people who oppose nuclear war to support TTAPS due to its antinuclear implications, and difficult to contradict for fear of appearing to dismiss the dangers of nuclear weapons. The physicist Freeman Dyson perhaps described it best when he said:

> [TTAPS is] an absolutely atrocious piece of science, but I quite despair of setting the public record straight....Who wants to be accused of being in favor of nuclear war?

9/11 Building Collapses

Date: September 11, 2001
Location: New York, New York
The Conspirators: The US government
The Victims: The American public

The Theory

During the attacks on September 11, 2001, New York's World Trade Center was destroyed, the Pentagon in Washington, DC, was severely damaged, and United Airlines Flight 93, said to have been en route to crash into the White House, went down, and all aboard died.

The most fanatical of all conspiracy theorists believe that these were not a coordinated attack by Islamic terrorists, but were in fact a false flag attack by the American government upon its own people, intended to create anger against Islamic states and breed support for a war. These theorists claim that the Twin Towers and Building 7 had all been rigged with explosives in advance by government agents and destroyed in a controlled demolition that was set to mimic a terrorist attack.

The Truth

All three buildings were destroyed by fire, the initial cause of which was the impact of the two airliners into the Twin Towers. There were no explosives used in any of them, the US government wasn't involved, and there was nothing unexpected about their collapses from an engineering perspective.

The Backstory

The historical tensions between Islam and Judaism go back more than 1,000 years, and are beyond the scope of this book. But the involvement of the United States in this conflict is much newer. When Israel was created after World War II, the United States was merely one of many nations sympathetic to their cause, but in the decades since, the United States has been Israel's most important supporter. Israel has received more financial aid from the United States than any other nation, and one big reason is its strategically important location inside the Middle East. Any bullet fired by Israel in a conflict against Islamic forces was likely paid for with American dollars; and accordingly, Islamic extremists have long had their eye on the United States as a target. The terrorist attacks of 9/11 were, quite probably, eventually inevitable.

As with so many national tragedies in the United States, conspiracy-mongering started immediately. The first was that 9/11 was perpetrated by Israel, in hopes of starting a holy war against Islam. This began with a story that was widely circulated in the alternative press that 4,000 Jewish people received warning not to report to their jobs at the World Trade Center and were thus saved. Within a few months the conspiracy theories evolved into some desperately complex stories implicating governments and individuals and money and oil; everything was thrown into the pot, no matter how self-contradictory or irrational, as long as it denied the actual events that everyone witnessed on that day.

Skeptoid® Says...

The 9/11 conspiracy community is best represented by an organization called Architects & Engineers for 9/11 Truth. On their website, more than 30,000 conspiracy theorists worldwide have signed a petition demanding that the events of 9/11 be reinvestigated. Of these, some 11 percent self-report some engineering background or education, though nearly all in irrelevant fields such as software, audio, or web design. Of those few with the expertise that the website highlights, most can be searched on the web and found to also promote other bizarre conspiracies. Suffice it to say that the main point communicated by their website is that their view is far out on the fringe.

Eventually three claims emerged that were specific enough to be testable. One was that the towers fell "faster than free fall"—presumably, the speed at which debris would fall if not connected to any supported structures—though it has never been made clear why this might be or what it would prove. Second was the fact that jet fuel—the principal accelerant that started the fires—burns at a maximum temperature of 1500°F and steel melts at 2750°F. Therefore, said the theorists, there is no possible way that the fires started by the airliner crashes could have caused the buildings' structures to fail. The third point emerged a few years later, when Larry Silverstein, owner of the lease on Building 7, said in a TV interview that he told the firefighters to "pull it," and the conspiracy theorists took this as an order to detonate the explosives. This, of course, indicated to them that Silverstein himself was a key member of the conspiracy.

The Explanation

Let's put the first conspiracy theory—about 9/11 being a Jewish plot—to rest right away. There was no email. No Jewish people or people of any other religious background stayed home because they had been forewarned about the attack. In fact, many Jewish people died on 9/11 along with people of every religion and nationality.

Also, the argument that the towers fell faster than free fall has never been made in a rational way. First of all, there is no one "free-fall" speed. A parachute has a much slower free-fall speed than, say, a bowling ball. Now, while the billowing dust clouds make it impossible to accurately say exactly how long it took each tower to collapse, most of these claimants say it took about sixteen seconds. Calculations show that a standard steel I-beam of the type used to form the structure of such buildings would take about nine seconds to fall the height of the Twin Towers. The videos of the Twin Towers collapsing make it clear that the beams from the sides of the building fall away much faster than the core collapses all the way down, which makes it easy to see that this theory is false. The cores of the buildings clearly collapsed more slowly than the debris coming off of them fell.

When it comes to the theory about the melting point of steel, let's just clarify and say that nobody ever claimed that the steel girders in the buildings had to melt (i.e., liquefy) for the buildings to collapse. They only needed to soften a bit. Blacksmiths prove that steel glows red and can be worked into any shape at only 560°F, far less than the 1500°F at which jet fuel burns. So there was nothing unexpected about all three buildings' structural failure from fire alone. There have been many other examples of this happening throughout history. For example, citywide firestorms triggered by attacks in World War II destroyed hundreds of tall, steel-framed buildings that were not otherwise damaged. Twisted steel girders and other reminders are on public display at the Edo-Tokyo Museum in Tokyo, Japan, the Imperial War Museums in London, England, and the Dresden City Museum in Dresden, Germany, for anyone who would like to personally inspect how dramatically fire alone can mangle a steel building structure.

Finally, on the claim that Larry Silverstein ordered the demolition triggered by telling the firemen to "pull it": a direct inquiry to Controlled Demolition, Inc. (the world's largest demolition contractor) revealed that they have never used that term for triggering a demolition, nor have they ever heard it used elsewhere in the industry. In a PBS interview, Silverstein recounted a phone call he received from the fire department commander as they were fighting the fires that raged inside Building 7. The firemen had reported structural groaning and an ominous bulge on the building's exterior between the 10th and 13th floors. Fearing an imminent collapse, the commander recommended pulling the battalion out of the building, which Silverstein agreed to as evidenced by the fact that those firemen were no longer in the building when it did collapse shortly thereafter. Silverstein recounted:

> I said, "We've had such terrible loss of life, maybe the smartest thing to do is pull it." And they made that decision to pull and then we watched the building collapse.

In any case, the claim had been illogical from the beginning. If the final go/no-go decision had been Silverstein's to make, the basic narrative would have been that a government conspiracy led by President George W. Bush and Secretary of Defense Donald Rumsfeld organized everything and had the building somehow surreptitiously wired with explosives, a multi-month job that nobody noticed. Then, on the day of the attack, they put the actual go/no-go decision into the hands of the building's owner (for some reason), and then had him go on national TV and reveal to the world that the demolition had been deliberate. If that was their strategy, it was not a wise one.

Skeptoid® Says...

The National September 11 Memorial & Museum opened ten years to the day after the attacks, and commemorates the 2,977 victims of 9/11 plus the six victims of the 1993 bombing. Its two pools are located in the footprints where the Twin Towers once stood.

The Pentagon and the Missile

Date: September 11, 2001
Location: Washington, DC
The Conspirators: The US government
The Victims: The American public

The Theory

On the morning of September 11, 2001, something flew into the Pentagon in Washington, DC, and destroyed a section of the building in a powerful explosion. All the evidence that exists shows that it was American Airlines Flight 77, a hijacked Boeing 757 that had just left Washington Dulles International Airport en route to Los Angeles. But a popular conspiracy theory states that this story is a false cover-up, and that there *was* no Flight 77. Instead, theorists say, what struck the Pentagon was a missile fired by the US government as part of an enormous "inside job" the government itself planned to carry out all of the 9/11 attacks.

The Truth

American Airlines Flight 77, a Boeing 757, was hijacked and crashed into the Pentagon in Washington, DC, killing 184 victims on the airplane and inside the building.

The Backstory

The attack on the Pentagon (and on the Twin Towers in New York City) took everyone by surprise. Before anyone had any idea what had happened, fire crews were arriving to fight the inferno and rescue dozens of people trapped in the rubble of the collapsed building. Only as the events of the day unfolded did anyone realize that this was part of the much larger 9/11 attacks. But within a few weeks, conspiracy theorists had amassed a number of claims that they believed constituted proof that 9/11 was an inside job, executed by the American government, and not by some group of what they believed were fictional terrorists.

First, they claimed that there was no aircraft wreckage at the Pentagon site. If an entire airliner had actually crashed there, the parts of an entire airliner would be scattered everywhere. Second, the radar track of the incoming object (whatever it was) was made public, and it showed radical maneuvers, and the conspiracy theorists claimed that this track was much too tight and unsafe for a 757 to have made. Only a small missile could have flown such a wild path, they said. Third, they said that the Pentagon's defense systems would have shot down any incoming threat, plane or missile, and because no such defense system appeared to have been used proves that the government allowed the attack to take place.

Finally, only one security camera video was ever found that actually showed the object impact the building. It was from a parking gate. Far off in the background of the camera's field of view, a small white streak flew in low—visible for only a single frame—and explosively struck the building. Conspiracy theorists who analyzed this streak claimed that it was clearly far, far too small to be a 757, and lacked a plane's tall vertical tail.

The Explanation

What happens in cases like this is usually that conspiracy theorists begin with their preferred conclusion—that the attack was perpetrated by the government against its own people—and then work backward looking for confirming evidence or anomalies and fitting them into their narrative. 9/11 Truthers tend to believe very deeply that the US government is actively engaged in open warfare against its own citizens, and so they begin with the conclusion that whatever happened here was *not* carried out by Islamic hijackers.

Two of the main pieces of evidence are simply false. There was plenty of aircraft wreckage at the crash site, and it's easy to find photos of it online. It was even visible in the live news footage, so it wasn't planted later. And as far as the Pentagon's defense systems, it never had any. In all of the thousands of aerial photographs of the Pentagon, it's plain to see that there are no antiaircraft batteries or other rooftop defenses.

Regarding the radar track of the approach that was taken, it was indeed a wild circle descent that would have been unsafe to perform in a 757. But that proves nothing. It was still well within a 757's capabilities, and the hijackers never had any intention of being safe. Moreover, missiles have no need to circle to lose altitude; they can simply go straight down. Large planes can't, not without breaking up from aerodynamic stresses.

As for the video of the incoming small white streak? No tail is visible because, in the one frame where the plane appears, it has not yet entirely entered the field of view, so its tail is still out of frame. Beyond this, the image is almost uselessly indistinct. The security camera was fitted with an ultra-wide-angle lens in order to capture the entire parking gate area. The Pentagon building itself appears deeply curved from the distortion of this lens. Anything far away, like the airplane, would be dramatically reduced in size. The fact that the white streak is as large as it is means that it has to be something as big as a 757. The video is absolutely consistent with how a 757 would appear to that lens.

As with all large conspiracy theories, we should consider the number of people who would have to be in on the truth in order to make it happen. What is the minimum number of people at American Airlines who would know if a nonexistent flight was added to their database? Consider all the people who worked at Washington Dulles International Airport, the flight's origin. The baggage handling and gate crews from all the American Airlines gates would have heard about the crash and quickly, by talking among themselves, have all learned that no such flight existed that day. They would have reported the inconsistency up their chain of command. Soon everyone with knowledge of American Airlines' flight schedules would have checked their books. At some level, virtually every one of American Airlines' 100,000 employees worldwide, 3,900 members of the Aircraft Mechanics Fraternal Association, 57,000 members of the Air Line Pilots Association, and 116,000 members of the Transport Workers Union of America would have heard about this discrepancy from their coworkers. More than a quarter of a million people would have had to be paid off or killed, without a single one of them coming forward to report this over more than a decade.

When a missile is fired—and we can assume this would have had to be a cruise missile launched either from the sea or from the air to avoid witnesses to its firing—how many people know about it? Certainly the crew of the boat or aircraft, but what about the teams responsible for the missile inventories, the civilian contractors who replace them, the civilian auditors who track everything? How many people know when a submarine's entire crew of 150 is paid off or threatened? At some point, it becomes an exercise in absurdity. The Pentagon was hit by American Airlines Flight 77, which was commandeered by terrorists. End of story.

Skeptoid® Says...

The Pentagon Memorial, situated at the crash site, has an inscribed bench for each of the 184 victims, arranged by birth date, from 1930 to 1998. It is open to the public twenty-four hours a day, 365 days a year.

PART 5
Suppressed Science

The Earth is flat. The cures for many common diseases have been created and tested. You can ditch your electric company and power your home for free. All this and more is true... if you're a conspiracy theorist, that is!

In this part we'll take a look at the conspiracy theories surrounding the business of suppressive science. Now, you'll often find made-up or mis-represented sciences used to explain technologies that exist only in our dreams. The expected result is an Internet filled with impossible-to-create machines and wild theories, all explained by tossed-together sciencey-sounding words with no real meaning. Closely related is the idea that "science doesn't know everything," which of course means that any-thing a person wants to believe to be true is true. The names of famous scientists like Nikola Tesla, Albert Einstein, and Galileo Galilei can almost always be found backing up these claims. These scientists' theories are almost always grossly misrepresented, but for people who want to believe, including these "proven" ideas helps back up any conspiracy theory. So let's take a look and find out what the theorists think about suppressed science.

The Hollow Earth Theory

Date: ca. 1600–Present
Location: The Earth
The Conspirators: World governments
The Victims: The world population

The Theory

You'd think that the idea of the Earth as a globe of rock with humanity living on its outside surface would seem to be an absolute given. Not for conspiracy theorists! In fact, there have been a number of groups throughout the centuries who claim that this accepted model of the Earth is absolutely false. These theorists believe in a hollow Earth and have claimed that the authorities—the mysterious and unnamed "powers that be"—are lying to the public in order to control us and prevent us from knowing the true geometry of the world.

There have been a number of divergent theories in the hollow Earth canon. In its most basic version, the universe consists of an infinite expanse of solid rock, and the surface of Earth consists of the concave surface of an empty bubble inside that rock. It is exactly the same surface area with the same surface features as the standard model of Earth, just turned inside out. Another variation, which is the more popular one that still survives today, has us living on the Earth's outer surface as in reality, but an alien civilization lives in the hollow, inner surface, and the aliens come and go through various openings in the Earth's poles in flying saucers. And, in yet another variation, the Earth is made up of concentric spheres with various civilizations living on each level, nested inside one another like gigantic Russian nesting dolls.

The Truth

The Earth is a globe and we live on its outer surface.

The Backstory

Claims of a hollow Earth have been as varied in their types of alternate geography as they have in their motivations, which, through the centuries, have sometimes been religious and sometimes political. Today, we know that Earth is a convex sphere because we can see it from space. Yet that does not stop modern authors from continuing to promote that it is hollow and filled with aliens who exit and enter Earth's surface through openings at the poles.

While this theory may be the most popular of those that survive today, it is not new. In the early 1800s, a former Army officer turned Hollow Earth promoter named John Symmes almost had the government persuaded to sponsor him on an expedition to find that north polar opening, in the hopes that the inner-world people could be persuaded to ally with the United States. The plan only died when President Andrew Jackson was elected and killed it, recognizing it as ridiculous.

The evidence that theorists cite as proof of this model has included the fact that birds migrate seasonally, and where else would they be headed but to those polar openings; and the fact that world maps have changed over the centuries, which is consistent with their belief in government suppression of the true geography of the world.

Even the model of nested concentric spheres has enjoyed serious scientific support at various times. In 1692 Astronomer Edmond Halley, after whom the famous comet is named, presented a paper to the Royal Society—Britain's leading scientific academy—suggesting that the Earth might consist of various concentric spheres, all held in place by gravity. Assuming the concentric spheres were free to rotate within each other, this would explain phenomena such as the way the magnetic poles move around. Additionally, luminous gases leaking out through the north polar hole (for Halley's model also had such holes) could explain the aurora.

But in 1870, it was Cyrus Teed, an American alchemist and pagan religious leader, who turned the world inside out, so to speak. His model said that the universe is an infinite expanse of solid rock with an Earth-sized bubble of air in the center, and all the world's oceans, continents, and people are on the inner surface of that vast bubble.

His book *The Cellular Cosmogony, or the Earth a Concave Sphere* described the universe as being inside out, with the world as we see it on the inside surface of a sphere, and all the heavens contained within. Teed established a church called the Koreshan Unity focused on this concept.

This concave sphere model of the Earth favored by Teed was famously put to the test by Ulysses Grant Morrow, a member of Teed's Koreshan Unity. Morrow had conducted many ocean-level optical studies to learn whether the surface of the ocean appeared convex or concave and had grown familiar with the optical distortions that sometimes make distant ships either visible above the horizon or invisible below it. Using this idea as a base, he contrived a proof that the Earth's surface curved upward that would not depend on sightings that he regarded as fallible and subject to optical illusions. Morrow reasoned that if he constructed an absolutely straight line four miles long and suspended it over the ocean, and that if it was absolutely level at one end, the far end would dip down toward the water, if the world was indeed concave and hollow.

In 1897, Morrow began his experiment at a stretch of straight beach near Naples, Florida. Because it wasn't practical to build a 4-mile-long object, he designed a set of four rigid H-shaped frames that he dubbed "rectilinears." They were built by the Pullman railroad car company, the most reliable builder he could find. Each was 12 feet long and 4 feet wide, made of mahogany and brass, and diagonally braced with steel bars to be absolutely rigid.

The first rectilinear was positioned just above sea level on rigidly anchored standards. It was leveled with four different types of level to be absolutely certain it was true. The next rectilinear was brought up beside it and bolted to it, and when it was secure, it too was fastened to a rigid standard. They continued down the beach this way, leap-frogging the last rectilinear and repositioning it at the front of the line. Caissons (watertight chambers) were placed in the water all along the way so the tides could be accurately measured and accounted for. Each measurement was checked and initialed by several people. Morrow went to great lengths to ensure that everything was absolutely correct.

In the true model of the Earth, with a convex surface, Morrow's line should have been about 2 percent higher off the ground at the far end, as the curvature of the Earth would slope down away from a perfectly straight line. However, in Morrow's model that curvature was exactly reversed, so his mathematics predicted the line would be about 2 percent closer to the water's surface. It took months of painstaking work, but when they reached the end of the line, the last rectilinear was exactly 2 percent lower than the first had been. His results? The concave sphere model was proven! Earth is indeed hollow, and we live on its concave inner surface.

Skeptoid® Says...

Today, a structural engineer can look at the one surviving rectilinear on display at the well-preserved Koreshan State Historic Site in Florida, a state park (www.floridastateparks.org) where you can see the Koreshan Unity's surviving buildings and workshops—not to mention their inside-out globe.

The Explanation

Let's start by taking a look at Morrow's "proof" of a hollow, inside-out Earth. With apologies to the engineers at Pullman, the rectilinears were built with an obvious geometric flaw. Although they were properly braced corner to corner, the point in the center where the diagonals crossed one another should have been fixed, with both diagonals fastened to the crossbar. Instead, the diagonals are free floating where they intersect the crossbar. This lack of attachment allowed the H-shaped frame to flex like an isosceles trapezoid. It is a testament to Pullman's exceptional build quality that this freedom to flex escaped unnoticed. For Morrow to have gotten the result he did, his line could have sagged no more than 4 percent over the full 4 miles, which adds to the impressiveness of the achievement. Had the rectilinears been braced across the top and bottom, and/or had the diagonals been fixed at the center of the frame, Morrow would have certainly got even less of an error.

Morrow could scarcely have predicted that in the future spacecraft would be able to see the convex blue sphere of the Earth in all its glory, but it is to his credit that, as wrong as he was, he made every effort to be as rigorous as possible in his science-based exploration of truth.

By gravitational studies, we know that the Earth is a solid ball and does not contain the vast cavities assumed by the other various Hollow Earth theories, and with our detailed air and ground surveys and imaging we know there are no great polar holes through which migrating birds, alien flying saucers, or anything else come and go.

The Flat Earth Theory

Date: ca. 1800–Present
Location: The Earth
The Conspirators: World governments
The Victims: The world population

The Theory

Out of all the conspiracy theories in the book, you've almost certainly heard this one before: the Earth is flat. The conspiracy theorists who believe this to be true think that the flat Earth is the greatest of all secrets, and that keeping it from the public is the ultimate act of control. As long as this most enormous of all possible truths is hidden from us, we remain under the control of the powerful elite, and are subject to whatever abuses they wish to impose. Many theorists who think the Earth is flat feel that it is their patriotic duty to believe; for if an immoral government is imposing a false claim on its people, resistance to that claim becomes a moral imperative, in their minds.

The Truth

The Earth is round.

The Backstory

Popular notions that ancient people believed the world was flat turn out to be almost universal, but are also almost universally false. Since the ancients first began forming concepts of the cosmos, humans have always understood the Earth to be a globe. Pythagoras noted this as early as the sixth century B.C.E., followed by Aristotle, Euclid, and others. More than 2,200 years ago, ancient computations had the circumference of the Earth to within 2 percent accuracy. Educated populations worldwide have always known that the Earth is round.

It was not until the 1800s in England that a significant number of otherwise well-educated people discarded the notion of a round Earth. This view rose from the world of biblical literalism. A few

Christian fundamentalists pointed to a number of Bible passages that they believed, when interpreted literally, proved the Earth must be flat. For example, references to "the four corners of the Earth" appear in Revelations 7:1, 20:8, and Isaiah 11:12, and references to "the ends of the Earth" appear in Psalms 67:7, 98:3, and Isaiah 45:22. All of which appear to suggest that the Earth has edges. Matthew 4:8 speaks of "all the world's kingdoms" being visible from a single mountaintop, which could only be the case if the whole Earth was a flat plain. Biblical flat-Earth enthusiasts continue these odd interpretations ad nauseam with further verses about waters, the sky, compass directions, you name it.

Skeptoid® Says...

A popular myth says Christopher Columbus had to persuade Ferdinand and Isabella to let him prove the Earth was round. This story is completely false. The spherical nature of the Earth had already been a fundamental of ocean navigation for a millennium. We also commonly believe Galileo was sent to the Inquisition for saying the Earth was round; but no, that had always been the prevailing view. Galileo was prosecuted for heresy, not for geography.

Most influential among these was a gentleman named Samuel Rowbotham, who called himself Parallax. Parallax decided that the promotion of a flat Earth should be his life's work, and he wrote, lectured, and debated about this idea tirelessly. He also came up with a number of experiments that were designed to prove the flatness of the Earth. He called his science Zetetic Astronomy (*zetetic* drawn from the Greek word for "inquiry") and, in 1865, published *Zetetic Astronomy: Earth Not a Globe*, which became the magnum opus of flat Earthism. In his view, expressed in the book, the North Pole lay at the center of the flat Earth, and Antarctica was an ice wall that surrounded its circumference. The sun was never more than 400 miles overhead, and the stars were some 1,000 miles away. Biblical literalists joined his Universal Zetetic Society in droves.

Flat Earthism languished for a few decades with no clear leadership until 1956, when English sign painter Samuel Shenton took up the torch and formed the International Flat Earth Research Society (IFERS), which worked to continue the ideas of the Universal Zetetic

Society. Shenton's view of the Earth was similar to Parallax's, but he also believed that the mythical ancient society of Atlantis was located under the North Pole and would occasionally launch flying saucers through a hole in the center of the city to periodically visit us. When astronauts working for NASA's Gemini program began sending back photographs of the Earth taken from space, Shenton developed convoluted explanations for everything in the sky that could be seen from the Earth. For example, although watching satellites passing overhead at night might prove to some of us that they are orbiting a spherical Earth, Shenton claimed in 1957 that Sputnik was merely circling overhead. In dismissing this as proof of a spherical Earth, he made the analogy of Sputnik to a sailboat, asking "Would sailing round the Isle of Wight prove that *it* were spherical?" Membership in the International Flat Earth Research Society dwindled to only twenty-four by the time Shenton died in 1971, insisting to the last that the Moon landings were fake.

Skeptoid® Says...

An early and infamous demonstration of this Zetetic Astronomy model was something called the Bedford Level Experiment of 1870. In this experiment, members of Parallax's Universal Zetetic Society bet £500 that a straight, 6-mile stretch of the Old Bedford River could be proven flat by surveyors with angle-measuring surveying instruments called theodolites. It was a great media circus with newspapers involved, and the various trials and retrials were debated, fell into disarray, and eventually ended in lawsuits.

For the next twenty-five years, the flat-Earth belief was led by Charles and Marjory Johnson, who lived in a remote desert homestead in California and called themselves the Covenant People's Church. They formed the International Flat Earth Research Society of America and took over where Shenton left off, publishing their periodical, *Flat Earth News*. The Johnsons pushed their fire-and-brimstone version of biblical literalism about as far as possible, but peppered it with broad-spectrum conspiracy-mongering. The Johnsons fervently promoted any and every crank theory of the universe, crank theory of physics, whatever, that came along—anything that would support their view that believed science is a deceit.

This was the Apollo era of the Moon landings, and the Johnsons spent a lot time disputing the validity of the Moon landings. The couple devoted much of their newsletter space to charging author Arthur C. Clarke and film director Stanley Kubrick, who cowrote the movie *2001: A Space Odyssey*, with faking the Moon landing, as had Shenton before his death. The Johnson's house burned down in 1995, leaving them destitute, and the publications ceased.

With the onset of the twenty-first century and the rise of the Internet, flat-Earth believers have had ample venues for propagating their beliefs. The biblical literalism angle has largely dwindled away, replaced by alternative science claims, conspiratorial distrust of authority, and ignorance-based ridicule of sciences such as global warming and quantum physics, which are all claimed to be part of the master plan to hide the greatest truth of a flat Earth.

Skeptoid® Says...

There was a sharp spike in interest in this conspiracy theory in 2016 when a rapper named B.o.B, who had been promoting the idea, was corrected over *Twitter* by famous astronomer Neil deGrasse Tyson. It actually escalated into a rap battle, with Tyson assisted by his musically inclined nephew. The whole phenomenon has take on a life of its own, spreading to NBA athletes and various other celebrities, all embracing the promise of forbidden knowledge and the exposure of the corrupt elite.

The Explanation

Although the Earth's spherical shape is a self-evident fact supported by so much blatantly obvious proof that it should be unnecessary to even discuss, it can still be an interesting intellectual exercise to find these proofs. Perhaps the best is the existence of time zones, and how we can pick up the telephone in the daytime and talk to someone in another country where it is dark. If the Earth were flat and the sun merely circled above it such that the region below it were most brightly lit, there can be no spot on that flat plane from where the sun would not be visible. That's not an illuminati lie, it's geometry.

With telescopes we can watch planets such as Jupiter and Saturn and see their cloud features rotate out of view and back in. We can watch the phases of the Moon change as its spherical surface rotates in and out of the sunlight, and we can even see the curved edge of the Earth's shadow darken part of the Moon during a lunar eclipse. And if we look at the stars at night and compare their positions simultaneously from different places around the world, there is no possible model to explain what we see except that of the observation being made from points on the surface of a sphere with a radius of 3,957 miles.

Although many obvious facts don't seem to be worth explaining, it's always interesting to learn how we know what we know.

Nikola Tesla

Date: 1856–1943
Location: United States
The Conspirators: World governments wishing to repress their citizens' access to technology
The Victims: Consumers worldwide who are robbed of advanced technologies

The Theory

If everything the Internet said about Nikola Tesla were true, we would all have flying cars and holodecks and transporters. This engineer has had his name co-opted by conspiracy theorists more than any other person. No matter what magical technology you wish were real, you can find someone who believes Tesla invented it. The form this usually takes is a vague claim that Tesla invented limitless electricity, free to everyone, forever. But since it would be impossible to meter and sell, nobody would invest in it; indeed, say the conspiracy theorists, his invention was actually suppressed by profit-driven utilities and regulators.

While limitless energy is the main invention that conspiracy theorists mention, his other inventions are treated the same way. They say his inventions were seized by the government and Tesla himself was written out of the history books. The claim that Tesla created fantastic inventions that are suppressed by governments to protect their profits remains a staple of Internet conspiracy culture.

The Truth

Nikola Tesla was a top-notch electrical engineer, but almost all of the fanciful inventions attributed to him by conspiracy theorists are fictional.

The Backstory

Nikola Tesla was almost thirty before he was finally able to immigrate to the United States from what is now Croatia. He'd been stuck in frustrating work as a telephone engineer in a remote European country with few resources or opportunities, while electrical technology was exploding elsewhere in the world.

Once Tesla arrived in the United States, he took a job in the laboratory of the great American inventor Thomas Edison, whom Tesla found to be gruff, unethical, and stingy. A contract dispute was the final straw that prompted him to head out on his own, but he had other (and better) reasons. He knew that Edison would have owned anything Tesla developed while in his employ, and Tesla had several good ideas that he wanted to keep for himself. So, on his own, Tesla filed a number of patents for an AC induction motor and for the distribution of alternating current via an electric grid. The acquisition of these patents by Westinghouse Electric & Manufacturing Company made Tesla's fortune and fame, and provided him with the resources he needed to do further research.

Tesla gained notoriety with photos of himself fearlessly sitting beside a giant Tesla coil, a high-voltage device popular today for its ability to throw off lightning bolts from a doughnut-shaped coil at the top. And, from his now-famous labs in Colorado Springs, Colorado, and New York State, Tesla plunged headlong into his more fanciful, theoretical work. He was obsessed with the idea of wireless power transmission. He did experiments with X-rays and radio, winning patents still in use today, but not really excelling in the business side of things. His next great investor, the industrialist J.P. Morgan, stopped financing Tesla when Italian engineer Guglielmo Marconi beat Tesla in successfully transmitting radio signals across the Atlantic Ocean.

Tesla sunk what funds he had left into building his great tower at Wardenclyffe in New York, with which he hoped to wirelessly transmit power around the world, and into his experiments in Colorado transmitting electricity through the ground. Some reports claim that he had success with this, but the losses were enormous, costing far more electrical power than could be successfully received.

Eventually Tesla ran out of money. His experiments came to an end and he moved into a New York hotel to live out the rest of his life as a recluse with odd habits, a deteriorating personality, and monomaniacal personal hygiene.

However, when he died, the United States was in the midst of World War II. Hoping to find some kind of weapon or useful invention, the government took advantage of Tesla's status as an immigrant and an obscure "alien property" act to seize all of his possessions. It took only three days to analyze what was there before issuing the following report:

[Tesla's] thoughts and efforts during at least the past 15 years were primarily of a speculative, philosophical, and somewhat promotional character often concerned with the production and wireless transmission of power; but did not include new, sound, workable principles or methods for realizing such results.

Sadly, after such a magnificent and promising career, Tesla's final gift to the world consisted of nothing more than useless, rambling notes.

The Explanation

No other name in history has been caked with as much false pseudo-science and false history as Nikola Tesla. It's true that he was a brilliant engineer, and he was certainly ahead of most of his colleagues in the field. Yet virtually every invention attributed to him was really just something that he was the first to patent in the United States.

Tesla is best known for the development of AC (alternating current), and his war with Edison who favored DC (direct current). Tesla's AC system is the one used worldwide today for transmitting power. However, experimental AC grids were already being tested in Europe when Tesla was still a young telephone engineer in Croatia. Tesla was simply the lucky first one to get the patents filed in the United States.

Tesla is also known as the inventor of the electric induction motor, a big improvement over the DC motors already in existence. Again, he was not the first: Galileo Ferraris had a prototype working two years before Tesla did. But again, Tesla was the first one to the United States patent office.

A clever showman, Tesla was keenly aware of his almost-magical reputation and knew to exploit it. The famous photographs of him sitting in his Colorado Springs laboratory surrounded by lightning bolts from his Tesla coil were double exposures made for publicity purposes. It would have been deadly to actually sit there.

Tesla's famous tower at Wardenclyffe, which he was never able to complete, is often characterized as a way to provide free electricity to everyone in the world by transmitting it through the air. However, even if it had worked, there would have been nothing free about it. The electricity would still have had to be generated somewhere, at the usual cost; Tesla's idea was only about *transmitting* it. Today we have a much better understanding of the ionosphere, and we now know that his Wardenclyffe Tower technology would not have worked. This is why there have been no serious attempts to replicate it.

In addition, many of his experiments with wireless power transmission were based on bad information. Tesla hoped that electromagnetic waves could be persuaded to work in a manner that we know today they don't. He hoped there would be no losses sending electricity through the Earth, losses that we know today are huge. In short, for much of his later work, he was simply wrong, dependent on crackpot mathematical ideas that were, even in his day, rejected by most mainstream mathematicians and physicists.

Tesla is also known for the creation of a powerful death ray. However, no corroborating information ever surfaced, either in his notes or from any of his lab assistants. This death ray was something he often spoke of, but only during the final years of his life, when he was destitute and consumed by his descent into obsessive compulsive disorder in a New York hotel.

However, Tesla does not deserve to be maligned in any way. He was massively productive and innovative, and spent his entire working career at the very forefront of his field. In order to patent working devices, he had to tweak or improve existing technologies to make his patent applications valid. Every textbook on electromagnetic theory rightly confers upon Tesla the enormous credit he deserves (contrary to the claims of conspiracy theorists who claim he has been "written out of history"). He was no slouch. He just didn't have the mystical, godlike powers that so many people attribute to him, and nothing he ever worked on remains a mystery to science today. Tesla was perhaps ten years ahead of his time...seventy-five years ago.

Free Energy

Date: Ever since the industrial age
Location: Worldwide
The Conspirators: Governments, energy companies, regulators
The Victims: Consumers worldwide

The Theory

If you are an authoritarian government, one easy way to control a population is to make them dependent upon a base necessity, like electricity. If people were able to generate their own electricity for free, and no longer had to buy it to heat their homes, drive their cars, get their news, or do almost anything else, they would no longer be dependent upon the establishment and would thus be more difficult to control.

Given this certainty, it is no surprise that a very vocal community of conspiracy theorists believes that this is exactly what has happened with electrical power generation and transmission. Many theorists believe that electricity can easily be generated for free, but that governments and industry suppress that knowledge for fear of losing their control over the population.

The Truth

Free energy machines do not and cannot exist, as the laws of physics make them impossible. Specifically, the laws of thermodynamics state that when energy is drawn from a system, the system is left with less energy. You can't drink water from a glass and have the glass still remain full.

The Backstory

Free energy is a compelling proposition. We all wish we could power our homes and cars with free, limitless electricity. The culture of crankery has responded, with centuries of proposals for free energy. Today these proposals often take the form of theoretical high-tech concepts, but for most of history, the idea of free energy has been based on mechanical perpetual motion machines.

The quest for perpetual motion has been around as long as humans have been using machines to do work. The first known concepts were called overbalanced wheels intended to spin forever all by themselves, and these were imagined in many different designs. One had spokes filled with mercury, curved in such a way that the mercury flowed outward as each spoke moved over the top of the wheel to provide more leverage on the downstroke. The mercury flowed back inward as the spoke moved under the bottom of the wheel to provide less leverage on the upstroke. Others used hinged levers to move weights in the same way. The idea was that if a wheel could be made to turn all by itself, it could be connected to a machine to do work, or to a generator to produce free electricity. No design has ever worked, but that's never stopped amateur engineers from trying.

Today the most common free energy device is a magnetic motor, with some arrangement of permanent magnets intended to keep a rotor always spinning, a ball always moving around some track, or some other mechanical action. No magnetic motor has ever been able to maintain its movement.

The term *perpetual motion* has gone somewhat out of favor for describing free energy machines, as it seems to suggest old-fashioned contraptions and clunky spoked wheels, rather than the finely machined devices that believers design today. These believers often cite complex mathematical concepts, or terminology from quantum physics, that they think might make their particular machine the first one to actually work. So the term generally used today is an *over-unity* device, suggesting that more energy comes out than goes in. This is exactly what perpetual motion means, but the new term sounds a bit more sciencey and promising to some in their quest to create a device to produce free energy.

Terminology has, in fact, played a significant role in the modern perpetual motion community. Because many of those who tinker with this stuff are nonscientific amateurs, some can be easily tempted by words that sound like support for their concept. One great example is the term *zero-point energy*, which suggests an untapped energy source sitting out there in space, just waiting for someone to come along and build the right kind of device to suck that power out and put it to work. The phrase "zero-point energy" can often be found in descriptions of today's free energy concepts.

One company in recent memory that gained a surprising amount of traction with a blatant claim of free energy production was called Steorn, formed in 2000 as a web design company. In 2006 they announced they were developing a "microgenerator." They named their device the Orbo but would say very little about how it worked, other than to say it produced free, clean, and constant energy. They asserted that it had been validated by eight independent scientists, but (unsurprisingly) would not name them or present them to the media for interviews.

Steorn did challenge an actual independent jury to test its device in 2007, but in 2009 the jury came back and announced that the production of energy had not been demonstrated. It soon became clear that the Orbo was simply one more attempt at a magnetic motor.

Skeptoid® Says...

In 2009–2010 Steorn put their free energy device on display in Dublin, Ireland, where it was powered by a battery—which didn't really impress anyone. They brazenly claimed that it was *charging* the battery rather than running off of it—which didn't really fool anyone. The company closed and went out of business in 2016.

The free energy community today is tightly wrapped up with the conspiracy theory community, and interestingly, with the UFO community as well—both communities sharing a belief that governments are keeping enormous secrets from the people. For a long time, UFO proponent Steven M. Greer has promoted what he calls the Disclosure Project, whereby he expects to compel governments to disclose all sorts of secret information about UFOs that he believes they are withholding. Increasingly he promotes free-energy technologies as well, and also calls on governments to disclose the devices he believes they are suppressing.

The Explanation

The fundamental reason that free energy machines can never work is hinted at in their name. They produce something from nothing. The way the universe works is defined by physical laws—and those laws don't work that way.

The first law of thermodynamics says that the energy level of any closed system remains constant. If we take energy out of it to do some work—for example, spinning a rotor—then we must put an equivalent amount of energy back in. (In point of fact, we must put *more* energy back in, because the act of doing these things would have consumed some energy as well.)

The second law of thermodynamics says that systems seek thermal equilibrium. Basically, heat energy will never flow on its own from a region of lower temperature to a region of higher temperature. If some of that heat energy is converted to work (spinning that rotor again, or some other job), energy from some other part of the system *must* flow to it as the system seeks equilibrium. You cannot extract work and still have the same amount of energy left. No way, no how, can any perpetual motion device (or any other "over-unity" claim) ever be possible. Physics is physics, and whether your device is an overbalanced wheel or the most precise magnetic motor yet derived, it can never work.

Of course, any company that *could* design and patent a functional free-energy machine would become fantastically wealthy, which is the basic logical reason that the conspiratorial claim of suppression is nonsensical. Why would anyone keep something that would make them rich under wraps?

Another reason that suppression can be trivially dismissed is that there does not appear to be any sort of suppression campaign in place. One need only glance at the Internet, especially *YouTube*, to see that free-energy devices are widely and freely discussed. They are most obviously not suppressed.

Zero-point energy—on which so many of these claims depend—is a real term, but it does not refer to a *source* of energy. It's a term in physics that refers to the minimum possible energy state of a system. Such a system is said to be at its ground state. Logically, energy could never be drawn from such a system, because it is already at its minimum. The example most often cited is so-called vacuum energy, which refers to the ground state of a pure vacuum, such as in outer space. The ground state of a pure vacuum is non-zero, because of quantum fluctuations—constant, minute changes in energy levels which are part of the universe's basic nature. That energy, which is vanishingly small, cannot ever be extracted, because doing so would leave the vacuum with an energy level that is less than its ground state, which is an impossibility. Yet, nonexperts will sometimes look at the words used and misconstrue that they mean a source of energy. You can't take speed away from a stopped car, and you can't take energy away from a system that is at its physical minimum.

Unless the fundamental laws of the universe are proven to be dramatically wrong, which seems unlikely, it's equally unlikely that we'll need to worry about governments suppressing perpetual motion machines.

The Big Pharma Conspiracy

Date: Era of modern medicine
Location: Worldwide
The Conspirators: Pharmaceutical companies
The Victims: People suffering from disease

The Theory

Half a billion people worldwide regularly take prescription medication, supporting a trillion-dollar industry. That's a lot of commerce—commerce that its beneficiaries might well like to protect. The conspiracy theory here is that those pharmaceutical companies could easily cure almost any disease with some simple natural cure, especially cancer. However, they choose to suppress these simple treatments because curing people would convert them from paying customers into noncustomers. Instead, the companies choose to offer only semi-effective drugs that they can patent and sell at the highest possible profit margin, and they keep the simple "real drugs" suppressed and off the market.

The Truth

There is no simple, magical cure for all cancers or all other diseases, and no rational reason to suspect one exists or would ever be suppressed. Treating all the thousands of diseases in the world is a complicated task and only variously effective, and something that we're always trying to improve.

The Backstory

Distrust of the pharmaceutical industry is very popular throughout all levels of society in many developed nations. This seems counterintuitive; if the most advanced nations are the ones doing the most advanced drug development, why would people in those same nations be distrustful of their own efforts?

The answer has to do with what was happening culturally when this particular conspiracy theory took root. Before the 1960s, the pharmaceutical industry was one in which many people took great pride. We saw dramatic successes like the polio vaccine and penicillin. But then, even as our medical technology advanced further, people began to view it with derision and suspicion. What changed?

It was largely the rise of the New Age and hippie movements in the 1960s and 1970s in the United States that shifted public attention away from pride in technical achievements and toward the spiritual, the natural, and the metaphysical. Sociologists call this the Western esotericism movement. The embrace of traditional natural healing and the rejection of science-based medical treatment were key to this movement. It was epitomized with the explosive interest in traditional Chinese medicine beginning in the early 1970s, and it continues today with anti-vaccination sentiment and naturalistic food fads like organic produce, trends that seek to vilify what we've learned through science. The time line of the rise of holistic medical treatments matches perfectly with the rise of the Big Pharma conspiracy theory, for reasons which seem clear, given the cultural context.

By now, this basic set of ideologies has become pretty solidly entrenched in Western culture. Thus, we can expect there will always be a native tendency among many to seek fault with science-based medicine in general, and with the pharmaceutical industry specifically. Given this climate, it was virtually inevitable that many adherents to these philosophies would be receptive to the idea of some remarkable all-natural herbal treatment, untainted by science, that would prove miraculously effective, while simultaneously proving that the pharmaceutical companies were corruptly suppressing it.

The Explanation

There is an obvious aspect to this conspiracy theory that makes it fundamentally illogical: it accuses Big Pharma of acting in a purely profit-motivated way, by doing something terribly unprofitable. If any pharmaceutical company could invent a single cure for all disease, it would be the most successful and profitable product in history. It would be disastrous from a business perspective for any company to suppress such a product, as doing so would risk having a multinational competitor launch it tomorrow, thus crushing them out of existence.

It is a fact that intense public demand for new medical treatments drives all segments of the pharmaceutical industry—from the huge international public companies to the independent, unregulated supplement maker—to innovate and release the best products. That all the world's competitors would agree to not release the Holy Grail of medicines, without a single opportunistic whistle-blower speaking up, doesn't make any sense.

The first thing that should tip you off that this conspiracy is improbable is that pharmaceutical executives and their families die of the same diseases everyone else does. If these executives truly had a secret vault with The Ultimate Cure to Everything inside, wouldn't they use it for themselves and their loved ones at least? Yet they don't appear to do any such thing.

The idea that a cure for cancer is suppressed is also trivially disproven, as there are, in fact, many cures for cancer on the market. Cancer is not a single disease, but many hundreds of different diseases with different causes and different treatments. There could never be one single cure for all cancers any more than there could be one single fix for all possible automobile mechanical problems, so this idea that there is a single wonder drug in some pharmaceutical company's vault is simply fiction.

There are many cancers that we have cured. When we catch them early enough, we have very successful treatments for breast cancer, most skin cancers, testicular cancer, Hodgkin's lymphoma, thyroid cancer, and some types of leukemia. Any of these is fatal if left untreated, and yet the supposedly suppressed cures for them are widely available from Big Pharma and widely used.

Unfortunately, there are also many cancers for which we have not made much progress, but many more for which we have made some amount of progress and we can slow or stop their spread. Taken as a whole, the history of cancer treatment over the past seventy-five years is one of the great success stories in the history of medicine. The claim that treatments are suppressed is blatantly at variance with easily observable facts.

Now, it is true that pharmaceutical companies prefer to sell patentable drugs for which they can own a monopoly for a time to recover development costs. However, this is not unique to the pharmaceutical industry; it is standard practice *in every manufacturing industry*. The need to be profitable is a foundational principle of all business. That its use in the pharmaceutical industry constitutes a conspiracy is a bizarre concept that could only be held by someone with a dismal naiveté of economic fundamentals.

Further, the belief that natural cures are more effective, but are suppressed because they cannot be patented, is both true and false. It's true that effective cures often come from nature, but false that they are not patentable and are thus suppressed. In fact, the study of molecules originally found in nature is a huge part of drug development. Pharmaceutical companies maintain research stations throughout the world, with researchers focusing on the most diverse possible set of compounds. The basic process is to take some plant or animal extract that researchers hope might be useful, and go through an exhaustive iterative process of testing its effect against various disease agents. When something useful is found, it is studied further. Then if it proves to be a useful treatment, it's generally synthesized if possible in order to bring production costs down and to maintain stricter control over quality, purity, and dosage. There are many drugs on the market that cannot be synthesized and where the natural compound itself goes through this process of purification and dose control. But at some level, virtually every drug on the market today traces its lineage to a natural compound.

While it's relatively harmless to society for a person to decide to avoid pharmaceutical drugs for themselves, it obviously poses a problem when people who are genuinely sick and need these treatments hear about the conspiracy theory and avoid going to the doctor as a result. When belief in the conspiracy theory is promoted—as we see happening with prominent Hollywood "shockumentary" films promoting natural cures and Big Pharma conspiracy-mongering—sick people suffer. It is far from a harmless conspiracy theory, but given that its roots are both deep and ideological, it is a sad probability that it will remain popular for generations to come.

Skeptoid® Says...

So who makes up "Big Pharma"? You'll recognize some familiar names at the top of the heap, like Johnson & Johnson, Pfizer, Merck, Bayer, Novo Nordisk, Eli Lilly, and more!

PART 6
Space Conspiracy Theories

Yes, NASA is real. But since much of its work is conducted in high-security laboratories and communication centers—and in outer space—NASA is a magnet for conspiratorial claims about UFOs, the Moon landing, and more. If you think about it, NASA is uniquely positioned to be able to pull off just about any nefarious task they want, in complete secrecy—and their reputation as a scientific agency means people will usually believe whatever they say.

For their part, of course, NASA denies secret UFO knowledge and fake Moon landings. Their job is to explore space, they say, not investigate hundreds of UFO reports. Sure, that might be true, but it also fits nicely into what the conspiracy theorists believe NASA would claim anyway. NASA can't win. Tell the truth, and it's regarded as a lie that confirms the conspiracy.

Let's take a look at what conspiracy theorists think is going on in space—and closer to home.

The Black Knight Satellite

Date: 11000 B.C.E.–Present
Location: Low Earth orbit
The Conspirators: NASA, unknown alien civilization
The Victims: Unknown

The Theory

According to conspiracy theorists, the Black Knight satellite is an artificial satellite of alien origin that has been orbiting the Earth for some 13,000 years. NASA and other space agencies know all about it, but they cover up its existence to prevent the general public from panicking from the knowledge of other civilizations. It is even alleged that there is at least one clear photograph of it, taken from the space shuttle *Endeavour.*

The Truth

There is no Black Knight satellite, and never has been. The photograph that allegedly exists of it actually shows a well-documented piece of debris from the space shuttle that took the picture.

The Backstory

Black Knight was first "discovered" by Nikola Tesla when he picked up a radio signal coming from space in 1899, a repeating click that was so regular that Tesla believed it had to have been artificially and intelligently created. He didn't know what it was at the time, and neither did anyone else. But the signal he received is still being transmitted today.

Then in 1928, Norwegian scientists experimenting with shortwave radio discovered a phenomenon called long delayed echoes (LDEs), and their explanation was that the radio signals were being reflected off something in orbit. This explanation seemed to be confirmed in 1954 when newspapers reported an Air Force announcement that at least two artificial satellites were currently in orbit around the Earth, at a time when no nation yet had such an ability. (It soon came out that this announcement was a hoax made up by an author trying to sell a UFO book, and that the Air Force had never made any such statement. There goes that evidence!)

In 1960, newspapers reported that another unknown object had been found in orbit. It was in an eccentric semi-polar orbit (an elliptical orbit that's almost, but not quite, in line with the Earth's North and South Poles), and it made a complete trip around this orbit every 104.5 minutes. Astronaut Gordon Cooper's 1963 flight on the Mercury-Atlas 9 mission brought a new dimension to the story. Over the radio, he reported seeing a strange, greenish object. NASA later reported that his CO_2 levels were wonky and he had been hallucinating. However, about 100 people at NASA's Muchea Tracking Station near Perth, Australia, also saw the object on the radar screens. Conspiracy theorists claimed that NASA was covering up whatever the object was.

Stories about Black Knight always give a special mention to Duncan Lunan, a Scottish researcher who set about finding the cause of the LDEs in 1973. In studying the Norwegian data, he found that by plotting the LDE on a graph, the graph ended up looking like a map of the stars. This map led to the star Epsilon Boötis, a double star in the constellation of Boötes. One principal star, Arcturus, was not where it is today, but rather where it was 12,600 years ago. Thus, the story was born that Black Knight came to us from Epsilon Boötes 12,600 years ago.

Skeptoid® Says...

The photos taken from the *Endeavour* space shuttle during the STS–88 NASA mission are widely available online; do an image search for "Black Knight satellite" to find them.

Rounding out the story were the photographs of Black Knight taken from the space shuttle. NASA's *Endeavour* launched in 1998, and on a space walk, astronauts reported seeing something. They took numerous high-quality photographs that were soon published on the NASA website; however, they were available only very briefly before being mysteriously taken down. They reappeared on the site later with different URLs and with new descriptions explaining them away as pieces of space junk. But it was too little, too late. The story of the Black Knight satellite had become essentially complete, evidence included.

All that remains unknown is why NASA is denying the existence of Black Knight, what its true purpose is, and who its alien creators might be.

The Explanation

Deconstructing the story of the Black Knight satellite is an exercise in trying to connect dots that don't line up very well. Even the name Black Knight doesn't seem to relate to anything! The name has been used many times in various nations' space programs, most notably by the UK. None of the events surrounding the satellite's discovery actually mention the name Black Night, though. So the name Black Knight was probably added in the modern Internet era.

That first dot to connect came from Tesla, who in 1899 did indeed pick up mysterious radio signals from space. They were regular, repetitive, and gave every indication of being artificially produced. Today, we know what he discovered: pulsars, which are stars that emit a beam of electromagnetic radiation. (These signals are so regularly timed that when they were rediscovered in 1967, researchers playfully named them LGMs, for Little Green Men.) So, as it turns out, Tesla's discovery had nothing to do with any alien satellite.

Nor, it transpired, did the Norwegian discovery of LDEs. As scientists have since learned, shortwave radio signals echo back about eight seconds after they're sent, and although the reasons are not fully understood, they have to do with effects from the Earth's ionosphere. LDE signals are not dependent upon, or correlated with, the existence or positions of any artificial satellites.

The object reported in 1960 to be circling the Earth on a semi-polar orbit was soon identified by the Air Force as the second of two casings from the *Discoverer VIII* launch. (Today, we know the Discoverer program was a cover for the Corona program, which launched spy satellites into polar orbits.)

And as much as Black Knight satellite proponents like to claim Duncan Lunan's LDE analysis as evidence for their apocryphal alien craft, he himself never expressed any such thing. He thought the

LDE reflections came from the Earth's L_5 Lagrangian point, a location 60° behind the Earth on its orbit around the sun. This clearly has no relation to an object in an eccentric semi-polar orbit around the Earth. Lunan himself later retracted his work, in fact, after finding errors in it. With that retraction went the support for the 12,600-year age of Black Knight and its connection with any specific star of origin.

Gordon Cooper's testimony is a bit different. He did report various UFOs during his long career, but he was always adamant that his Mercury-Atlas 9 sighting of a greenish object in 1963 was a total fabrication by UFOlogists. He claims he saw nothing at all, and indeed no official records confirm a radar sighting by 100 people at the Australian tracking station (we do know, however, that nowhere near 100 people could have physically fit in front of the tiny radar screen, so that part of the story is certainly false).

And all of this brings us to the final piece of evidence, those photographs of Black Knight taken by the crew of the *Endeavour*. These photos were indeed taken by the shuttle crew, but there is nothing mysterious about them. During the space walk, a piece of thermal blanket came detached from the inside of the cargo bay and floated out of reach. The astronauts documented it with their cameras. We can also say with certainty that the photos are not of anything on a semi-polar orbit. The shuttle orbited on a semi-*equatorial* orbit, so the shuttle and the debris would have passed each other at about 36,000 kmh if the debris had been on a semi-polar orbit—far too fast to be seen, and much too fast for anyone (let alone a spacesuit-clad astronaut) to take a picture. The fact that multiple pictures were taken is incontrovertible proof that the object was nearby and following the shuttle on its exact same orbit.

All in all, it's an intriguing story, but unfortunately, no useful evidence can be found to support the existence of any Black Knight satellite, nor of a conspiracy by NASA to cover it up.

Roswell

Date: 1947
Location: Roswell, New Mexico
The Conspirators: US Army Air Forces, other military branches
The Victims: Unclear

The Theory

The story of Roswell is the most famous cover-up conspiracy in all of UFOlogy, and it's based on actual events that UFO authors have strung together into a cohesive narrative of aliens and deception. Strange debris found in 1947 near Roswell Army Air Field was initially described as a "flying disc" in the *Roswell Daily Record*. Even though the story was corrected the next day to identify it as material from a weather balloon, conspiracy theorists thought there might be more to the story. Imaginative authors in the 1970s claimed that the debris was actually a crashed flying saucer containing alien bodies, and that story has become the stuff of conspiracy legend. Today, conspiracy theorists feel that no intelligent person would believe the ludicrous explanation of "weather balloon" to explain a crashed flying saucer with alien bodies, and so their general belief is that the Air Force's explanation was a cover-up.

The Truth

No flying saucer has ever been found crashed at Roswell. What was found in 1947 was debris from a weather balloon, and was well known to the New York University researchers who launched it, and to the Roswell Army Air Field officers who retrieved it.

The Backstory

The Roswell story began when rancher Mac Brazel found some strange debris on the Foster Ranch property 75 miles northwest of Roswell, New Mexico, in 1947. He reported it to the sheriff, who passed the report along to Major Jesse Marcel at nearby Roswell Army Air Field

(RAAF). Marcel released a statement to the *Roswell Daily Record* newspaper, which ran the headline "RAAF Captures Flying Saucer on Ranch in Roswell Region."

However, the next day, the *Roswell Daily Record* printed a correction, stating that it was merely debris from a weather balloon, and this has been the official position of the Air Force ever since (in September of 1947, the US Army Air Forces became the US Air Force).

Skeptoid® Says...

Some believe that the mysterious debris was taken to government-owned facilities for examination—part to the highly classified Area 51 in Nevada for testing, and part to Hangar 18 at Wright-Patterson Air Force Base in Ohio.

Although later accounts have varied considerably, the debris that was initially found consisted of some 5 pounds of aluminum and foil. Army Air Force officials immediately identified it as part of a long, low-frequency antenna train suspended from a weather balloon as part of Project Mogul, intended to detect Soviet nuclear tests by their low-frequency radio burst. The photographs of the debris being examined by Marcel and other officers show material consistent with the Mogul balloon trains. Some have accepted this explanation, and others have not.

Skeptoid® Says...

Talk about the power of suggestion: Mac Brazel had just been reading about UFOs, so he reported the debris he found to the sheriff as such. The sheriff didn't know any better, so he reported it to the Army as such. And, apparently, the reporter from the *Roswell Daily Record* didn't know any better either, and so printed the headline.

Regardless, the story was essentially dormant and largely unknown until 1978, thirty-one years later. The *National Enquirer* tabloid decided to reprint the original uncorrected article from the *Roswell Daily Record*, which identified the debris as a flying saucer. UFOlogist Stanton Friedman, assuming the first story to be the true account, interviewed everyone he could find who was still alive to try and piece together the story, but there wasn't much new information. Two other UFOlogists published the book *The Roswell Incident*, which also didn't add very much.

It wasn't for another eleven years that the story finally took on a life of its own. The TV show *Unsolved Mysteries* devoted a 1989 episode mainly to Friedman and his work. One viewer was a retired mortician, Glenn Dennis, who had worked in Roswell in 1947. Dennis contacted Friedman to share his recollections. Together, the two reconstructed what they believed was an accurate time line of extraordinary events, based entirely upon Dennis's forty-two-year-old memories. This reconstruction forms the entire basis of the modern Roswell mythology, including alien bodies, multiple crash sites, and an aggressive military cover-up. The 1991 book *UFO Crash at Roswell* details the complete reconstructed tale, based on Friedman's interviews with Dennis. This book captures all the out-of-this-world theories you've ever heard about the Roswell incident.

The Explanation

It turns out that Glenn Dennis's memory wasn't very good, and Friedman was perhaps a little too eager and imaginative.

Under tremendous pressure from UFOlogists and the general public to reveal these alien discoveries, New Mexico Congressman Steven Schiff made an official request through the General Accounting Office, and the Air Force detailed Col. Richard L. Weaver and 1st Lt. James McAndrew to dig up everything they could to explain the extraordinary claims in the book. Their findings were compiled into the book *The Roswell Report: Fact versus Fiction in the New Mexico Desert*, which was made freely available to the general public. It is highly entertaining—you should definitely check it out.

Weaver and McAndrew were indeed able to concretely identify all of Dennis's memories—but it turns out they did not occur in one single event in 1947, but were many unrelated events over a twelve-year period. Most of them happened in the 1950s.

For example, Dennis recalled going to the base one day on business and finding everyone very upset for some reason unknown to him. He remembered a tall, red-haired colonel, accompanied by a black sergeant, who angrily threw Dennis off the base and threatened him. This incident is usually pointed to as part of the cover-up effort. Whatever this incident was, however, could not have happened in 1947, because the

Air Force did not begin racial integration until 1949—and the only red-haired colonel ever stationed there, Lee Ferrell, didn't start until 1956.

Dennis also recalled an Air Force nurse friend being very upset over the autopsy of three small bodies that were mangled, burned black, and emitted fumes so noxious they had to be moved. The nurse soon disappeared and Dennis was not able to learn what happened to her. In fact, these bodies came from a 1956 crash of a KC-97G aircraft, which killed all eleven crew in an intense cabin fire. Little remained of the bodies. Three of the charred corpses were soaked in fuel and had to be moved from the military base because of the strong fumes, and they were autopsied instead at Dennis's mortuary. The nurse friend who disappeared was Lt. Eileen Mae Fanton, who was taken to a hospital in Texas in 1955 and medically retired—but the dates prove that these incidents were unrelated. (Dennis had been unable to learn her fate simply because of privacy regulations.)

The most amusing of Dennis's recollections concerned a humanoid creature with a huge head walking under its own power into the base hospital. Even this story was tracked down. Captain Dan Fulgham was struck on the head by a balloon gondola in 1959 and developed a magnificent hematoma, which made his forehead and face swell up. But he said he felt all right, and smoked a cigarette and hung around like that for a while before heading into the hospital for treatment.

Weaver and McAndrew's report also contains extensive documentation of the debris that was collected. Army Air Forces officers recognized it immediately as a rawin target (short for radio-wind and pronounced RAY-win), a battery-powered telemetry instrument that is lifted by a weather balloon. Although the purpose of Project Mogul was classified, the actual materials its rawin was made of were commonplace, so they were not difficult for the officers to identify.

In short, ample evidence exists that the full scope of the Roswell incident was the recovery of some boring weather balloon equipment that was quickly identified and then forgotten. Zero evidence supports the modern reinterpretations of this event, such as multiple crash sites, alien spacecraft, alien bodies, and death threats and cover-ups by a military conspiracy. After more than seventy years, it's unlikely that anything new will emerge.

Area 51

Date: 1955–Present
Location: Nellis Air Force Base, Nevada
The Conspirators: US Air Force and other unspecified US government divisions
The Victims: Not specified

The Theory

Way off in a remote corner of nowhere in the Nevada desert is a great, flat, dry lake bed with an Air Force base sprawling at its edge. As it's inside the vast boundaries of Nellis AFB, it is off limits to civilians, and fenced off with signs warning against trespassers. No small wonder that such a facility draws the curious into suspecting a conspiracy.

The conspiracy theorists call it Area 51, and they claim that the government denies that it (most famous military facility in the world) exists. They believe that an alien spacecraft crashed at Roswell in 1947, and the wreckage was brought here and has been developed by the US government for use as a weapon. They also believe that secret Nazi weapons, including a vehicle very much like a flying saucer, were brought here and their development has continued as well. Even darker, they believe that trespassers who only want to know the truth are often seized and never heard from again. What could the government actually be doing inside this most inner sanctum, the very heart of black ops?

The Truth

Area 51 is actually the National Classified Test Facility, and is used for test flying both new designs for the Air Force, and captured foreign aircraft. There are no alien flying saucers in its hangars.

The Backstory

Area 51 is an actual place. Formally, it is called the National Classified Test Facility inside Nellis Air Force Base in Nevada, and its existence has always been public. The large, flat surface of dry Groom Lake makes it an ideal place for long runways. The test facility was founded in 1955 by Lockheed design chief Kelly Johnson, who needed a place for the Air Force to develop and test his new U-2 spy plane. He gave the remote location a nice name to attract civilian workers: Paradise Ranch. At the time it was public knowledge.

Skeptoid® Says...

Informally, Area 51 has been called The Ranch, Groom Lake, Dreamland, or simply The Site. Radio traffic inside Nellis has referred to it as The Box, Red Square, Homey Airport, and Home Plate. Regardless, Area 51 has emerged as the public's favorite name. (The name comes from its parcel number from when the US Atomic Energy Commission subdivided land to create the National Proving Grounds in 1950, for the testing of nuclear weapons.)

Once the highly classified, top-secret "black programs" began operating there, the veil of secrecy was pulled over Area 51, its employees, and its activities. It's a large facility, easily visible, and yet the Air Force would say nothing about it officially. Conspiracy theorists therefore jumped on it—after all, whenever the government is up to something secret, it's got to be something nefarious.

Much of the modern pop-culture hype about Area 51 is the result of one man who came forward, claiming to have been an employee working on captured alien technology. In 1989, a guy named Bob Lazar told a Las Vegas TV reporter that he had been a civilian engineer at Area 51 assigned to study alien field propulsion systems. He quickly became the darling of TV documentaries looking to sensationalize Area 51, and spoke very openly of his work and his background.

The Explanation

The problem with supporting the conspiratorial claims about Area 51 is that its actual history is pretty well documented, while its conspiratorial history is without any evidence at all, and certainly without scientific plausibility. The types of propulsion technologies described by Lazar aren't simply nonexistent, they're based on purely fictional misrepresentations of physics.

To start, one glaring red flag characterized Lazar's commentary about his secret work, and it's a common one that we see with many such people who claim some insider position. In Lazar's version of Area 51, everything was top secret, and employees were told never to reveal their work. Yet Lazar actually spoke quite freely and openly about his alien propulsion systems. It seems unlikely for both to be true: that Lazar had actually worked there under a threat not to reveal the fact, and that he now traveled around telling his stories openly to anyone who would listen.

However, it seems only the TV producers took Lazar seriously. Amateur investigators immediately discovered that he lied about his educational credentials (he said he graduated from Cal Tech and MIT, yet he never attended either school, much less earned a degree). Actual physicists who listened to Lazar's descriptions of some basic physics revealed that he had no idea what he was talking about, and probably had no physics education whatsoever. For example, he did not appear to understand the difference between gravity and particles; he said that gravity and the strong nuclear force were one and the same, which they're not; and he claimed that an equivalent mass of antimatter could be created by bombarding conventional matter with protons, a flagrant violation of basic arithmetic, as well as a fundamental violation of conservation of energy. Basically, Lazar tossed together a "word salad"—language that sounds sciencey because the words are impressive to a layperson, but that mean nothing to anyone who understands them.

Skeptoid® Says...

Despite declassified files, conspiracy theorists continue publishing strange beliefs about what happens at Area 51, even making claims now proven to be false. In 2011, author Annie Jacobsen published *Area 51: An Uncensored History of America's Top Secret Military Base*, which repeated the claim that the nonexistent "flying saucer" recovered at Roswell in 1947 had been studied at Area 51.

As far as secret projects go, in 1991, the Air Force declassified Project OXCART, and the complete development history of the A-12 and SR-71 spy planes became a matter of public record. We now know that after these programs, Area 51 was mainly the development base for the F-117A stealth fighter (project names HAVE BLUE and SENIOR TREND), as well as a test site for various new technologies. This shows us that Area 51 was quite busy on actual, earthly projects throughout the 1960s, 1970s, and 1980s, and had scant time or resources for anything else.

Adding to the pile of official information about Area 51's activities was the 2007 release of former Area 51 employees from their confidentiality agreements. They're all now free to speak quite openly about all the work that was done there, and they often do. So far, nothing beyond the projects that we know were developed there—and that we've talked about in this chapter—has ever come up in conversation. (Unsurprisingly, the employees' unofficial association, Roadrunners Internationale, does not count hoaxers like Bob Lazar among their membership.)

Despite all of this transparency about what happened at Area 51, some conspiracy theorists say that it's still possible that advanced craft, possibly using alien technology, may still have been tested there. The problem is that this claim can't be reconciled because both the aircraft and their budgets are eventually declassified, and the aircraft end up in museums. Plus, aviation writers and researchers are relentless. We have access to the entire global history of aviation, and although national test programs are littered with aircraft that never made it into production, very few of them differ substantially from conventional aircraft. Nothing using "field propulsion," or anything else from the annals of science fiction, has ever materialized.

The technology currently being developed at Area 51 remains classified, of course, so we don't know what it is. Industry speculation points to various unmanned aerial systems and possibly hypersonic vehicles. But we *still* have never found any reason to suspect anything unworldly.

The Lucifer Project

Date: 1968–?
Location: Outer solar system
The Conspirators: NASA
The Victims: Unclear

The Theory

Large gas giant planets like Jupiter are sometimes called failed stars—they contain all the elements necessary to undergo fusion and become stars, but they lack sufficient mass to collapse under their own gravity and produce sufficient pressure and heat to ignite the process. Hypothetically, if we could somehow make it happen, having a second star in our outer solar system might turn some of the larger moons of Saturn or Jupiter into habitable worlds.

Despite those pesky laws of physics, there is a group of believers who say that NASA has already attempted to do this at least twice, and may do so again. These alleged previous attempts were the *Galileo* probe, which crashed into Jupiter in 2003, and the *Cassini* probe, which crashed into Saturn in 2017. Both probes were powered by RTGs (radioisotope thermoelectric generators), which contain plutonium. Believers say that plutonium can cause a thermonuclear reaction inside the gas giants that should initiate a chain reaction to turn them into stars.

Theorists haven't given any particular reason NASA might have done this, other than the fanciful notion that it might be fun to have some other warm planetoids in the outer solar system.

The Truth

It would be impossible for our solar system's largest gas giants to sustain fusion and become stars, and NASA has never attempted such a ludicrous feat.

The Backstory

The idea of turning a gas giant into a star appears to have originated with Arthur C. Clarke's book *2001: A Space Odyssey*. In this book, he used Saturn as an example, but the movie version (and most subsequent theories) have used Jupiter. Jupiter is far more massive than Saturn, so is a better candidate for the gravitational confinement needed to create sufficient pressure and heat to sustain a chain reaction. In Clarke's stories, the new star was named Lucifer.

When *Galileo* was about to end its mission by crashing into Jupiter, a Dutch engineer and conspiracy theorist named Jacco van der Worp went on the *Coast to Coast AM* radio program to explain his belief that this scheme is exactly what NASA had in mind. The RTGs on *Galileo* were chosen instead of more conventional solar power, van der Worp believed, because the true hidden purpose of the mission was to ignite Jupiter into a star, and NASA needed the thermonuclear potential of the RTGs. Van der Worp called NASA's plan the Lucifer Project.

Nothing happened, of course, when *Galileo* finally did crash into Jupiter in 2003. However, a few months later, a dark spot was observed on the planet's surface. Other conspiracy theorists like Richard C. Hoagland were quick to claim that this was the result of *Galileo's* thermonuclear explosion—which, for some unknown reason, had not successfully triggered the desired chain reaction.

The 2017 collision of *Cassini* into Saturn also produced no dramatic change from planet to star, and at this point it's unclear if theorists believe that NASA intends to try again.

The Explanation

NASA employs people who understand physics pretty well, and unfortunately for proponents of the Lucifer Project, the laws of physics dictate that such a project would never work.

Gravitational confinement is the main problem. In order to sustain a thermonuclear reaction, a star needs to have a mass greater than about 0.08 solar masses, otherwise it will not have enough gravity to squeeze its core into a mass hot and dense enough. Jupiter is only 0.001 solar masses, and Saturn is only 0.0003. So neither planet is remotely close enough to ever sustain a chain reaction. Even if we somehow did trigger a thermonuclear device inside them, the fusion reaction would involve only critical masses of fuel inside that device.

Back here on Earth, we have detonated thermonuclear devices many, many, many times greater than what could be achieved using the plutonium from an RTG. The largest was the Soviet Union's 1961 Tsar Bomba hydrogen bomb test with a yield of 50 megatons. You'll note that Earth was not converted into a small sun when this happened. One of the reasons is that the Earth is not hot and dense enough, and because it is too small to achieve the required gravitational confinement. The same lack of chain reaction would result if a device was exploded on (or in) another planetary body, like Jupiter or Saturn, that is also too small.

Skeptoid® Says...

Arthur C. Clarke knew that his scheme couldn't work within the confines of the laws of physics. In fact, in his book, one of the characters said he "can see a dozen objections" to the plan. That's why Clarke's fictional execution of Lucifer required the intervention of powerful aliens, who had some presumed power of creation beyond physical laws.

The other major problem with the Lucifer Project theory is that an RTG cannot explode like a nuclear bomb. First of all, it uses the wrong grade of plutonium. An RTG uses reactor-grade plutonium, while a bomb uses weapons-grade plutonium. The difference is the relative proportions of Pu-238 and Pu-240. Conspiracy theorists say that this alone does not make it impossible because in 1962, the United States did successfully detonate a weapon using reactor-grade plutonium. The yield was low, but it worked.

The second reason the Lucifer Project cannot happen has to do with the structure of an RTG. A nuclear explosion requires a quantity of fissile material sufficient to reach critical mass. For Pu-238, this quantity is about 10 kg. To trigger it, it must be imploded by a single instantaneous explosive force striking it from all directions. This crushes it together enough that the fusion reaction is triggered. The shape of this mass and of the implosion force must be exactly right, or it won't work.

The RTGs used in *Galileo* and *Cassini* were the GPHS-RTG, General Purpose Heat Source RTG. This design uses seventy-two marshmallow-sized pellets of Pu-238 for a total of only 8.1 kg, short of critical mass. Each pellet is individually clad in iridium, separated by membranes, and each group of four is encased in a graphite impact shell. These impact shells are stacked into sleeves. Eighteen of these shells make up the GPHS. Because of this intricate design, there is no plausible scenario in which all the Pu-238 could magically become separated from the other materials in the structure and then somehow be grouped together into a single mass. Even if that *did* happen, there is not enough plutonium there for a critical mass, and no explosive material at all is included in the design to provide the implosive force.

Some conspiracy theorists have posited that the heat of reentry into the thick atmosphere of the gas giant would create sufficient heat and pressure to trigger the thermonuclear detonation. This is not true, and even if it were, pretty much everything else is missing from the equation that would make a detonation possible.

Claims that solar panels are usually used for these missions are also just plain wrong. In deep space, there is not enough sunlight for solar panels to power the spacecraft. Enter RTGs, which function reliably for decades with no moving parts and no dependence on sunlight. That's why NASA always uses them for deep space missions.

From the beginning to the end, every single link in the chain required to make this conspiracy possible is broken. The RTGs cannot explode, the planets cannot burn as stars, and NASA's scientists know these facts very well. So clearly the *Galileo* and *Cassini* missions were not covers for the Lucifer Project, which would never be attempted— at least by people who know what they're doing.

The Moon Landing Hoax

Date: 1969–1972
Location: An undisclosed movie set
The Conspirators: NASA, unknown filmmakers
The Victims: Soviet Union

The Theory

Despite overwhelming historical and physical evidence, a moon-rock-solid community of believers worldwide hold that NASA's Apollo missions did not actually land any humans on the Moon. Some believe the spacecraft did actually launch, but were unmanned; others say the astronauts did fly, but never went farther than Earth's orbit; still others say the *Apollo* spacecraft merely orbited the Moon and returned; and yet another group insists that nothing was ever actually launched at all. The only thing they seem to agree on is that the official acknowledged history of the Apollo program is false, and no humans have ever set foot on the Moon. They claim the pictures and videos were faked on a movie set, and that all the other evidence is fake as well.

Why do they think the Moon landings were hoaxed? Because the United States was in a Cold War with the Soviet Union, and wanted the ultimate propaganda victory.

The Truth

NASA's Apollo missions did land twelve Americans on the Moon, a fact that even the Soviets don't dispute.

The Backstory

Doubting the Moon landings has its roots in an unexpected place: Christian fundamentalism. The original International Flat Earth Research Society was dedicated to proving the literal truth of the Bible, and some do interpret a few Bible passages as meaning that the Earth is flat. The Society's founder, Samuel Shenton, first began arguing against the reality of the Gemini program—which preceded the

Apollo Moon program—as soon as we started to get the first photos of the Earth taken from space.

The hoax narrative did not really go mainstream until 1976, when Bill Kaysing, who had been a publications analyst at Rocketdyne (a rocket engine design and production company) in the early 1960s, self-published a pamphlet titled *We Never Went to the Moon: America's Thirty Billion Dollar Swindle.* In it, he proposed a plot that was echoed in Peter Hyams's 1977 movie *Capricorn One* about a fake Mars launch, in which the astronauts sneak out of the capsule and transfer to a safe location to make counterfeit TV transmissions.

Skeptoid® Says...

Kaysing sued Hyams for copyright infringement of his theory. Though the lawsuit was unsuccessful, it brought a lot of attention to his version of the story, and from then on, the Moon landing hoax belief has been taken seriously by some 6–7 percent of Americans, and by about four times as many Europeans, according to one 2009 study done by the UK's Institution of Engineering and Technology.

As far as evidence, theorists point to the photos taken on the Moon and note the following:

- Light seems to be coming from angles that could only be consistent with studio lighting and not a distant sun.
- Dust behaved impossibly, including not having been blown away by the rocket motor.
- American flag flaps in a wind that is supposed to be nonexistent in space.

One science-based argument that many Moon hoax believers make is that the Earth's Van Allen radiation belts are a region of space too lethal for humans to pass through. If true, it would be impossible for humans to ever fly outside of a low Earth orbit.

The Explanation

The very best proof that humans went to the Moon is the rocks that were brought back. They bear physical proof of having been in space, specifically on the Moon, and brought to Earth in a protected artificial environment. The characteristics of these rocks aren't even things NASA can fake:

- Using rubidium-strontium dating, the rocks are shown to be 4.46 billion years old, older than any on Earth. We have no way to fake this result.

- They also bear what are called zap pits, microscopic craters from impacts with micrometeors at up to 80,000 kph. We don't have any way to fire projectiles that fast on Earth.

- They contain cosmogenic nuclides, which are isotopes that damage the crystals in the rocks. These cosmogenic nuclides can only be created by bombardment from high-energy cosmic rays, but the Earth's atmosphere blocks cosmic rays from doing this to rocks on Earth.

- We know these rocks didn't come to Earth naturally as meteors, because their pitted surfaces are pristine. All meteors that pass through Earth's atmosphere are covered in fusion crusts, or a melted outer layer.

Perhaps the best certification of the Moon rocks' authenticity comes from foreign scientists who have studied them. Even the United States' enemies at the time couldn't dispute them (the Soviet scientists especially would have loved nothing better than to prove them fake, but they couldn't).

Apollo 12 astronauts also retrieved about 10 kg of pieces from *Surveyor 3*, an unmanned probe that landed on the Moon in 1967. The glass from its camera lens shows the same type of cosmic ray damage found in the rocks, incontrovertible proof that men brought it back from space.

It is true that traveling through the Van Allen radiation belts does expose the astronauts to high levels of radiation, but people can survive going through it. The Apollo engineers chose a trajectory that carried the astronauts through a narrow part of the radiation belts as quickly as possible. Nevertheless, they were exposed for about an hour. This exposes astronauts to about 1 rem, which is what you get from about 100 chest X-rays. That's only about 1 percent of what you'd need to get the first signs of radiation sickness.

Once on the Moon, the astronauts place retroreflectors on the ground at each landing site. A retroreflector is a panel covered with little cubical right-angled mirrors that reflect laser light back at exactly the same angle it came in. During the Apollo program, many nations, including the Soviet Union, verified these retroreflectors by shining their own lasers at them.

Skeptoid® Says...

Interestingly, the mere presence of retroreflectors doesn't prove that any humans were actually on the Moon, because unmanned probes have also taken retroreflectors to the Moon. But it does prove beyond all doubt that all the Apollo missions flew and landed exactly where NASA says they did, because *something* brought the retroreflectors there.

For a long time, hoax believers questioned why there were no photographs of the Apollo landing sites taken from Earth. Surely our best observatories' telescopes should be able to see that, including the Hubble space telescope. The science here is actually a bit surprising. In fact, the Apollo landing sites are too small for Hubble to see them. Hubble is great at seeing things extremely far away, so long as they are incredibly enormous—the size of a star, nebula, or galaxy. The biggest objects we left on the Moon are no bigger than a car— simply too small to be seen from Earth, even using our biggest telescopes. It wasn't until 2009 that the *Lunar Reconnaissance Orbiter* spacecraft was able to take close-up photos of the sites from lunar orbit. Why was its camera able to see what even Hubble could not? Simple: the LRO was 17,000 times closer to the Apollo sites than Hubble. Although Hubble's telescopic lens is much bigger and better than the LRO's smaller telescopic lens, it isn't 17,000 times better.

Perhaps the most important takeaway from any discussion of the Moon landing hoax is that no scientific rebuttal will ever be able to keep up with every claim made by the conspiracy theorists. That's why you will easily find loads of information online that claims to prove the Moon landings were faked that is not addressed here. Unfortunately, pseudoscience will always spread faster and more aggressively than science.

The Face on Mars

Date: 1976
Location: Cydonia, Mars
The Conspirators: NASA
The Victims: Unknown

The Theory

When the Mars probe *Viking I* sent a set of photos from Mars in 1976, one shot in particular set off wild speculation that life was or had been present on Mars. One photo appeared to be a human face, perhaps even sculpted, about a full square kilometer in size. It is no exaggeration to say that it set the world abuzz. Skeptics dismissed it as a fun coincidence, a hill with shadows that, at first glance, did look a bit like a face. But others claimed the resemblance was far too close to be anything but a deliberate artificial carving and that NASA degraded or Photoshopped the new images in order to cover up the existence of the civilization that built the face. Conspiracy theorists pointed out that many other constructions in the immediate vicinity also appear to be artificial, including pyramids and geometrically shaped buildings. The region of Mars is called Cydonia, and if you believe the conspiracy, NASA seems determined to block humankind's first contact with this enigmatic race that has tried so hard to signal their existence to us.

The Truth

As we know from recent high-resolution photographs, the hill on Mars that some believe is a carefully carved face has no interesting features at all; it only appeared so in the earliest photo because of black dots where data was missing.

The Backstory

When NASA engineers first discovered the face, they thought it was pretty funny. All of *Viking*'s photos were speckled with black dots, which were places where the camera didn't capture data. It is thanks to the fortuitous placement of about eight such dots that the hill looks reminiscent of a face. NASA published the photo, never imagining that people would think it was actually a face. Much to their dismay, they soon discovered they'd created a whole subculture of people who believed there was an advanced civilization of megasculptors on Mars.

This group was led by Richard C. Hoagland, a conspiracy theorist who spent much of his career trying to publicly associate himself with the US space program or famous planetariums or *anyone* who would listen to his various alternate theories. He has proposed something he calls "hyperdimensional physics" in which all fundamental understandings of the universe are wrong, and only he is right (despite having no academic credentials). He claims the Face on Mars is only one feature in what is a great citadel of pyramids and other monuments, despite a total lack of evidence and voluminous contradictory evidence proving that no such citadel exists.

Skeptoid® Says...

Hoagland has even tried to claim that he was the creator of the plaque attached to the *Pioneer 10* space probe, when there is abundant true history to show it was created by Carl Sagan and others, and that Hoagland had no remote connection to it. The plaque shows a male and female figure and some information about where the ship came from. It is intended as a peaceful communication to any extraterrestrial life that might see it.

In 1987, Hoagland published *The Monuments of Mars: A City on the Edge of Forever*. This book has become something of a Holy Bible for ancient monuments constructed on Mars, the Moon, and other places. It is full of conspiratorial gobbledygook, flagrant pseudoscience, and outright untruths about the solar system.

In 1998 and 2001, the *Mars Global Surveyor* spacecraft took dramatically improved pictures of the Cydonia region with a resolution of only 1.5 m per pixel, and it became immediately clear that the Face on Mars did not look anything like a face. It was an unremarkable knoll without any especially distinguishing features. And then as if that wasn't enough, the High Resolution Imaging Science Experiment

(HiRISE) on board the *Mars Reconnaissance Orbiter* spacecraft (launched in 2005) took a picture five times sharper, all the way down to about 30 cm per pixel. Still no face. We now have excellent radar and 3-D data of Cydonia, and none of the features hold up to the initial expectations so many were hoping for. No pyramids, no buildings, no giant sculpted faces.

What we *can* tell from the 3-D data is that when the light is hitting the hill from a certain angle, two contours fill with shadow and look generally like an eye and a mouth on one half of a face. The other half of the face is in complete shadow.

Despite all this substantial evidence, Hoagland has not slowed down. The conspiracy community now claims that the NASA images have been "degraded" to obscure the face's true details, which is silly because the hill's features are clearly visible in great detail. Still absolutely insistent that it is an artificial face, Hoagland has also moved on to other structures throughout the solar system that he believes were constructed by advanced civilizations, including skyscrapers on the dark side of the Moon.

The Explanation

In science, we often point to the law of large numbers when confronted with a manifestation that appears unlikely. This law refers to the mathematical probability of highly unlikely events popping up at predictable intervals. The Face on Mars is about 1 square kilometer, and the entire surface of Mars is about 150 million square kilometers. If we posit that the likelihood of any given patch of surface looking somewhat like a face is one in a million, then the probability is that there are some 150 such faces on Mars.

Believe it or not, there are certainly many, many such faces on Earth. In 2013, a company called onformative created a program that automatically scanned *Google Earth* looking for natural features that look like faces, and many of the results were striking. Alberta, Canada, is home to the Badlands Guardian, which when viewed from the air appears to be an astonishingly realistic depiction of a Native American seen in profile, wearing a full feathered headdress. A natural gas well and road that were put in happen to make it look exactly like he's listening to an iPod (trust me—head to *Google* for a picture). France has its Apache Head of Ebihens, a face jutting out from a hillside. There is the Queen's Head in Taiwan, the sleeping giant of Pedra da Gávea in Brazil, the Hoburgsgubben in Sweden, and the Devil's Head in North Carolina. And, of course, there is the most famous natural face of all: the Man in the Moon.

Skeptoid® Says...

The tendency of our brains to spot faces in ordinary objects is called pareidolia. It is an evolved trait in all animals to help us recognize our parents and others of our kind. If we didn't have pareidolia, we would never be able to recognize cartoon characters as being people. Two dots and a line don't actually look much like two eyes and a mouth, but our human brains make the connection instantly.

We can safely conclude that the existence of a conspiracy by NASA to cover up an advanced civilization on Mars is nonsense. There's also no rational reason why NASA (or anyone else) would do such a thing. The law of large numbers and the phenomenon of pareidolia sufficiently account for any perceived similarity of the Cydonia formation to an actual face, and as the modern imaging proves, it doesn't actually even look like a face!

PART 7
Urban Legend Conspiracy Theories

Who doesn't love a good urban legend? They tend to be lighthearted mysteries that many of us have heard of, but are often more mainstream and relatable than hardcore political conspiracy theories. Sometimes they involve a story heard from a friend of a friend of someone who was involved, but they nearly always reference something that you vaguely remember hearing in the news and that has the air of plausibility—something that *could* happen to you. Sometimes they're funny, sometimes they're weird, sometimes they're scary.

It's the familiarity that is key to urban legends' tendency to spread. We're all much more likely to pass on a story we've heard if the person it happened to was a friend of a friend, or if it happened nearby, or if it involved a service we all use or something we're all familiar with. Urban legends spread virally nowadays, because nothing travels faster on the Internet than a cool story.

Is that arcade game you've always played really a way for the government to spy on you? Is it possible that Finland isn't a real place? Was TWA Flight 800 shot down by the United States? Urban legends—believe them or not—will always at least get your attention.

Hearst and Hemp

Date: 1930
Location: United States
The Conspirators: William Randolph Hearst, DuPont, Federal Bureau of Narcotics
The Victims: The hemp industry and marijuana users

The Theory

Cotton and timber are planted in much higher amounts than hemp. Yet many marijuana enthusiasts claim that hemp is a superior industrial product to both cotton fiber and wood fiber, so why is its planting so marginalized?

The answer, they say, is that newspaper publisher William Randolph Hearst lobbied against hemp to protect his vast wood-fiber paper holdings. That's why many states went so far as to make marijuana illegal.

The Truth

Hearst was a buyer of paper, not a seller. He would have benefited from increased competition in the paper market from hemp. The reason hemp wasn't planted in greater amounts is that hemp is a terrible fiber for newspaper, and most other products that need finer, softer threads. Hearst had nothing at all to do with laws to ban marijuana, which were in place long before he came along. States had been banning marijuana largely as an action against immigrant classes, who were its main users. The war on marijuana was driven by racism, not a newspaper magnate.

The Backstory

The story of Hearst lobbying to get hemp and marijuana banned to protect his holdings did not exist until 1985, when pro-marijuana activist Jack Herer published a small book called *The Emperor Wears No Clothes.* Herer's book is still popular today. In it, Herer expanded upon two popular beliefs and invented a third. He greatly exaggerated the industrial value of hemp, and he greatly exaggerated the medicinal value of cannabis. The myth that he invented was that Hearst and his "vast timber holdings," along with the DuPont family that produced nylon, were allegedly afraid of hemp competition.

In fact, Hearst did briefly own one processing mill, the Dexter Sulphite Pulp and Paper Company in New York, in the hopes that it would provide him with cheap paper; but the paper it produced turned out not to work well for newspapers, so he sold it to Kimberly-Clark.

The only significant land holdings Hearst owned were a 270,000-acre ranch in San Simeon, California, a lease on the 50,000-acre Wheeler Ranch in Northern California, and the 900,000-acre Babícora Ranch in Mexico. Neither San Simeon nor Babícora were ever used for logging. After Hearst's death, his trustees did do limited logging on Wheeler Ranch. In his lifetime, however, Hearst never sold a splinter of wood for paper manufacturing. He simply wasn't in that business.

Nearly all of his newsprint was imported from Canada. By 1939, its rising prices seriously impacted Hearst. Had there been a viable alternative in the market, the competition would have helped drive down paper prices for him. Hemp was never that alternative. Its fibers are coarse and suitable for products like cardboard, but it simply doesn't work for finer paper products.

Skeptoid® Says...

There is another popular urban legend that says when George H.W. Bush was shot down in World War II, his parachute and its lines were both made from hemp; his shoes were stitched from hemp; his plane's engine was lubricated with hemp seed oil; and the ship that picked him up had rigging, lines, and fire hoses all made from hemp. So far as researchers have determined, none of this is true. The United States was using cotton for most of these products and had little hemp fiber on hand. Plus, Bush was rescued by the submarine USS *Finback*, not by a ship with rigging.

World War II did see a surge in the demand for hemp fiber; in fact, a 1942 war propaganda film titled *Hemp for Victory* intended to encourage its planting. The vast majority of industrial hemp in the United States had been imported from overseas, and when war with

Japan hampered those imports, cotton had to do double duty. The calls for increased domestic hemp production were too little, too late, and when the war ended, the industry had not materialized in any meaningful way.

The Explanation

While Herer's efforts to promote marijuana by touting hemp may have fallen flat, he was not entirely wrong that powerful forces played a role in the banning of recreational marijuana. It's just wasn't Hearst or the DuPont family.

Marijuana's doom came from two fronts in the early twentieth century: the institutionalized racism inherent in the criminal justice system, and the evangelical Christianity that triggered Prohibition. Throughout World War I, anti-immigrant sentiment ran high in the United States. Making the lives of immigrants harder was one way that law enforcement tried to discourage them from coming here. Marijuana use was high among Chinese immigrants in California (for whom cannabis was a common traditional remedy) and in many poorer black and Latino communities nationwide. After Prohibition was passed, marijuana use skyrocketed, notably among Mexican farm workers who could no longer have a drink to relax after work. Volumes of historical research published in such journals as the *Virginia Law Review*, *Contemporary Drug Problems*, and *Public Health Reports* reveal that enforcement of laws against marijuana was almost entirely against minority ethnic groups.

Harry Anslinger, commissioner of the Federal Bureau of Narcotics, was one of the most powerful crusaders against marijuana. It was Anslinger who began calling it marijuana, a Spanish word, so that it would be perceived to be associated with low-class or criminal immigrants. Before 1930, it was called Indian hemp, or *Cannabis indica*.

Anslinger's assault was multipronged. Educational films such as *Reefer Madness* in the 1930s cemented public sentiment against marijuana. Anslinger fed newspapers a constant feast of hysterical press releases blaming murders and many other crimes on people using the drug.

Anslinger's swan song was the Marihuana Tax Act of 1937 (yes, spelled with an H). This provided a legal way for farmers to sell hemp (so long as they paid the tax) but simultaneously made the sale of recreational marijuana (which was, of course, done without taxes) a federal crime. It was opposed, unsuccessfully, by the American Medical Association, as medicinal uses of marijuana were indeed on the rise—until the act passed.

All of this was going on completely independently of William Randolph Hearst. The closest connection he had to the decline of either hemp or marijuana was that his newspapers, like all newspapers in the country, eagerly trumpeted Anslinger's press releases. But the forces that were already in motion to ban recreational marijuana were virtually unstoppable. Industrial hemp was doomed to find its own place as a fair material for some uses, mainly boutique clothing and food products, but not a very good one for many.

There Is No Finland

Date: 1945
Location: Eastern Sweden
The Conspirators: Japanese and Russian governments
The Victims: Residents of Eastern Sweden

The Theory

It sounds almost too bizarre to believe, but some people think that the country of Finland (which separates Russia from the Baltic Sea) is actually not there—instead of the landmass shown on maps, it is actually just more Baltic Sea. Thus, people who believe themselves Finns living in Finland are actually located in eastern Sweden, north of where they think they are. The story states that all governments are complicit in agreeing to alter maps and GPS data in order to fool everyone into thinking that this section of the Baltic Sea is the fictional country of Finland.

The Truth

Finland exists.

The Backstory

Much of this claim depends on the alleged backstory of Japanese overfishing in their local waters in the late 1940s, and the consequent need to find new fishing grounds. A glance through the pages of a history book tells us this is not very likely because prior to the 1960s, the idea of overfishing in the ocean didn't really exist. There hadn't been any decline in any fishing stocks—not counting certain species of whales—and no nations had ever had to do anything about it. So it's very doubtful that the Japanese faced critical shortages as early as 1950.

Prior to World War II, Japan had a thriving fishing industry, one of the strongest in the world. But the war effort devastated it, and they actually experienced severe famine in the closing year of the war.

After the war, rebuilding their fishing industry was a major priority for the occupying forces. The Allies invested in it heavily—so successfully that by 1952, the revitalized Japanese fishing industry exceeded its pre-war size. Thus, this "need to find new fishing grounds" around 1950 can't be accurate. So much for the fundamental motivation of the alleged conspirators.

Another facet of the overfishing narrative is that after World War II, Russia had starvation problems, and because Japanese waters were overfished, the two nations hatched a plan to solve both of their issues. Japan would fish in the Baltic Sea, and would share its catch with Russia. Russia would construct the Trans-Siberian Railway for Japan to transport the fish. Win-win!

Skeptoid® Says...

To support the conspiracy, the theory claims that the Trans-Siberian Railway was built after World War II, but the fact is that its first transcontinental route had been completed during World War I, some thirty years earlier.

The grandest part of the plan was the strategy to protect the Japanese fishing boats from international regulators: the two nations would pretend that there is no Baltic Sea in that area—that instead it is some new country called Finland; thus, no regulators would think to check there for fishing boats. All the other nations of the world agreed to alter their maps and GPS data as a gesture of goodwill toward these two nations, which had both suffered so terribly during World War II.

The Explanation

Finland has a long history, stretching back some 9,000 years to when it was first settled as the glaciers receded from the Ice Age. Plenty of evidence proves that Finland existed as a nation, by name, for many centuries. Just about every ancient text in Scandinavia mentions Finland by name. There is an immense amount of ancient documentation of the early Finnish wars from the thirteenth and fourteenth centuries. There is also an eleventh-century runestone named U 582 on which *Finland* is carved, and also a thirteenth-century runestone named G 319 that bears the name as well.

But these only prove that a region called Finland existed; it doesn't prove that it is located where the maps say it is. Proving that is even easier. Go to the coast of Estonia, maybe to its capital city, Tallinn, and look north. On practically any clear day, you can actually see Finland; it's only about 37 miles away. One other method proves Finland is there: at night, the bright city lights of Finland's capital city Helsinki cast a glow in the sky over what the maps show is Helsinki, but what the conspiracy theory claims is open ocean. That's a lot of lights for a smattering of Japanese fishing boats.

It turns out that the only history that's related to this conspiracy happened in 2014 on the online forum *Reddit*. There was a discussion in which people were sharing stories of things they learned from their parents that they grew up assuming were normal, only to later discover that they weren't. One user, using the online name Raregan, answered:

> My parents never believed in Finland, I grew up to never believe in Finland until I researched it further. It's a pretty heated topic in my family.

Asked why, he continued:

> Well firstly they say that the actual "place of Finland" is just Eastern Sweden. Helsinki is in Eastern Sweden and when people fly there it's not like they would notice.
>
> World maps are altered as it's a UN conspiracy to keep people believing in Finland. And the idea that an entire country is made up seems so bizarre that nobody would ever believe it, making it easy to do.
>
> Finland's main company, Nokia, is apparently owned by the Japanese and they're a main player in this.
>
> Now as for "why" people would want to invent Finland as a country that's a bit more in depth and there's a few reasons as to why Sweden and Russia go along with it but it's mostly to do with Japanese fishing rights.
>
> You see the Japanese love their sushi but tight fishing regulations and public outcry mean they can't fish as much as they want. So after the Cold War they agreed with Russia to create

a "landmass" called Finland where they could fish. After all, if people thought there was a country there nobody would expect the Japanese to be harpooning whales would they?

The fish is then transported through Russia where a small percentage of the food is given to the population (they were of course starving at the time of Finland being invented), and then is shipped to Japan under the disguise of "Nokia" products. Japan is apparently one of the world's largest importers of Nokia products despite the fact that "nobody there owns a Nokia phone" apparently.

The crux of all this however, and my favourite part, is the homage that the Japanese gave to this entire conspiracy theory.

What do fish have? Fins. Therefore they named their imaginary country Finland.

So far as anyone has found, this one *Reddit* post constitutes the entirety of the evidence that Finland doesn't exist.

But if you still find this one old *Reddit* post more persuasive than everything about Finland in the entire world, then simply board the Tallinn to Helsinki ferry from Estonia. In about two hours, you'll be in Finland. By 2030 you will be able to drive there through the Helsinki to Tallinn Tunnel.

Men in Black

Date: 1956–Present
Location: Worldwide
The Conspirators: Unknown government or alien agencies
The Victims: UFO eyewitnesses

The Theory

Ever since the flying saucer phenomenon became a part of pop culture in the 1950s, there has been a parallel belief in Men in Black. Their descriptions vary somewhat, but all share the black clothing, usually a plain black suit. Often they are very large, and often their facial features have something just a little bit unusual. Some believe they are government agents; others believe they are alien beings trying to look like humans. All believe their purpose is to intimidate UFO witnesses into staying silent, to protect the secret knowledge of alien visitors to the Earth.

The Truth

Although some government agents have no doubt worn black suits at certain times in their career, there has never been any reliable evidence of anyone matching the descriptions and described behavior of Men in Black. At least, that is, not outside the realm of blockbuster movies.

The Backstory

The stories often go something like this:

> Standing at the door were two tall men, but only one spoke, while the other made only odd twitches of his head. The strange man repeatedly asked in broken sentences to come in and discuss Peter's UFO sighting. Peter asked who they were, but instead of identifying themselves they simply repeated the request to come in. They had no eyebrows, no stubble, no blemishes,

almost as if their skin was plastic. No matter what Peter asked them, they could only repeat the same broken sentences.

Or this:

They were young men, tall, and dressed poorly in very cheap suits that didn't quite match. They wore black sunglasses and their hair was so greased it appeared to be a single mass. I refused their request to come in and they seemed to quickly get nervous, and when I asked another question or two, they suddenly turned and scurried back to their car. It looked like a long black Cadillac, but made no noise as it drove away. I ran out and copied the license plate number, which I gave to the police to report the men as suspicious. The next day when the police came by, they told me that plate number was invalid, and to call again if the men ever came back. I am certain I copied it down correctly.

Or this:

The visitor would only stand in the middle of the lawn, and ignored our invitation to come up into the light. He seemed to be having trouble breathing, and kept asking to learn about the UFO we reported. As we spoke I noticed he had some kind of red wire coming out of his leg which appeared to go up under his shirt. Soon my wife went back into the house, and right away he began backing away toward the street. A dark car came along with no headlights and stopped precisely when he stepped backward off the curb. He reached behind himself to get into the car, which seemed to be illuminated inside with a green light. The car drove away into the night, still with no headlights.

The reports have come from eyewitnesses to UFOs, and even to some who only heard about UFO sightings, since the 1950s. There don't seem to be any reports of people being harmed, only frightened, called upon, and followed. There are no photographs of Men in Black; something seems to go wrong with security cameras whenever they appear.

These foreboding characters were first reported in the 1956 book *They Knew Too Much about Flying Saucers*, a nonfiction collection of stories, compiled and published by UFO writer Gray Barker. The book tells of a number of UFO researchers, once prominent, who went silent, one by one, after being visited by the Men in Black.

Barker had been in a unique position to collect these stories. In 1952 he began writing for a periodical called *Space Review*, which had previously been the one-man show of a UFO writer named Albert K. Bender, who referred to himself as the International Flying Saucer Bureau.

In 1953 the CIA released the *Robertson Panel Report*, which analyzed the Air Force's Project BLUE BOOK, an effort in the 1950s and 1960s to collect and classify as many UFO reports as possible. The report concluded that UFOs did not appear to constitute any threat to national security. However, the *Robertson Panel Report* did make an ominous mention of UFO researchers:

> The Panel took cognizance of the existence of such groups as the "Civilian Flying Saucer Investigators" (Los Angeles) and the "Aerial Phenomena Research Organization" (Wisconsin). It was believed that such organizations should be watched because of their potentially great influence on mass thinking if widespread sightings should occur. The apparent irresponsibility and the possible use of such groups for subversive purposes should be kept in mind.

It was like a switched flipped in Bender's mind. He notified the newspapers that he was closing his International Flying Saucer Bureau immediately, and he withdrew from the publishing of information about UFOs. In November 1953 the *Bridgeport Sunday Herald* newspaper reported:

> Bender said "three men wearing dark suits" came to his home, flashed credentials showing them to be representatives of the "higher authority," and asked him many questions about the IFSB....They told him "not roughly, but sternly and emphatically," to stop publishing flying saucer information.

At that point, Barker took over from Bender. Bender's story, and the stories of others who reported similar experiences, became the centerpieces of Barker's *They Knew Too Much about Flying Saucers.*

Coupled with the publicly known fact that Project BLUE BOOK actually was sending Air Force personnel out into the world to personally interview UFO eyewitnesses, the revelations in Barker's book became the foundation of modern Men in Black conspiracy theories.

The Explanation

Sadly for the legend, it turns out that Gray Barker never believed a word that he wrote—he made most of it up and exaggerated the rest. He was also something of an unsavory character who didn't mind making crank calls to provoke reports, and if his crank call didn't produce any interesting reports, he'd invent something and write it up anyway. He once telephoned UFO author John Keel and disguised his voice to make a false UFO report. How do we know he did this?

John Sherwood is an author who got his start under Barker's tutelage, and he later wrote a series of articles for *Skeptical Inquirer* magazine after Barker's death revealing the lengths Barker would go to for a great story. Barker would often encourage Sherwood to make up or sensationalize his stories. Sherwood wrote that Barker:

hawked his books and magazines by embellishing stories and encouraging others to fabricate more. He launched hoaxes, joined others' deceptions, and manipulated people's beliefs.

Barker's book, though it claimed to be nonfiction, was in fact anything but. It was indeed inspired by Bender's report of what happened to him, but "inspired by" should be taken pretty loosely. After publishing his own version of Bender's experience, Barker persuaded Bender to write his own book about it (which Barker then published). It was titled *Flying Saucers and the Three Men.* In it, Bender revealed what he really meant when he told the newspapers about his visit from the Men in Black.

Their visit, he wrote, had not been an actual one by three men dressed in black suits. Instead, it had been a psychic visitation. They came from Antarctica, where the aliens had their secret base. The aliens came in three genders. Bender learned of all this by astrally projecting himself there. Sadly, Bender probably suffered from delusional disorders and might have even needed psychiatric treatment. Barker unfortunately took advantage of the situation to make some money.

Are strange Men in Black—who might be from the government, or might be aliens—actually going around to the homes of UFO witnesses and trying to compel them to remain silent? Nope. It was the fictional invention of a fraudulent author, who highlighted a mentally ill man's delusion to make it even more sensational. If you ever are lucky enough to have a UFO sighting, you can focus on the extraterrestrials and not the Men in Black.

Polybius

Date: 1981
Location: Portland, Oregon
The Conspirators: Unknown government agencies
The Victims: Portland arcade customers

The Theory

This legend claims that government agents conspired to construct an arcade game to collect information about players for some unknown purpose, a game which had the collateral effect of sickening the players. It is said to have been installed in a few video arcades in Portland, Oregon, in 1981, whereupon several players fell ill or committed suicide. Government agents would collect player data from the machines, then one day—as mysteriously as they appeared—the games were all taken away.

The Truth

Although some parts of the legend are based on real events, the *Polybius* game itself is completely fictitious and never existed.

The Backstory

Tales of how *Polybius* worked and what it did are a bit scattered, but most follow the same general theme.

Sometime in 1981, people claim a few *Polybius* consoles appeared in arcades in suburbs of Portland, Oregon. The games were wildly addictive—teens would line up to play them. But then some players began having serious side effects after playing, ranging from insomnia to hallucinations. There are even stories of suicides and permanent insanity resulting.

To add to the intrigue, mysterious government agents, sometimes described as Men in Black, would apparently come to the arcades and download data from the *Polybius* games, but seemed uninterested in collecting any money from them. This happened for about a month, and then suddenly, all the games disappeared, removed from the arcades by government agents.

Nobody has ever unearthed an actual *Polybius* console game, although quite a few people have built replicas, and there is now even a standard logo that's always used and descriptions of how the game was played. Some enterprising coders have actually written 1980s-style gaming code to make their *Polybius* consoles functional, though they just made up a game themselves.

Due to its dark and compelling history, the game has become a fixture in arcade culture. It was famously seen in a 2006 episode of *The Simpsons* where Bart went into an arcade. It has had various other appearances in media since: comics, TV, and even as a meta reference in other video games.

The Explanation

There don't appear to be any references to the *Polybius* legend until decades later. In fact, there is a handy time machine that allows us to go back and verify with certainty that there was never any such arcade game anywhere in the early 1980s. *Electronic Games* was an industry magazine that covered every minute detail of gaming and arcades. If it happened in arcade culture, it was covered in this magazine. All its issues from 1981 through 1984 are available and electronically searchable, and there is neither any mention of *Polybius* nor any of the events associated with the urban legend. For all practical purposes, case closed.

Nevertheless, we can go back and find specific events that likely inspired the legend. Newspapers reported that two arcade players had gotten sick after playing at the same arcade in Portland on November 29, 1981. One was twelve-year-old Brian Mauro, who was at the tail end of an attempt to beat the *Asteroids* record, with local TV crews on hand. After playing for twenty-eight hours straight, Mauro became ill with stomach cramps, attributed to anxiety from all the attention coupled with the prodigious volume of Coca-Cola he'd been consuming.

In a separate event, police were called to a scene where teen Michael Lopez was found collapsed on a stranger's lawn. He had been playing *Tempest* at the same time and the same place as Mauro, but had developed a severe migraine and left. Unfortunately, he didn't make it all the way home before falling. Two players, arguably both taken out of action by arcade games in Portland in 1981. That's kind of suspicious, right?

But there was more to come. Unrelated to the two boys, authorities had been scoping out Portland area arcades for some time for illegal gambling activity. Some older arcade games could be rigged with hardware counters to total up game scores, and some arcades would make cash payouts to players who reached certain high scores, as a way to attract more players. The legality was disputed; arcades said these were games of skill, but the Feds said it was illegal gambling. And so, ten days after Mauro and Lopez went down, multiple law enforcement agencies made raids at several Portland arcades, seizing cash and rigged games. And thus was another element of the urban legend satisfied: government agents removing video games.

There is even a close match for a true historical event referencing the name of the game. It was called *Poly Play* (close to *Polybius*). *Poly Play* was a crappy East German console game that was a rip-off of eight popular Western games, and sold to Eastern Bloc arcades in 1985. But they broke a lot, and with the dissolution of the Iron Curtain, were suddenly subject to copyright claims. So the factory, VEB Polytechnik, recalled them all and destroyed them.

Skeptoid® Says...

A movie and a book from 1984 may have inspired the *Polybius* legend. The movie is *The Last Starfighter*. In this film, a mysterious "man in black" recruits a teenage gamer by planting arcade consoles all around the world, looking for that one most skilled player. Another is the novel *Arcade* by Robert Maxxe, which features a nearly identical arcade game except it's called *Spacescape* instead of *Polybius*, and turns out to be a government mind control project.

Digging through all possible archives and resources, the earliest reference to the *Polybius* video game that anyone's found so far is an entry on www.coinop.org, which is sort of a *Wikipedia* of video games. An anonymous author posted the basics of the *Polybius* legend. The post is dated August 3, 1998, but some researchers believe that date is fake and the post was not actually created until February 6, 2000. It included the game's publisher, Sinneslöschen. There was no actual software publisher of that name, and it's not even quite proper German. Loosely translated, it means something like "lose your senses" and is a word you might come up with if you didn't know any German but had access to a German–English dictionary. If this is indeed the earliest published mention of the game, then it's likely that this anonymous poster was the originator of the urban legend.

Sometime after that, Coinop.org owner Kurt Koller advised *Game-Pro* about the post. *GamePro* magazine ran an article in 2003 called "Secrets and Lies," and the urban legend took hold.

Suppose the author of the Coinop.org entry saw *The Last Starfighter* or read *Arcade*, and/or had heard about the Portland arcade raids, and/or the teens being sickened. The story practically writes itself. And that's probably how this urban legend was born.

HAARP

Date: 1993-2014
Location: Gakona, Alaska
The Conspirators: US Air Force, US Army, DARPA, University of Alaska
The Victims: Civilian populations worldwide

The Theory

HAARP is the High-Frequency Active Auroral Research Program, a remote facility in Alaska built by the US Air Force, US Army, and the Defense Advanced Research Projects Agency (DARPA) in partnership with the University of Alaska. It's a 33-acre lot with 180 high-frequency antennas, each 72 feet tall, with a maximum transmission power of 3,600 kilowatts (about 75 times the power of an average commercial radio station). It is designed to energize a patch of ionosphere high above, for purposes as diverse as atmospheric studies, characterizing radio communications during atmospheric events, and extremely low frequency radio communication with submarines. It can even produce a faint artificial aurora, though too faint to be seen with the naked eye.

Ever since it was constructed, conspiracy theorists have claimed that HAARP has been "weaponizing" the weather by creating destructive hurricanes (like 2005's Katrina), is able to trigger earthquakes at will (like Sichuan in 2008), and can beam mind-control waves to any part of the globe for some unspecified nefarious purpose.

The Truth

Communications are important to the military, and there are a lot of things in the atmosphere than can disrupt communications, both natural and man-made. So of course the military would build an atmospheric research program focused on communications. The fact is that the physical and electrical properties of the ionosphere are crucial to communication and navigation systems (like GPS) that rely on the transmission of radio signals, and the ionosphere can be altered a lot by space weather. HAARP allows researchers to temporarily create various conditions in the small patch of sky directly overhead, so that these technologies can be tested and adapted. It's certainly not creating deadly hurricanes thousands of miles away.

The Backstory

The conspiratorial beliefs about HAARP first become widely known when Nick Begich Jr., son of a former Alaska congressman and career police state conspiracy theorist (and who inexplicably calls himself "Dr." Nick Begich), self-published a book called *Angels Don't Play This HAARP* in which he laid out most of the basic claims of the urban legend.

As with most conspiracy theories surrounding strange military projects, this one was warmly received by its target audience. Theorists quickly dug up what has been called the "HAARP patent," filed by physicist Bernard Eastlund in 1985, claiming all kinds of powerful abilities using a "method and apparatus for altering a region in the earth's atmosphere, ionosphere, and/or magnetosphere."

It sounded very compelling to some. Even a few legitimate academics—in fields outside of atmospheric physics, of course—have voiced their fears over what HAARP might be able to do.

The absurdity reached its peak in 2007 when the *YouTube* video "Crazy Sprinkler Lady" went viral, in which a woman pointed her camera at a rainbow made by her yard sprinkler, and explained her belief that the rainbow effect was caused by HAARP.

But some took it far more seriously. As late as 2016, two years after the facility had been shut down, two men were arrested in Georgia with a large arsenal of weapons intended to destroy HAARP to save humanity. They said that God had told them to destroy the machine so the souls of all the people trapped in it could be released.

The Explanation

Unfortunately for the conspiracy, HAARP has virtually none of the capabilities they imagine. Even Eastlund's patent was for a theoretical device which bore no resemblance to HAARP, was *one million* times as powerful, *and* would have been at least 14 miles on a side. Neither he nor his patent ever had any connection with HAARP.

The actual intent of HAARP has been clear from the beginning— to better understand and address potential communications interruptions caused by atmospheric influences. Certain space weather events can disrupt activity on Earth. Some of the better-known include solar flares, which produce X-rays that can actually black out whole bands of the radio spectrum; solar radiation storms that bombard satellites with energetic protons, potentially knocking out their circuitry; coronal mass ejections causing geomagnetic storms on Earth that can bring down power grids; and crucially, powerful geomagnetic storms that can degrade GPS signals enough that they become useless for military or civilian operations.

At any rate, HAARP is now wholly owned and operated by the University of Alaska. Neither the US Air Force nor DARPA have any involvement anymore.

Skeptoid® Says...

HAARP was only very rarely actually turned on. Its power requirements are immense and expensive, and it was only active during brief experiments. Once it's turned off, HAARP's effects on the ionosphere directly above are no longer detectable after only one second to ten minutes, depending on the experiment performed. That fact pretty much shuts down claims from people who blamed HAARP for chronic problems like migraines or even climate change.

HAARP's abilities to affect the Earth's environment are limited by what it actually is: a big radio transmitter, pointing straight up, only good for frequencies up to 10 MHz, far short of what it would take to do microwave heating. There is also no mechanism by which it could direct its energy anywhere else in the world. It is located where it was built, and can study only that one patch of sky directly overhead. It cannot trigger some event in the earthquake faults beneath China any more than the cell phone towers in your neighborhood can redirect an asteroid.

As a radio transmitter, HAARP has no potential to impact the atmosphere at all, so there go any ideas about controlling the weather.

Its electromagnetic signal can only interact with the charged particles in the ionosphere, far above atmospheric weather systems. This is the same reason we don't see TV broadcasts or cell phone signals changing the weather.

Also, let's have some humility. Humans are smart and we can do a lot, but we can't compete with nature when it comes to electromagnetic radiation. The maximum signal strength HAARP can generate in the extremely low frequency band is less than one ten-millionth of the Earth's natural background field. It's also useless during the daytime, because natural solar radiation energizes the ionosphere far more than HAARP can, so its effects are completely negated.

Finally, nothing about HAARP has ever been secret. The research performed there was done by faculty and students at the University of Alaska, Stanford, Penn State, Boston College, Dartmouth, Cornell, University of Maryland, University of Massachusetts, MIT, Tomsk Polytechnic University, UCLA, Clemson, and the University of Tulsa. For most of the years it was operating, HAARP even held an open house each summer for the general public.

In 2015 HAARP was turned over to the University of Alaska, which plans to continue making its facilities available to atmospheric researchers...not nefarious government agents.

Skeptoid® Says...

HAARP is not even a unique device. There are a number of similar research stations around the world, namely the Sura Ionospheric Heating Facility in Russia, EISCAT in Norway, the Arecibo Observatory in Puerto Rico, and the HIPAS observatory near Fairbanks, Alaska, which is operated by UCLA.

TWA Flight 800

Date: July 17, 1996
Location: Atlantic Ocean just outside New York City
The Conspirators: US Navy, other government agencies
The Victims: 230 passengers and crew of Flight 800

The Theory

TWA Flight 800 took off out of New York's John F. Kennedy International Airport in 1996 and almost immediately crashed, killing everyone on board. Conspiracy theorists believe it was shot down by an American missile.

The Truth

TWA Flight 800 was destroyed by a spark of unproven origin from the plane's electronics inside the center fuel tank. The National Transportation Safety Board (NTSB) reconstructed the wreckage and was easily able to rule out a missile strike and found no evidence of any foul play. Sometimes bad things just happen.

The Backstory

TWA Flight 800 was a Boeing 747 headed for Rome with 230 passengers and crew. The takeoff just before sunset was uneventful, but twelve minutes later the plane exploded and broke up in midair over the open ocean. Rescuers found no survivors.

Many eyewitnesses on the shore saw what they believed was a missile streaking upward and then striking an aircraft with a tremendous boom, so conspiracy theorists immediately said the plane was downed by a missile fired by the government. Some claimed the missile had been fired from a ship (either accidentally or deliberately), and some believed that a shoulder-fired missile could have been launched from either a boat or the shore. Either way, they claimed that an American missile was what must have destroyed it.

Another TWA pilot, Robert Stacey, and journalist James Sanders became so persuaded that a missile had brought down the plane that they actually managed to steal bits of wreckage from the NTSB reconstruction site, hoping to find proof. They were, of course, convicted of the theft of government property. Sanders wrote two books claiming the United States shot down Flight 800 with a missile, *The Downing of TWA Flight 800* (1996) and *Altered Evidence* (1999).

In addition, William Donaldson, a retired naval officer who referred to himself as the "Associated Retired Aviation Professionals" (why this was plural was never explained), wrote a 127-page manifesto titled *Interim Report on the Crash of TWA Flight 800 and the Actions of the NTSB and the FBI*. He went on to promote it as the Donaldson Report. He considered two scenarios: an accidental shootdown by the US military and a terrorist shootdown using a missile fired from a boat, both of which he described in great detail, though entirely speculatively. He considered the terrorist scenario more likely. Donaldson's explanation for why the government would cover this up was the upcoming presidential elections, though this was not persuasively argued.

After the NTSB investigation found no evidence of any missile interference, the theory morphed into that of a government cover-up. The government must have known, they reasoned, that they had shot down the plane themselves, thus the NTSB investigation would be a sham.

The Explanation

In one of the most amazing debris recoveries in all of history, the NTSB managed to retrieve the bodies of all the victims, as well as 95 percent of the aircraft wreckage. Investigators were incredibly able to reconstruct a 93-foot section of the fuselage where the explosion had happened, allowing detailed study of the wreckage.

Unfortunately, what was eventually learned was that the cause of the explosion will probably always remain unknown.

Damage to the aircraft structure reveals a lot about the way it was damaged. Investigators were able to easily rule out any type of missile strike or external cause, as these would have left unambiguous evidence that is clearly not there. They were also able to rule out a bomb on board the plane, as this would have also left clear signs.

What was learned for certain is that the explosion came from inside the plane's 17,000-gallon center fuel tank, which sits beneath the floor right under the wing. Vapor in the tank was ignited by an electrical spark, but the exact source of the spark could not be determined. Conspiracy theorists often interpret this to mean that there *was* no possible source, thus leaving the door open for some outside influence. But all it means is that of the many possible sources, no one could be proven to be the one responsible. It could have been any one of many. The NTSB described the most probable as:

> a short circuit outside of the CWT (center wing fuel tank) that allowed excessive voltage to enter it through electrical wiring associated with the fuel quantity indication system.

They were also able to rule out the following alternate causes:

> A lightning or meteorite strike; a missile fragment; a small explosive charge placed on the CWT; auto ignition or hot surface ignition, resulting from elevated temperatures produced by sources external to the CWT; a fire migrating to the CWT from another fuel tank via the vent (stringer) system; an uncontained engine failure or a turbine burst in the air conditioning packs beneath the CWT; a malfunctioning CWT jettison/override pump; a malfunctioning CWT scavenge pump; and static electricity.

Skeptoid® Says...

The reconstructed 93-foot section of Flight 800's fuselage is now a permanent teaching tool at the NTSB training center in Ashburn, Virginia, helping tomorrow's investigators prevent future air disasters.

The explosion blew the nose off the aircraft. Suddenly tail-heavy, the plane pulled sharply upward. Burning heavily, it rose in the darkening sky (this was about seven minutes after sunset) and could have looked very much like an ascending missile. Its wings then broke up, releasing much more fuel that bloomed in a massive fireball, and the plane made its final dive into the ocean.

Theorists claim that the witness accounts tell a very different story. This is part of a typical account (from Witness 73), as included in the NTSB report:

> While keeping her eyes on the aircraft, she observed a "red streak" moving up from the ground toward the aircraft at an approximately 45-degree angle. The "red streak" was leaving a light gray colored smoke trail….At the instant the smoke trail ended at the aircraft's right wing, she heard a loud sharp noise which sounded like a firecracker had just exploded at her feet.

The reason we know that what she saw and heard could not have been a missile going up and striking the plane has to do with physics: the speed of sound, in this case. The plane was about 9 miles out to sea and about 2.5 miles up when the center fuel tank exploded, as proven by the flight data recorder. This placed the aircraft just about one minute away from the nearest eyewitnesses on the coast, measured by the speed of sound. When this witness saw a red streak going up and then terminating with a boom, physics tells us that the boom happened a minute *before* the red streak went up.

Other witnesses at various distances described turning to look only *after* hearing the explosion, and saw a red streak ascend and terminate in a fireball. Many of them interpreted this to be a missile, but the time and distance make their observations consistent with the already-halved airplane ascending and then the fireball when the severed wing tanks burned.

Although these eyewitness reports were the only evidence that a missile had been fired, the FBI still followed up on all the possible leads. Shoulder-fired missiles were dismissed, because there are none in the world with anything remotely like the range needed. There were a few military assets that had been in the area, including a Navy P-3 Orion aircraft and a US Coast Guard cutter, but neither had any missile-firing capabilities.

Malaysia Airlines MH370

Date: March 8, 2014
Location: Indian Ocean
The Conspirators: Various
The Victims: 239 passengers and crew on board the plane

The Theory

Malaysia Airlines Flight MH370, a Boeing 777 with 239 people on board, disappeared on March 8, 2014. Conspiracy theories range from a suicide by the pilot to a Russian state operation to an abduction by time-traveling aliens.

The Truth

We have no idea what happened to MH370, but we have no reason to believe it was anything more extraordinary than a typical mechanical failure.

The Backstory

Taking off just after midnight on the morning of March 8, 2014, Flight MH370 began normally, leaving Kuala Lumpur en route to Beijing. About forty minutes after takeoff, they were over the South China Sea, about halfway between Malaysia and Vietnam. Leaving the Malaysian air traffic control area, the pilots signed off with a "good night" message, and stopped their transponder from squawking, as is normally done. At this point they were no longer inside radar coverage, and the only ongoing contact with the outside world was the ACARS system, which periodically used the plane's satellite data connection to send maintenance information back to the airline.

What happened thereafter remains unknown, but very shortly after signing off, the plane made a U-turn to head back toward Malaysia. This is known only by sporadic military and secondary radar contacts. The plane overflew Malaysia and turned right, heading west over the Andaman Sea, west of Thailand. Their last known maneuver was to turn south onto a heading that the plane appears to have followed until it ran out of fuel. Near the end of that path, a satellite made a brief handshake connection to the aircraft but no data was transmitted or received. Inmarsat, the company that operated the satellite, was able to derive a particular arc over the Indian Ocean, somewhere along which the plane was when their satellite made that brief handshake. And then, there was no more contact.

The lack of any radio communication throughout these obviously controlled movements aroused suspicion immediately among conspiracy theorists; questions persisted. Perhaps the plane had been hijacked, but then where did it go? Perhaps it was a suicide plan by the pilot, but then why the elaborate maneuvers?

Serious investigation first focused on the pilot, Zaharie Ahmad Shah. There were claims that he was distraught over separating from his wife, and that he had no future appointments written in his calendar. This line of inquiry was eventually dropped when it became clear that there was no evidence of suicidal thoughts or tendencies. He also had a number of unusual routes on the flight simulator on his home computer, which the press made much of, but they were not substantially different from funky flight paths that many pilots fly when they're relaxing on their computer.

Skeptoid® Says...

There were all kinds of other crazy ideas about the flight. One (unscientific) poll on the CNN website found that 9 percent of respondents believed one of several supernatural fates had taken the plane, including alien abduction, a time warp, or some parallel dimension.

One theory held that the plane was hijacked to the island of Diego Garcia, a British territory in the western Indian Ocean where the British and Americans both have military and intelligence facilities. According to some theorists, it landed there and the passengers were killed for some unclear nefarious purpose; according to others, it was shot down as it approached. French author and former airline executive Marc Dugain has been a staunch proponent of this theory, and pointed out that residents of the Maldives claimed to see a plane fly low over their country early that morning. However, the Maldives are not on the way to Diego Garcia, and there do not appear to have been any such reports from islanders until some three months after the disappearance.

The Russians have been implicated in at least two conspiracy theories. One holds that Russia hijacked the plane and had it secreted away in Kazakhstan to retaliate against the United States for sanctions, but that theory is odd because MH370 was not an American plane. Another theory is that a Russian satellite detected the plane crash, but Putin would not reveal the location to anyone to protect the secret of the satellite's existence.

Even North Korea has been suggested as the mastermind. In one theory, North Korea hijacked the plane and brought it there in order to reverse engineer it to benefit their own struggling aircraft industry. Another suggests MH370 was being used to deliver a nuclear weapon to North Korea, so the Americans shot it down in flight.

All of these hijacking theories are, of course, in direct violation of what's known about the plane's flight path.

The Explanation

Within just a few days of the disappearance—and well outside of the conspiracy theory community—airline pilots were already writing about what they believed had happened, and it's a much more plausible scenario without Russians, aliens, or time warps. All of those weird things about the flight that confused conventional reporters fit right into the pilots' theory. All it required was a minor electrical fire.

If pilots smelled smoke in the cockpit, the very first thing they would do is shut down all the electronics they could possibly spare. This would include the ACARS and the radio. They would even physically pull out the fuses if they could. Thus, the automated communications stopped. The voice communications would stop too, but mainly because pilots are trained that communicating is the last priority when dealing with an emergency. Aviating—keeping the plane flying—is always the first priority, and this meant doing whatever was necessary to keep the plane safely in the air. If a fire was suspected, putting it out would have taken precedence over anything else. The second priority is to navigate—to make sure that wherever the plane is headed is actually a useful direction to go. In this case, Shah was probably heading not back to Kuala Lumpur, because of its mountainous terrain, but to a preferred backup airport at Pulau Langkawi, with longer runways and easier access. That their first turn put them on this course tells us a lot about what was happening on board.

After a pair of later turns that eventually left them headed south on autopilot from a position just west of Thailand, the pilots eventually became incapacitated, either from carbon monoxide or possibly from decompression. The plane, which by then could well have been a flying tomb, made it at least as far as the Inmarsat arc before it ran out of fuel or a fire did sufficient damage to bring it down.

The third priority, communicating, is something they obviously never got around to. Thus their lack of radio communication is not suspicious, but rather it is telling. It tells us they had more important things to worry about before calling for help.

From the expert perspective—that of pilots who saw what the plane did and recognized that it was exactly what they themselves would have done—there is no mystery surrounding the loss of MH370. Unfortunately, we can't know exactly what happened without seeing the wreckage. And that particular riddle remains as deep as the ocean.

PART 8
Conspiracy Theories That Turned Out to Be...True?

We've spent the preceding parts of the book looking at conspiracy theories that were just too crazy to be true. A large majority of theories fall into this bucket. But there are real conspiracies, and people go to jail for them every day. And if you're a conspiracy theorist, the fact that *some* conspiracies are real makes you think that the theory that you believe in is real as well.

Of course most conspiracy theories that have been proven to be true didn't actually have a theory attached to them until they were proven by investigators. But surely there must have been some, right? Surely the conspiracy theorists must have been proven right in at least a few cases? It is the most common question received by researchers of conspiracy theories: which are the ones that have been proven true? It is an eager search for validation by our naturally conspiratorial brains; it's the hope that knowing previous theories turned out to be true in the past will mean that some of our current theories will turn out to be proven true in the future.

What follows are a few theories that are most often *claimed* to be the ones that turned out to be right—we'll look at each of them to see how true that is.

Numbers Stations

Date: 1914–Present
Location: Worldwide
The Conspirators: Government intelligence agencies
The Victims: Governments who get spied on

The Theory

Ever since World War I, but most especially during the Cold War when the United States and the Soviet Union were engaged in an arms race and all its accompanying espionage, the airwaves have carried dozens of mysterious radio broadcasts. These broadcasts come over shortwave, a radio frequency band notable for its extreme long distance capability. Each of these mysterious radio programs has certain specific days and times on which it broadcasts. Typically, the broadcasts consist of a spoken voice reading long strings of nonsense letters and numbers. Conspiracy theory hypotheses have abounded for years about what these mysterious radio stations might be, but the leading theory is that they are governments transmitting information to spies located in foreign countries.

The Truth

In this case, the conspiracy theory is spot on. In at least some cases, stations have been proven to be encrypted communications to spies.

The Backstory

Encrypted transmissions via Morse code began to be widely used during World War I, allowing militaries to communicate over long distances without their broadcasts being understood by the enemy. Over the decades, these encrypted Morse code broadcasts gradually evolved into what we now call a numbers station. It's now a spoken voice reading off numbers instead of those characters being sent as Morse code, but all work the same way: Important information is encrypted into nonsensical letters or numbers, then transmitted via shortwave radio, and received and decrypted on the other end back into readable text.

During the Cold War, amateur shortwave operators began finding and cataloging these encrypted broadcasts, which they called numbers stations because most of them broadcast long strings of numbers, in groups of five at a time. Nobody knew what they meant, and all of these broadcasts were on unlicensed stations. Amateur investigators used direction-finding technology to try and locate the sources of the numbers stations. Many of them turned out to be broadcast from inside secure military bases.

Skeptoid® Says...

Many of the discovered encrypted broadcasts had unique characteristics. One named "Yosemite Sam" would start with an audio clip of the famous cartoon character shouting "Varmint, I'm a-gonna blow you away." Another named the "Lincolnshire Poacher" began with a short musical clip from the English folk song of the same name.

One popular alternate hypothesis has been that numbers stations are utility broadcasts, which typically include info like weatherfax data (a system for sending satellite pictures of storm fronts) and ice warnings to ships at sea, fishery fax data, oceanographic buoy data, and other such things. But most utility stations send data signals consisting of dots or blanks that come out as visual images on the receiving end, not encrypted strings of spoken numbers. So this hypothesis never seemed to fit very well.

Eventually, a series of high-profile arrests proved the true explanation for number stations:

- In 1989, a Czech spy was arrested in the UK, caught receiving and decoding numbers stations broadcasts from Romania.

- In 1998, five spies called the Cuban Five were arrested in Miami, having received communications for years from a Cuban numbers station nicknamed Atención.

- Nine days after September 11, 2001, in an event that might have been overshadowed by other news, the US Defense Intelligence

Agency arrested one of its own senior analysts, who was also found to have been decrypting messages from the Cuban station, Atención.

- In 2009, a retired US State Department official and his wife were arrested in Washington, DC. For years, they had been spying for Cuba, and had received instructions via a Cuban numbers station using a shortwave radio given to them by the Cubans.

- A ring of ten Russian spies headquartered in New York City were arrested by the FBI in 2010, having been caught listening to a numbers station and writing down all the numbers.

- In 2011, a Russian couple was arrested for espionage in Germany, having received information via a Russian numbers station for more than twenty years. Interestingly, they were caught only after upgrading to more modern encrypted satellite communication gear.

So it does appear, after all, that the conspiracy-theory version of numbers stations turns out to be the true one: governments communicating worldwide with spy networks.

The Explanation

Shortwave is used for numbers stations and other services that require a signal to be carried over very great distances, even all the way around the world. While most radio bands have ranges limited to line of sight, shortwave can reflect and refract from the ionosphere, allowing them to propagate as far as needed. If the transmitter is powerful enough, you can rest assured a shortwave signal will get there.

Shortwave also has a number of other important and unique benefits. First, it's virtually impossible to determine who might be listening to a radio station, and there is no practical way to find an active receiver because they don't transmit anything back. Compare this to Internet signals, which go through routers and servers and get logged.

This radio band is also immune to massive infrastructure failure, since it doesn't depend on the Internet, or physical wires, or satellite communications. All you need is a transmitter and a receiver, and a shortwave radio will work very well anywhere in the world. The receivers are widely available worldwide. Anyone can buy one at a thrift or surplus store for very little money, even in underdeveloped nations, and they can even be built relatively easily. They are the ultimate untraceable receiver.

Most numbers stations transmit numbers in blocks of five digits, and the voice usually repeats each block of five once. There can be any number of five-digit blocks, depending on the length of the message. The use of five-digit blocks is simply a convention in encryption. There are any number of encryption schemes out there, but a transmission in groups of five characters is the standard. It makes it easy for the recipient to write them down or type them into a computer. Each block is repeated to minimize transcription errors, and it also helps for times when the signal strength isn't great. Seeing that the numbers stations transmit in this form gave a very big clue that they were sending some encrypted message.

Some encryption schemes can be decrypted with pen and paper by a recipient who has the key, typically a single-use key called a one-time pad. This is a long string of random text for which the number value of each letter is added to the number value of each letter in the message to be encoded. It is only ever used once, making it impossible for a cracker to find common patterns. While low-tech, a code encrypted with a one-time pad is essentially unbreakable. The downside is that the recipient will need to have some kind of book or list of one-time pads, and that's evidence that could be used against him. On the other side of things, it's very easy for the intended recipient who has the correct keys to use computer software to decrypt a message from a numbers station, but again, the presence of this program on a computer is evidence that can be used against the spy. However, such a program can use more advanced encryption like RSA, the modern standard used today that powers web browser encryption and financial transactions.

The question of whether numbers stations are a conspiracy theory that was proven true is a sticky one. While even the most conspiratorial interpretation of them has been proven true, what's not clear is that a conspiracy theory ever existed before the first spies who used these numbers stations were arrested. Yes, the use of these stations in espionage has been documented since World War I, but this hasn't always been public information. Newspaper reports of arrests, on the other hand, have freely discussed how the numbers station was employed by the spy and how it constituted evidence against him. So, while it isn't really appropriate to credit conspiracy theorists for having uncovered this one, we can certainly give them credit for their interpretation being the correct one.

Skeptoid® Says...

Most often cited as proof that conspiracy theories often come true is the conspiracy to murder Julius Caesar in the year 44 B.C.E. It is a historical fact that he was murdered by a conspiracy. However, it's quite a stretch to regard this event as proof of a conspiracy theory that was proven to be true. Why? Well, it never existed as anyone's conspiracy theory until after it had happened. If anything, it was an example of a successful conspiracy that eluded all discovery—until the conspirators themselves went public.

MKULTRA

Date: 1953-1973
Location: United States
The Conspirators: US Central Intelligence Agency
The Victims: Unwitting test subjects

The Theory

Mind control is the ability to make people think or act differently than they normally would. For twenty years, the conspiracy theory says, the CIA attempted to achieve successful mind control by conducting unethical experiments on human subjects both with and without their knowledge and consent—using drugs, psychology, and combinations of both. This twenty-year series of experiments was called MKULTRA. They were top secret and nobody was ever punished for them. MKULTRA was most notable for giving LSD to people without their knowledge.

True believers in the conspiracy theory think that MKULTRA lasted for so long because it was successful, and that the government can, in fact, cause people to think and act in certain ways.

The Truth

The CIA did fund MKULTRA and did perform experiments for twenty years hoping to find something like mind control, but were never remotely successful. A small percentage of these experiments were extremely unethical, especially by today's standards.

The Backstory

As soon as World War II ended, the United States found itself fighting a new kind of war: the Cold War. This conflict was more about intelligence and espionage than about weapons. The CIA was on the lookout for new tools that could be used in this type of warfare.

Two particular events triggered the CIA's interest in mind control. The first was the arrest of Cardinal József Mindszenty for treason by

Communist authorities in Hungary. The CIA knew him to be innocent, but they watched him make a very mechanical confession to a list of absurd crimes. The second event was when American fighter pilots who were shot down over North Korea and captured made strange robotic anti-American statements on TV. The CIA figured that some kind of mind control must have been causing these people to think and act differently than they usually would and they decided that they needed to learn all they could on the subject. And Project MKULTRA—which focused on the study of LSD and its effects—was born!

Skeptoid® Says...

There were many programs aside from MKULTRA that were also studying mind control—both in the CIA and at other agencies. They were all trying to learn how to make the enemy think and act in some desired way. Project ARTICHOKE was one, as were MKSEARCH, MKOFTEN, Project BLUEBIRD, and Project CHATTER. Some of these projects involved pharmacological experiments, others used psychological persuasion. All of them did ultimately result in important research and increased our knowledge in the relevant fields, but none of them ever provided the useful mind control the CIA hoped for.

The world's top experts in LSD and mind control aren't found at the CIA, but at universities and research institutions. So when the government runs a program like MKULTRA, they fund a research project at a university. With MKULTRA, they set up front organizations to disguise their true identity, and used those organizations to fund various research projects. The "Society for the Investigation for Human Ecology" was one of front groups. It funded research projects at as many as eighty-six institutions, including universities, hospitals, and prisons. Without realizing it, scientists all over were fighting the Cold War on a very subtle front, trying to see if they could exert finely tuned influence on the minds of the enemy.

Today we regard much of what was done as highly unethical, mainly because the ethical standards of the day were far more lax than they are today. At McGill University, community members who came in for routine psychotherapy were instead given radical treatment such as electroshock therapy at much higher voltages than normal,

LSD, and other experimental or illegal drugs. Some suffered lifelong disabilities as a result.

The Addiction Research Center at the Public Health Service Hospital in Lexington, Kentucky, gave similar treatments. Massive doses of LSD, heroin, methamphetamine, and psychedelic mushrooms were given and the effects were studied, all under the protection of the CIA's license. In the most extreme example, seven volunteers seeking treatment for addiction were given high doses of LSD for seventy-seven days in a row.

There are two particularly disturbing specific claims made by MKULTRA conspiracy theorists. One was that the CIA tested aerial spraying of LSD over a village in France in 1951. Many residents experienced severe symptoms that included convulsions, insomnia, pain, hallucinations, and delirium. Several people died, and a number were committed to insane asylums. The second claim concerns a microbiologist named Dr. Frank Olson. He was working in an MKULTRA-funded research program, but expressed misgivings about working in germ warfare and asked to be transferred out of the program. Just a couple of days later, he fell to his death from a thirteenth-story window. Many have claimed that he was murdered for threatening to reveal details about the program.

Skeptoid® Says...

Government websites can sometimes be hard to navigate, so it's often easier to find released government reports at privately run sites like TheBlackVault.com. Such sites often contain "unusual" information as well—such as purported proof of Bigfoot—but you can get the congressional report on MKULTRA at http://documents.theblackvault.com/documents/mindcontrol/hearing.pdf.

The CIA terminated MKULTRA in 1973 following the Watergate scandal. Nothing useful to the CIA had been learned, and CIA director Richard Helms saw no reason to risk getting busted over the program's clear human rights violations. Helms ordered all MKULTRA records destroyed, which was a common practice for classified programs.

When the Senate's Church Committee investigated abuses by the nation's intelligence agencies in 1975 (an investigation prompted largely by *The Washington Post's* revelations about COINTELPRO, which is discussed in the following entry), a cache of about 20,000 MKULTRA documents that had escaped destruction were revealed and investigated in congressional hearings in 1977. Some of them have since been declassified and are now even available online, and it's from these documents that we know most of what we know about MKULTRA.

The Explanation

What we've learned in the decades since MKULTRA is that its entire premise was scientifically flawed. We now know that concepts such as brainwashing and deprogramming were fictional concepts that are not a part of actual psychology. But what about all of the stories that conspiracy theorists tie back to MKULTRA?

Well, Cardinal Mindszenty was finally able to tell his story when he was freed in the Hungarian Revolution after spending eight years in prison. He said that his confession had not been the result of mind control, but of torture. He had been beaten with rubber truncheons until he agreed to make the confession. The same story emerged from the American fighter pilots who made confessions from their North Korean prison cells. They had simply been tortured and coerced into making the statements. Not one of them reported being "broken" or having their mind changed.

And as for that village in France that theorists say had been sprayed with LSD? What happened there was in 1951, two years before MKULTRA was funded, so it couldn't have been connected anyway. Also, that same year the *British Medical Journal* published an article explaining the strange effects on the village's population. It had been a case of ergot fungus contamination of the food supply. Ergot contains the same chemical precursor as LSD (ergotamine), so it's likely that some conspiracy theorists tried to make this the connection.

The death of Dr. Frank Olson was, however, most likely tied to MKULTRA. He and a number of MKULTRA colleagues were at an employee retreat in Maryland when they were all given LSD without their knowledge. Again, this was unethical, but it was at a period in the program when it was common for participants to experiment on one another, with or without their consent. Olson's reaction to the LSD was paranoia, depression, and self-doubt. And a week later he did indeed ask to leave the program. It was in this condition that he fell from the hotel window and died. His death was officially termed a suicide. Unofficially, it was very likely prompted by the LSD.

Skeptoid® Says...

After the revelations about MKULTRA were made public, Dr. Olson's family sued the government and reached a settlement. Later, when his body was moved to a different grave, the family took the opportunity to ask for a new autopsy. Some on the forensic team felt that the body bore injuries suffered in the hotel room before the fall. The family tried twice more over the years to have the case reopened, but the terms of the previous settlement caused the new cases to be dismissed.

Whether MKULTRA can be considered a conspiracy theory that was proven true is problematic. There is no evidence that MKULTRA was suspected by anyone with any reasonable specificity until it was revealed by the congressional investigation...which, of course, means that it never existed as a conspiracy theory, therefore it cannot be considered one that was later proven true.

COINTELPRO

Date: 1956–1971
Location: United States
The Conspirators: Federal Bureau of Investigation
The Victims: Progressive political factions

The Theory

During the civil rights era, the FBI under J. Edgar Hoover aggressively and systematically conducted covert operations that were intended to subvert and/or sabotage various domestic groups with Communist ties through a program called COINTELPRO (Counterintelligence Program). These operations included illegal surveillance without warrants; planting of false rumors and news stories to create suspicion of these groups; and work with local police stations to conduct raids against targets, some of which resulted in violence and death.

What really makes COINTELPRO controversial is that its operations gradually expanded to include targeting progressive movements that Hoover considered "subversive," including antiwar protesters, civil rights groups, feminist organizations, the Black Panthers, gay rights groups, and even Martin Luther King Jr. The most conspiratorial claims charge that beatings and even direct assassinations were performed against American citizens to intimidate and silence America's progressive voices.

The Truth

The FBI did systematically harass and threaten certain factions in the United States, and got away with it until they were exposed by investigators.

The Backstory

The COINTELPRO program was started in 1956 by J. Edgar Hoover's FBI specifically to disrupt the Communist Party USA, a legitimate political party that still exists today, little different from other minor political parties (Libertarian Party, Green Party, etc.). The FBI got quite creative. They had the IRS conduct unwarranted audits against them. They made up stories about some members and sent the stories to other members. Rifts within the party were sought and fed.

But over the next fifteen years COINTELPRO drifted away from its original goal. It's no secret that J. Edgar Hoover regarded pretty much everyone he didn't like (immigrants, liberals, members of the African-American and LGBTQ communities, etc.) to be Communists, so COINTELPRO's mission expanded to harass those groups as well—anyone who could have the label of "Communist" slapped on them.

COINTELPRO's cover was blown almost by accident. A group of eight Vietnam War protesters, calling themselves the "Citizens' Commission to Investigate the FBI," were responsible for unveiling the program to the world. They spoke of the United States' "war against Indochina" and criticized the United States for war profiteering. Some of them had formerly been members of the Camden 28, a group which in 1971 raided and destroyed a New Jersey draft board office, where Vietnam War draftees were processed. The Citizens' Commission planned a similar raid on an FBI office in Pennsylvania, hoping to reveal evidence of crimes they believed the FBI was committing against American citizens. What they stumbled into revealed COINTELPRO to the world.

The Citizens' Commission selected an FBI field office in Media, Pennsylvania, and kept it under surveillance to figure out when it was most likely to be vacant. Finally they broke into the office in the middle of the night and seized more than 1,000 pages of documents. From the office, they went directly to a public pay telephone, called the Reuters news agency, and read a statement. It said in part:

> As long as the United States government wages war against Indochina in defiance of the vast majority who want all troops and weapons withdrawn this year, and extends that war and suffering under the guise of reducing it. As long as great economic and political power remains concentrated in the hands of a small clique not subject to democratic scrutiny and control. Then repression, intimidation, and entrapment are to be expected.

The burglars made copies of the stolen documents and sent them to major newspapers nationwide, but initially nobody published them. Not only were the newspapers uncertain of whether the documents were real, but they risked publishing information about ongoing FBI operations and potentially jeopardizing agents. Finally, after two weeks, *The Washington Post* broke the story.

Skeptoid® Says...

The Citizens' Commission to Investigate the FBI chose March 8, 1971, as they day they would break into the FBI office. Why? This was the date of Muhammad Ali and Joe Frazier's "Fight of the Century" in New York City, and they hoped that the building security would be paying more attention to the fight than to their job.

Meanwhile the FBI was trying to figure out who broke into their office. Two hundred agents spent five years trying to catch the thieves, but they never made any progress. The statute of limitations expired, and the investigation was ultimately dropped, unsolved. It wasn't until 2014 that a journalist, Betty Medsger, interviewed all eight of the burglars—five men and three women. Her book, *The Burglary: The Discovery of J. Edgar Hoover's Secret F.B.I.*, told the complete story, and identified all the burglars, now safe from prosecution due to the expiration of the statute of limitation. Two used pseudonyms.

The Explanation

COINTELPRO was a real operation. It formally began in 1956, but the FBI had been following similar policies to a lesser extent for some time. Who the real targets of COINTELPRO were depends somewhat upon who you ask. The program was created to disrupt the activities of Communist infiltrators in the United States, but according to the FBI, it was eventually expanded to other subversive groups, namely the Ku Klux Klan, the Socialist Workers Party, and the Black Panthers, groups that arguably do have some subversive elements. But if you ask most other people they will name mainly peaceful civil rights groups. It seems that almost everyone's version of who COINTELPRO targeted is an effort to color history by emphasizing the FBI's actions against whatever groups they personally support. But the shocking reality is that the FBI *did* take actions of one kind or another against nearly all of these groups, so in effect, just about anything you want to criticize about COINTELPRO is true.

Skeptoid® Says...

COINTELPRO's name is short for Counterintelligence Program. Counterintelligence refers to actions taken domestically against foreign spies. During the years of COINTELPRO, the Soviet Union and other hostile nations absolutely did have spies inside the United States, and so this part of the program was indeed well justified.

So does this count as a conspiracy that's been proven true? It's still a difficult argument to make. The eight burglars were mainly interested in protesting the Vietnam War and didn't have any idea of the scope of the documents they ended up finding (though it's doubtful that they were surprised). On the other hand, J. Edgar Hoover's attitudes toward what he saw as the "subversive left" were well known, and it was something of an open secret that the FBI did the kinds of things described in the COINTELPRO documents. Their discovery of the documents simply put a name on it, and confirmed its activities and existence.

Although the specifics of the program may have been lacking until the discovery of the documents, the fact that the FBI, CIA, and other government agencies were doing this kind of thing had been general knowledge for a long time. In 1975, the US Senate formed the Church Committee to investigate the specific revelations from the stolen COINTELPRO documents.

Perhaps one of the most shocking actions undertaken as part of COINTELPRO was a letter written by the FBI and sent anonymously to Martin Luther King Jr. It threatened him, insulted him, and advised him to commit suicide. The Church Committee found a copy in J. Edgar Hoover's personal documents. The letter concluded:

King, there is only one thing left for you to do. You know what it is. You have just 34 days left in which to do (this exact number has been selected for a specific reason, it has definite practical significant [sic]). You are done. There is but one way out for you. You better take it before your filthy, abnormal fraudulent self is bared to the nation.

When all was said and done, the most important result of the Church Committee was the establishment of the US Senate Select Committee on Intelligence, made up of rotating members from a broad spectrum of the Senate, charged with overseeing the activities of the intelligence agencies.

The Gulf of Tonkin

Date: August 1964
Location: The Gulf of Tonkin
The Conspirators: US Navy, President Lyndon B. Johnson, Secretary of Defense Robert McNamara
The Victims: The North Vietnamese

The Theory

The United States' entry into the Vietnam War was triggered by the second of four alleged attacks by North Vietnamese fast torpedo boats against US naval forces in the waters off North Vietnam, called the Gulf of Tonkin. The conspiracy theory is that this second attack was either fictional or was perpetrated by clandestine US forces as an excuse to draw the United States into the war. These theorists say that this attack was either fabricated or faked entirely for the purpose of giving Congress a reason to order entry into the conflict.

The Truth

The second attack did not, in fact, happen, but this wasn't clear at the time. US naval forces did open fire on targets that appeared sporadically on their radar screens, but nobody ever actually saw anything and no inbound fire was ever received.

The Backstory

In August of 1964 the American Navy and North Vietnam found themselves in an uneasy standoff. American ships were off the Vietnamese coast and tens of thousands of American troops were with the South Vietnamese as advisers. This was a proxy war between Communism and capitalism, between East and West. As the Soviets and Chinese were arming and funding North Vietnam to spread Communism throughout Southeast Asia, the Americans' Truman Doctrine compelled them to contain its spread, and they were determined not to let South Vietnam fall to the North.

On August 2, 1964, the American destroyer USS *Maddox* was provocatively engaged in electronic surveillance just outside the boundary of international waters as recognized by the rest of the world, but inside the boundaries claimed by North Vietnam. The *Maddox* was approached by three North Vietnamese fast torpedo boats that had been stalking it for more than a day. The *Maddox* fired three warning shots across the bows of the torpedo boats, which prompted these boats to attack. The *Maddox* opened fire with its guns while the Vietnamese boats began launching torpedoes and firing their machine guns. Some distance away, the aircraft carrier USS *Ticonderoga* launched four planes, which joined in the attack. By the time it was all over, one of the torpedo boats had been sunk, two had been damaged, and four North Vietnamese sailors were dead and six wounded. The *Maddox* and one of the aircraft each suffered a single bullet strike with no casualties.

In the early hours of August 4 the seas were high and the weather rough. Radar, sonar, and radio signals received by the *Maddox* were interpreted as signaling another attack, and the gunners opened fire in the direction of radar targets that had been spotted. This continued for some four hours, even into the daylight, when it finally became clear that nobody had actually seen any enemy boats. The sonar signals that had been received, which sounded like the propellers of launched torpedoes, were actually the *Maddox*'s own engines. Having assessed the situation, Captain John J. Herrick of the *Maddox* cabled Washington:

> Review of action makes many reported contacts and torpedoes fired appear doubtful. Freak weather effects on radar and overeager sonarmen may have accounted for many reports. No actual visual sightings by *Maddox*. Suggest complete evaluation before any further action taken.

But despite Herrick's review of the situation, Secretary of Defense Robert McNamara, who favored escalation against North Korea, continued to persuade President Johnson that this second attack had been a real one. As more cables from Herrick came in walking back the initial reports of an attack, Senator Wayne Morse (an opponent of the war) reported Herrick's cables to the press and lobbied other congressmen to block any attempted escalation by Johnson.

But it was too late. President Johnson, influenced by McNamara, had made up his mind. He ordered air strikes against North Vietnamese targets, which were then launched from carriers in the area. He then drafted the Gulf of Tonkin Resolution, which was passed by Congress within the next two days after impassioned testimony from McNamara, who exaggerated the Vietnamese aggression and greatly downplayed the role of the *Maddox*. The resolution authorized the president to do whatever he deemed necessary to assist the South Vietnamese.

Of course, throughout the debate over the resolution, evidence suggesting that no such attack had taken place was brought up. But by then, it didn't matter.

The Explanation

It is no secret that McNamara, and much of the rest of the US government, was eager for any excuse to bomb Ho Chi Minh's Communist North Vietnam in the early 1960s. This was widely understood at the time, and has been ever since. The United States was already secretly engaged in operations against the North, having paid for unmarked Norwegian fast patrol boats and skippers crewed by South Vietnamese sailors. For about three years prior to the Gulf of Tonkin, these boats had been launching strikes against the North Vietnamese. And of course, there were already tens of thousands of American troops stationed in South Vietnam to support their defense against a potential invasion from the North.

The *Maddox* was stationed off the coast of Vietnam to intentionally provoke the North. This strategy included having the clandestine Norwegian boats make nighttime strikes against the North Vietnamese coast, not really to cause any damage, but simply to get the North Vietnamese to turn on their coastal radars. This accomplished two goals: first, it allowed the *Maddox* to see where those radars were located; and second, it showed the North Vietnamese that the *Maddox* was right there off their coast!

Because of the Cold War between the Communist Bloc and the West, many in the US government were determined to escalate the American presence in the Vietnam War, and were looking for any pretext to do so. People who were against this escalation, like Senator Morse, were keenly aware of this, and were actively on the lookout for anything that would get the United States into the war under false pretenses. The newspapers had been exhaustively covering this conflict of interests for years, and it was an absolutely well-known, public fact.

All the important facts about the incident were publicly known as they happened. Even as the *Maddox* was firing, and even as Captain Herrick was radioing to Washington that there was no attack taking place, and even as Senator Morse repeated this to Congress and to the press, Johnson was already drafting the Gulf of Tonkin Resolution, and everyone knew it. There was never any moment when this fictional naval battle existed as a conspiracy theory. Instead it is evidence that real conspiracies do happen and are discovered all the time, and nothing more.

Military Dolphins

Date: 1964–Present
Location: Worldwide
The Conspirators: US Navy
The Victims: Marine animals and enemy divers

The Theory

Given the speed and agility of dolphins underwater, it's always seemed reasonable that they might be trained to attack enemy divers. And in fiction they've been used to attach limpet mines to ships. So for a long time, there was speculation that the US Navy (and other navies) were doing just these things with dolphins and keeping it a secret both to prevent enemy spies from learning about it, and also to keep the public from knowing about its inhumane treatment of the animals.

The Truth

Dolphins and other aquatic mammals such as sea lions, pilot whales, and belugas have, in fact, been used by many navies worldwide for just about any task you can imagine. Their current duties are relatively benign and humane, but in the past, this was not always the case.

The Backstory

There are good reasons for navies to look at dolphins and other aquatic mammals for a great variety of underwater tasks. Dolphins are far faster and more agile than either divers or any underwater vehicles. They are inexpensive, they go very deep very fast, their echolocation is far superior to anything we've developed, and they are intelligent enough to train.

In 1967 a French novel came out that put the idea of military dolphins into the public consciousness. The novel, titled *Un animal doué de raison* (A Sentient Animal), was about a virtuous couple who studied and trained dolphins, but then the government came in and used their dolphins for violent purposes. The novel was turned into a popular movie, 1973's *The Day of the Dolphin*.

When the movie came out, the media instantly began seeking experts to interview, and they got them. The two most public faces were Dr. James Fitzgerald, a sonar expert who was the godfather of the US Navy's dolphin program; and Michael Greenwood, a former CIA agent who had worked under Fitzgerald, but had resigned when he became disillusioned with the inhumane aspects of the work. Both men were interviewed on separate episodes of the TV news program *60 Minutes* in 1973.

What was revealed in these broadcasts was that dolphins had never been weaponized. They might retrieve lost objects or find mines or perform underwater sentry duties, but attacking divers and attaching mines to ships was never something that was done. Dolphins can't be trained to make decisions, both experts said, so it would be too risky to arm them.

Skeptoid® Says...

Throughout the Middle East conflicts, the US Navy Marine Mammal Program has been used extensively to guard ships, to find mines, and to clear lanes for beach landings. Although bottlenose dolphins and California sea lions do all the work today, in the past the US Navy program has experimented with at least nine other species of cetaceans (including killer whales) and five other pinnipeds (including giant elephant seals).

The Explanation

Once Fitzgerald and Greenwood said their piece, the public's interest in the military's use of dolphins died down a bit. But then it roared back in 1977 with information that has kept the story in prime time ever since. *Penthouse* magazine published a long and detailed article that told a much more sordid tale than the one told in 1973. *Penthouse* used Greenwood as its main source, and while Greenwood confirmed that Fitzgerald had never been able to reliably get dolphins to attach limpet mines to ships, he said that the government had used them to attach listening devices. In one specific story, a CIA boat disguised as a Caribbean rumrunner released a dolphin through an underwater door; it then swam to a nearby Russian nuclear ship and attached a listening device to its hull. The article also revealed that Fitzgerald had attempted to sell the dolphin technology he'd developed for the CIA to Mexico, Peru, Colombia, Chile, Argentina, and Brazil.

As this was basically charging him with espionage, Fitzgerald sued *Penthouse* for libel. But in the lawsuit, it was revealed that he had in fact done those things, and he lost the case. Greenwood then became much freer on the interview circuit, and revealed that dolphins were in fact trained to kill, armed with either a knife or a modified version of an anti-shark weapon called a Shark Dart, a dagger-like weapon charged with CO_2 to blow up a victim. This was in stark contrast to what Fitzgerald and other official sources had always claimed, which was that dolphins had been trained to rip off a diver's air mask and force him to surface, but nothing more violent than that.

This use of marine mammals was dramatically demonstrated during the Vietnam War, when American and Soviet special forces would sometimes clash...if unofficially. The records of Soviet Spetsnaz (special forces) reported that two divers of an underwater demolition team called Delfin (ironically, the Russian word for dolphin) were killed in Vietnam by a dolphin when they were trying to mine an American ship. In response to this, Delfin training thereafter included underwater defense techniques against dolphins. Records show that Delfin divers successfully killed a number of these militarized dolphins off the coast of Nicaragua during the 1970s.

Over time, much of the US Navy Marine Mammal Program (but not all) has by now been declassified. A primary mission of Navy marine mammals—which include not only dolphins but also sea lions—is port surveillance and defense against enemy divers. In one program called SWIDS (Shallow Water Intruder Detection System), which is attached to the mission, sea lions are trained to "mark" enemy divers, which involves spearing their leg with a barbed harpoon to which trackers or other devices can be attached. Human divers then go in to determine what else needs to be done (and, presumably, to do it).

Is this a conspiracy theory proven true? It has sometimes been cited as one, but it's not really a conspiracy. We all know that the military does a lot of what they do in secret; they have to, just as they often spread a smoke screen about their exact capabilities. Calling standard military secrecy a conspiracy cheapens the definition of what a conspiracy really is.

Skeptoid® Says...

It turns out that if you wanted to see the wildest examples of trained dolphins, you'd have to look at the former Soviet Union. In 1998 a Western dolphin expert, Doug Cartlidge, was invited to go see what they had. Soviet dolphins had been trained to find and attach markers with a lethal remote-triggered CO_2 device to enemy divers. Soviet dolphins had also been trained as kamikaze bombers, delivering explosives to ships or submarines. Finally, there were dolphin paratroopers. Dolphins in fabric slings attached to parachutes could be dropped from as high as 3,000 meters, with whatever hardware they were to use once in the water.

CIA Drugs for Guns

Date: 1980s
Location: Nicaragua
The Conspirators: CIA, drug cartels, Contra rebels
The Victims: American drug addicts, Sandinistas

The Theory

Nicaragua had long been ruled by the US-backed Somoza Administration. But in 1979, Somoza was overthrown by the Socialist Sandinistas in the Nicaraguan Revolution, who then took control. The CIA then funded and trained the right-wing Contra rebels to try to retake control from the Sandinistas. Both the Sandinistas and the Contras had ties to the drug cartels, but the CIA looked the other way and knowingly continued funding the Contras despite their cartel connections.

However, conspiracy theorists take this indirect relationship between the CIA and the drug cartels to another level. These theorists believe that the CIA assumed a leading role in the actual transport and sale of the cartel's drugs to American citizens, whom they purposefully got addicted to crack cocaine in order to maximize profits, resulting in more money to buy guns for the Contras. Media revelations and Senate hearings, conspiracy theorists claim, have endorsed their view and proven them right.

The Truth

The relationship between the Contras and the cartels existed with or without the CIA, and the CIA never participated in the sale of drugs to Americans to fund the Contras.

The Backstory

Since the United States didn't want a Socialist government in Nicaragua, the CIA began funding and training the Contra rebels in 1981. The United States' war against Socialism in the Western hemisphere, fought on the ground between the Contras and the Sandinistas, was the basic background for this whole conspiracy theory.

It was impossible to ignore the fact that factions on both sides had ties to the major drug cartels; the drug economy was simply woven into the fabric of Nicaragua during those turbulent times. But the CIA didn't really care, because their main concern was getting the Socialist Sandinistas out of the way. However, the abundance of drug money as a source of funding for the Contras did conveniently fit into their plans, since it was a funding source that didn't have to be funneled through Washington.

Newspapers began reporting the ties between the Contras and the drug cartels in 1984, and this reporting increased through 1986. The association with drug cartels was something of a public relations nightmare for the United States. The Reagan administration downplayed the ties, saying that they were minor, that they were without the knowledge of Contra leaders, and that they'd already severed any such ties, but few people were persuaded.

In 1986 the Senate Foreign Relations Committee held a series of hearings and ultimately prepared what became known as the Kerry Committee Report. This report essentially confirmed what everyone basically already knew: that narcotics trafficking and Contra activities were intertwined. They shared resources, business relationships, and supply operations. The cartels provided direct support to the Contras including cash, weapons, planes, pilots, air supply services, and other materials. By then, Nicaragua had begun general elections, and in 1990 a coalition of anti-Sandinista parties assumed power. The CIA's war with the Sandinistas was over. From then on, things on the "CIA drugs for guns" front were essentially quiet. But everything changed in 1996, when the modern conspiracy theory received its greatest boost.

In 1996 reporter Gary Webb published a series of articles in the *San Jose Mercury News* titled "Dark Alliance," which he later expanded into a book. Webb's premise was that the crack cocaine epidemic among the African-American population in South Central Los Angeles was the direct work of a handful of major drug dealers tightly connected to the CIA, and that the CIA was fully complicit in a solid pipeline of cocaine from the Contras to these dealers and to Los Angeles. Getting

African Americans in Los Angeles addicted to crack was, Webb claimed, fundamental to the CIA's plan to fund the Contras.

Skeptoid® Says...

Gary Webb's *Dark Alliance* book and articles remain a topic of debate. While Webb's reporting contained a number of factual inaccuracies, he correctly captured the general truth of the entire affair, according to most analyses: that the CIA was more concerned with overthrowing the Socialists than with the welfare of American drug addicts.

There was a tremendous response to Webb's series from all quarters, very little of it positive. *The Washington Post*, *The New York Times*, and the *Los Angeles Times* all assigned teams of reporters to scrutinize the "Dark Alliance" articles and found Webb's claims to be poorly supported and greatly exaggerated. The African-American community was especially outraged at Webb's claims. California senators and the Justice Department demanded that Webb's claims about the CIA be investigated. Three major federal investigations were launched, plus one by the Los Angeles County Sheriff's Department. These investigations found little to substantiate Webb's claims that went beyond what was already known from the Kerry Committee Report. The CIA did work with parties they knew to be connected to the cartels, but there is a lack of evidence that the CIA took any active role in the drug trade.

The Explanation

Although theorists love to claim the "CIA drugs for guns" debacle as a victory for conspiracy theories being proven true, there are two major problems with this: First, the links between the Contras and the cartels had been public information almost from the very beginning, as the newspapers were all reporting it. Conspiracy theorists can hardly claim credit for revealing something that they read in the papers.

Second, what they claim today widely misses the mark. The conspiracy theories trumpeted today are of activities that were investigated and then dismissed. The theorists claim that the CIA was involved in selling cocaine to Americans and even actively trying to get them addicted in order to sell more, but not even Gary Webb ever alleged that anything like that happened, and there was certainly never any evidence of it. The crack epidemic in Los Angeles had no connection to the CIA and was not caused by them, but in fact had myriad complex real causes. Conspiracy theorists can hardly claim vindication for believing something that is demonstrably wrong.

Ample evidence proves that the CIA was aware that the Contras they worked with were linked to the drug trade. The CIA knew that much of the Contras' supplies were financed by drug money. Although this would have been the case even if the CIA had never become involved, the CIA did get involved to a higher degree. They authorized and made payments to people they knew to be drug traffickers. They used their influence to protect Contra officials from prosecution for drug-related crimes. They even hired drug trade professionals to perform certain tasks, such as aerial transport.

But as far as taking an active role in the drug trade and taking actions to distribute drugs in Los Angeles and get African Americans addicted, there is no evidence whatsoever that anything like this took place.

Resources

In this section, you'll find resources that will allow you to take a deeper dive into each topic discussed in the book. These resources are books, websites, and periodicals that include authoritative original sources and/or expert analysis. This section is divided by part number and section title to help make the information easy to find and digest when you want to learn more.

PART 1: THOSE WHO RUN THE WORLD

The Knights Templar

Barber, M. *The Trial of the Templars.* Cambridge: Cambridge University Press, 1978.

Clow, E. "The Knights Templar and the Holy Fictionalization of History." *Skeptic North.* January 9, 2010. www.skepticnorth.com/2010/01/the-knights-templar-and-the-holy-fictionalization-of-history/.

Ralls, K. *Knights Templar Encyclopedia: The Essential Guide to the People, Places, Events, and Symbols of the Order of the Temple.* Franklin Lakes, NJ: New Page Books, 2007.

The Rothschild Family

Ferguson, N. *The House of Rothschild: Money's Prophets, 1798–1848.* London: Weidenfeld & Nicolson, 1997.

Kaplan, H. *Nathan Mayer Rothschild and the Creation of a Dynasty: The Critical Years, 1806–1816.* Stanford: Stanford University Press, 2006.

Neal, L. "The Financial Crisis of 1825 and the Restructuring of the British Financial System." *Review* 80, no. 3 (May/June 1998): 53–76.

The Bohemian Club

Domhoff, G. *The Bohemian Grove and Other Retreats.* New York: Harper & Row, 1974.

Ronson, J. *Them: Adventures with Extremists.* New York: Simon & Schuster, 2002.

Weiss, P. "Inside Bohemian Grove." *Spy,* November 1, 1989, 59–76.

The Bilderbergers

Bilderberg Meetings. "Meetings." Accessed 22 Sep. 2010. www.bilderbergmeetings.org/conferences.html.

Burnett, T. *Conspiracy Encyclopedia: The Encyclopedia of Conspiracy Theories.* New York: Franz Steiner Verlag, 2006.

Radford, B. "Fidel Castro's Conspiracy Theories: Worth Considering?" *LiveScience.* August 19, 2010. Web. 21 Sep. 2010. www.livescience.com/10036-fidel-castro-conspiracy-theories-worth.html.

The North American Union

Grubel, H. "The Case for the Amero: The Economics and Politics of a North American Monetary Unit." *Fraser Institute Critical Issues Bulletin,* September 1999. www.americansov.org/news/amero/art_amero_1999jan01.html.

Pastor, R. *Toward a North American Community: Lessons from the Old World for the New.* Washington, DC: Institute for International Economics, 2001.

Security and Prosperity Partnership of North America. "SPP Myths vs Facts." SPP. August 2006. https://web.archive.org/web/20080701112402. www.spp.gov/myths_vs_facts.asp.

The Denver Airport Conspiracy

TheDenverChannel.com. "DIA Cracked Plane Windshields Mystery Solved." February 28, 2007. www.thedenverchannel.com/news/dia-cracked-plane-windshields-mystery-solved.

Denver International Airport. "Art." City & County of Denver Department of Aviation. February 23, 2010. www.flydenver.com/art.

Li, A., R.B. Williamson, F.P. Mulvey, L.E. Hegg, T.B. Baird, S.N. Calvo, J. Furutani, S.K. Gupta, M.S. Panwar, K.A. Rhodes, F.W. Sutherland, and A.D. Trapp. *New Denver Airport: Impact of the Delayed Baggage System.* Washington, DC: US General Accounting Office, 1994. www.gao.gov/products/RCED-95-35BR.

The Reptoids

Bosquet, J. "Lizard Peolpe's[sic]Catacomb City Hunted." *Los Angeles Times,* January 29, 1934.

Lewis, T., and R. Kahn. "The Reptoid Hypothesis: Utopian and Dystopian Representational Motifs in David Icke's Alien Conspiracy Theory." *Utopian Studies* 16, no. 1 (Spring 2005): 45–74.

Rhodes, J. "Basic FAQ's." Reptoids Research Center. November 14, 2009. www.reptoids.com/basic_faqs.htm.

PART 2: GOVERNMENT OPPRESSION

Vaccines

Centers for Disease Control and Prevention. "Ingredients of Vaccines—Fact Sheet." US Department of Health & Human Services. Updated February 22, 2011. www.cdc.gov/vaccines/vac-gen/additives.htm.

Doja, A., and W. Roberts. "Immunizations and Autism: A Review of the Literature." *Canadian Journal of Neurological Science* 33, no. 4 (November 2006): 341–346.

Ribeiro, C., and V. Schijns. "Immunology of Vaccine Adjuvants." *Methods in Molecular Biology* 626 (January 2010): 1–14.

Water Fluoridation

Estupiñán-Day, S. *Promoting Oral Health: The Use of Salt Fluoridation to Prevent Dental Caries*. Washington, DC: Pan American Health Organization, 2005.

McKay, F. "Mass Control of Dental Caries Through the Use of Domestic Water Supplies Containing Fluorine." *American Journal of Public Health and the Nation's Health* 38, no. 6 (June 1948): 828–832.

World Health Organization. *Inadequate or Excess Fluoride: A Major Public Health Concern*. Geneva, Switzerland: WHO, 2010.

Plum Island

Cella, A. "An Overview of Plum Island: History, Research, and Effects on Long Island." *Long Island Historical Journal* 16, no. 1-2 (September 2003): 176–181.

Rather, J. "Plum Island Reports Disease Outbreak." *The New York Times*, August 22, 2004.

US Department of Agriculture. "An Island Fortress for Biosecurity." *Agricultural Research* 43, no. 12 (December 1995): 4.

FEMA Prison Camps

Falkenrath, R. *Problems of Preparedness: U.S. Readiness for a Domestic Terrorist Attack*. Boston: International Security, 2001.

Irons, P. *Justice at War*. New York: Oxford University Press, 1983.

Jacobs, J. *Socio-Legal Foundations of Civil-Military Relations*. New Brunswick, NJ: Transaction, Inc., 1986.

The Branch Davidian Assault

"Children of the Cult." *Newsweek*, May 16, 1993.

Colloff, P. "The Fire That Time." *Texas Monthly Magazine*, April 1, 2008. www.texasmonthly.com/articles/the-fire-that-time/.

Danforth, J. *Final Report to the Deputy Attorney General Concerning the 1993 Confrontation at the Mt. Carmel Complex, Waco, Texas*. November 8, 2000. https://upload.wikimedia.org/wikipedia/commons/8/85/Danforthreport-final.pdf.

Chemtrails

Cairns, R. "Climates of Suspicion: Chemtrail Conspiracy Narratives and the International Politics of Geoengineering." *Geographical Journal* 182, no. 1 (April 2014): 70–84.

Rasch, P., S. Tilmes, R. Turco, A. Robock, L. Oman, C. Chen, G. Stenchikov, and R. Garcia. "An Overview of Geoengineering of Climate Using Stratospheric Sulphate Aerosols." *Philosophical Transactions of the Royal Society A*. 366, no. 1882 (November 2008): 4007–4037.

West, M. "How to Debunk Chemtrails." *Contrail Science*. June 29, 2011. Web. 14 Feb 2018. http://contrailscience.com/how-to-debunk-chemtrails/.

PART 3: SUSPICIOUS DEATHS

Amelia Earhart

Dunning, B. "Finding Amelia Earhart." *Skeptoid: Critical Analysis of Pop Phenomena* (podcast). January 31, 2012. https://skeptoid.com/episodes/4295.

Strippel, R. "Researching Amelia: A Detailed Summary for the Serious Researcher into the Disappearance of Amelia Earhart." *Air Classics* 31, no. 11 (October 1995): 20.

US Navy/US Coast Guard. *U.S. Navy Report of the Search for Amelia Earhart, July 2–18, 1937.* July 31, 1937. https://catalog.archives.gov/id/305240.

JFK

Bugliosi, V. *Reclaiming History: The Assassination of President John F. Kennedy.* New York: W.W. Norton, 2007.

NBC. *Seventy Hours and Thirty Minutes, as Broadcast on the NBC Television Network.* New York: Random House, 1966.

Wood, M., K. Douglas, and R. Sutton. "Dead and Alive: Beliefs in Contradictory Conspiracy Theories." *Social Psychological and Personality Science* 3, no. 6 (November 2012): 767–773.

Paul McCartney

Glenn, A. "'Paul Is Dead!' (said Fred)." *Michigan Today,* November 11, 2009. http://michigantoday.umich.edu/a7565/.

Polidoro, M. "The Walrus Was Paul!" *Skeptical Inquirer* 30, no. 1 (January/February 2006). www.csicop.org/si/show/the_walrus_was_paul.

Reeve, A. *Turn Me On, Dead Man: The Beatles and the Paul Is Dead Hoax.* Bloomington, IN: AuthorHouse, 2004.

Elvis Presley

Chan, M. "Elvis Presley Died 40 Years Ago. Here's Why Some People Think He's Still Alive." *Time,* August 15, 2017. http://time.com/4897819/elvis-presley-alive-conspiracy-theories/.

Federal Bureau of Investigation. "Elvis Presley, Parts 1 through 12." FBI Records: The Vault. February 14, 2018. https://vault.fbi.gov/Elvis Presley.

Lacy, P. *Elvis Decoded: A Fan's Guide to Deciphering the Myths and Misinformation.* Bloomington, IN: AuthorHouse, 2006.

Tupac Shakur and The Notorious B.I.G.

Runtag, J. "The Truth Behind Tupac Shakur's 1996 Murder: 'It Was Simple Retaliation,' Reveals an LAPD Source." *People,* September 13, 2017. http://people.com/music/tupac-shakur-murder-gang-retaliation-lapd/.

Smith, B. "Everything You Need to Know about the Murders of 2Pac and the Notorious B.I.G." Oxygen: Crime Time. November 3, 2017. www.oxygen.com/blogs/everything-you-need-to-know-about-the-murders-of-2pac-and-the-notorious-big.

Sullivan, R. *LAbyrinth: A Detective Investigates the Murders of Tupac Shakur and Notorious B.I.G., the Implications of Death Row Records' Suge Knight, and the Origins of the Los Angeles Police Scandal.* New York: Grove Press, 2002.

Princess Diana

Baker, S. *Coroner's Inquest into the Deaths of Diana, Princess of Wales and Mr. Dodi Al-Fayed: List of Likely Issues.* London: Judicial Communications Office, 2007.

BBC News. "Point-by-point: Al Fayed's claims." February 19, 2008. http://news.bbc.co.uk/2/hi/uk_news/7251568.stm.

Metropolitan Police. *The Operation Paget Inquiry Report into the Allegation of Conspiracy to Murder Diana, Princess of Wales and Emad El-Din Mohamed Abdel Moneim Fayed: Report.* London: Metropolitan Police, 2006.

PART 4: THE WORLD AT WAR

Nazi Wunderwaffen

Cornwell, J. *Hitler's Scientists: Science, War, and the Devil's Pact.* New York: Viking, 2003.

Gallagher, T. *Assault in Norway: Sabotaging the Nazi Nuclear Program.* Guilford, CT: The Lyons Press, 2002.

Pauwels, L., and L. Bergier. *The Morning of the Magicians.* New York: Stein and Day, 1963.

Holocaust Denial

Fleming, G. *Hitler and the Final Solution.* Berkeley: University of California Press, 1984.

Shermer, M., and A. Grobman. *Denying History: Who Says the Holocaust Never Happened and Why Do They Say It?* Berkeley: University of California Press, 2009.

Zimmerman, J. *Holocaust Denial: Demographics, Testimonies, and Ideologies.* Lanham, MD: University Press of America, 2000.

Attack on Pearl Harbor

Borch, F., and D. Martinez. *Kimmel, Short, and Pearl Harbor: The Final Report Revealed.* Annapolis, MD: Naval Institute Press, 2005.

Carroll, R.T. "Philadelphia Experiment." *The Skeptic's Dictionary.* Updated November 21, 2015. http://skepdic.com/philadel.html.

Central Intelligence Agency. "Memorandum for the Director of Central Intelligence: Intelligence at Pearl Harbor." August 22, 1946. www.cia.gov/library/readingroom/docs/DOC_0000188601.pdf.

Clausen, H., and B. Lee. *Pearl Harbor: Final Judgement.* New York: Crown, 1992.

The Philadelphia Experiment

Goerman, R. "Alias Carlos Allende: The Mystery Man Behind the Philadelphia Experiment." *FATE* 33, no. 10 (October 2, 1980).

Vallee, J.F. "Anatomy of a Hoax: The Philadelphia Experiment Fifty Years Later." *Journal of Scientific Exploration* 8, no.1 (October 1994): 47–71.

Nuclear War and Nuclear Winter

Sagan, C. *The Demon-Haunted World: Science as a Candle in the Dark.* New York: Random House, 1995.

Thompson, S., and S. Schneider. "Nuclear Winter Reappraised." *Foreign Affairs* 62 (June 1986): 981–1,005.

Turco, R., O. Toon, T. Ackerman, J. Pollack, and C. Sagan. "Nuclear Winter: Global Consequences of Multiple Nuclear Explosions." *Science* 222, no. 4630 (January 1983): 1,283–1,292.

9/11 Building Collapses

Dunbar, D., and B. Reagan. *Debunking 9/11 Myths: Why Conspiracy Theories Can't Stand Up to the Facts.* New York: Hearst Books, 2006.

9/11 Commission. *The 9/11 Commission Report.* New York: W.W. Norton & Company, 2004.

Sunder, S., R. Gann, W. Grosshandler, H. Lew, R. Bukowski, F. Sadek, F. Gayle, J. Gross, T. McAllister, J. Averill, J. Lawson, H. Nelson, and S. Cauffman. *NIST NCSTAR 1A: Final Report on the Collapse of World Trade Center Building 7.* Washington, DC: US Government Printing Office, 2008.

The Pentagon and the Missile

Roberts, S. "Photos of Flight 77 Wreckage Inside the Pentagon." Rense.com. December 4, 2002. http://rense.com/general32/phot.htm.

Scott, J. "Pentagon & Boeing 757 Engine Investigation." Aerospaceweb. May 6, 2006. www.aerospaceweb.org/question/conspiracy/q0265.shtml.

Snopes. "Hunt the Boeing!" Updated August 21, 2016. www.snopes.com/rumors/pentagon.asp.

PART 5: SUPPRESSED SCIENCE

The Hollow Earth

Gardner, M. "Notes of a Fringe-Watcher: Occam's Razor and the Nutshell Earth." *Skeptical Inquirer* 12, no. 4 (July 1988): 355–358.

Ohnemus, C. "Dr. Cyrus Teed and the Koreshan Unity Movement." *Cultural Resource Management* 24, no. 9 (January 2001): 10–12.

Teed, C. *The Cellular Cosmogony, or The Earth a Concave Sphere.* Chicago: The Guiding Star Publishing House, 1898.

The Flat Earth Theory

Gardner, M. *Fads and Fallacies in the Name of Science.* New York: Dover Publications, 1957.

Garwood, C. *Flat Earth: The History of an Infamous Idea.* New York: St. Martin's Press, 2007.

O'Neill, B. "Do They Really Think the Earth Is Flat?" *BBC News.* August 4, 2008. http://news.bbc.co.uk/2/hi/uk_news/magazine/7540427.stm.

Nikola Tesla

Cheney, M., and R. Uth. *Tesla: Master of Lightning.* New York: Barnes & Noble, 1999.

O'Neill, J. *Prodigal Genius: The Life of Nikola Tesla.* New York: I. Washburn, 1944.

Tesla, N. *Colorado Springs Notes, 1899–1900.* February 14, 2018. www.bibliotecapleyades.net/tesla/coloradonotes/coloradonotes.htm.

Free Energy

Gardner, M. "Perpetual Motion: Illusion and Reality." *Foote Prints* 47, no. 2 (January 1984): 21–35.

Quinn, G. "The Patent Law of Perpetual Motion." *IP Watchdog.* October 11, 2011. www.ipwatchdog.com/2011/10/11/the-patent-law-of-perpetual-motion/.

Simanek, D. "Perpetual Futility: A Short History of the Search for Perpetual Motion." *Donald Simanek's Pages.* December 14, 2012. www.lockhaven.edu/~dsimanek/museum/people/people.htm.

The Big Pharma Conspiracy

Blaskiewicz, B. "The Big Pharma Conspiracy Theory." *Medical Writing* 22, no. 4 (November 2013): 259–261.

Higgins, M. "Is There Really a Conspiracy to Suppress Cancer Cures?" *Cancer Treatment Watch.* October 24, 2007. www.cancertreatmentwatch.org/q/conspiracy.shtml.

Novella, S. "Demonizing Big Pharma." *Science-Based Medicine.* April 22, 2010. http://sciencebasedmedicine.org/demonizing-big-pharma/.

PART 6: SPACE CONSPIRACY THEORIES

The Black Knight Satellite

"Dark Satellite Remains Mystery; Unclaimed by All." *The Southeast Missourian.* February 11, 1960.

Oberg, J. "Phantom Satellite?" October 21, 2014. www.jamesoberg.com/sts88_and-black-knight.pdf.

Van der Pol, B. "Short Wave Echoes and the Aurora Borealis." *Nature* 122 (December 1928): 878–879.

Roswell

Nickell, J. *Real-life X-Files: Investigating the Paranormal.* Lexington: University Press of Kentucky, 2001.

Saler, B., C. Ziegler, and C. Moore. *UFO Crash at Roswell: The Genesis of a Modern Myth.* Washington, DC: Smithsonian, 1997.

Weaver, R., and J. McAndrew. *Roswell Report: Fact versus Fiction in the New Mexico Desert.* Washington, DC: United States Air Force, 1995.

Area 51

National Reconnaissance Office. *Comparison of SR-71 and A-12 Aircraft.* Washington, DC: NRO, 1967.

Roadrunners Internationale. "Memories of the Cold War." Last modified September 29, 2008. http://roadrunnersinternationale.com/coldwarstories.html.

US Department of Energy. *Origins of the Nevada Test Site.* Washington, DC: US Department of Energy, 2000.

The Lucifer Project

Blanchard, A. *Updated Critical Mass Estimates for Plutonium-238.* Aiken, SC: Westinghouse Savannah River Company, 1999.

NASA. "Spacecraft Power for Cassini." NASA Fact Sheet. January 16, 2010. http://georgenet.net/hubble/cassini_pdf/power.pdf.

O'Neill, I. "Project Lucifer: Will Cassini Turn Saturn Into a Second Sun? (Part 1)." *Universe Today.* Updated December 24, 2015. www.universetoday.com/2008/07/24/project-lucifer-will-cassini-turn-saturn-into-a-second-sun-part-1/.

The Moon Landing Hoax

"*Apollo 11* Hoax: One in Four People Do Not Believe in Moon Landing." *The Telegraph.* July 17, 2009. www.telegraph.co.uk/news/science/space/5851435/Apollo-11-hoax-one-in-four-people-do-not-believe-in-moon-landing.html.

Keel, W. "Telescopic Tracking of the Apollo Lunar Missions." *Space Bits.* University of Alabama, August 1, 2016. Web. 30 August 2016. http://pages.astronomy.ua.edu/keel/space/apollo.html.

Plait, P. *Bad Astronomy: Misconceptions and Misuses Revealed, from Astrology to the Moon Landing Hoax.* New York: John Wiley & Sons, 2002.

The Face on Mars

Morrison, D. "MGS Photographs 'Face on Mars.'" *Skeptical Inquirer* 25, no. 3 (May 1998): 65.

Philips, T. "Unmasking the Face on Mars." *NASA Science.* May 24, 2001. http://science.nasa.gov/headlines/y2001/ast24may_1.htm.

Posner, G. "The Face Behind the Face on Mars: A Skeptical Look at Richard Hoagland." *Skeptical Inquirer* 24, no. 6 (November 2000): 20.

PART 7: URBAN LEGEND CONSPIRACY THEORIES

Hearst and Hemp

Bonnie, R., and C. Whitebread. "The Forbidden Fruit and the Tree of Knowledge: An Inquiry Into the Legal History of American Marijuana Prohibition." *Virginia Law Review* 56, no. 6 (October 1970): 971–1,203.

Swanberg, W. *Citizen Hearst*. New York: Charles Scribner's Sons, 1961.

Wishnia, S. "Debunking the Hemp Conspiracy Theory." *AlterNet*. February 20, 2008. www.alternet.org/story/77339/debunking_the_hemp_conspiracy_theory.

There Is No Finland

Bestor, V., and T. Bestor. "Japan and the Sea." *Education about Asia* 19, no. 2 (October 2014): 50–56.

Encyclopaedia Britannica, s.v. "Trans-Siberian Railroad." Updated May 9, 2017. www.britannica.com/topic/Trans-Siberian-Railroad.

Lamoureux, M. "This Dude Accidentally Convinced the Internet That Finland Doesn't Exist." *Vice*. December 9, 2016. www.vice.com/sv/article/this-dude-accidentally-convinced-the-internet-that-finland-doesnt-exist.

Men in Black

Barker, G. *They Knew Too Much about Flying Saucers*. New York: University Books, 1956.

Bender, A. *Flying Saucers and the Three Men*. Clarksburg: Saucerian Books, 1962.

Sherwood, J. "Gray Barker: My Friend, the Myth-Maker." *Skeptical Inquirer* 22, no. 3 (January 1998): 37–39.

Polybius

DeSpira, C. "Reinvestigating Polybius." *Retrocade* 1, no. 2 (April 2012): 141–148.

"Tummy Derails Asteroids Champ." *Eugene Register-Guard*, November 29, 1981.

"Video Games Gambling Count Admitted." *The Oregonian*, December 9, 1981.

HAARP

Eastlund, B. "Method and Apparatus for Altering a Region in the Earth's Atmosphere, Ionosphere, and/or Magnetosphere." United States Patent and Trademark Office. August 11, 1987. http://tinyurl.com/328mdn4.

Ratcliffe, J. *An Introduction to the Ionosphere and Magnetosphere*. London: Cambridge University Press, 1972.

University of Alaska Fairbanks Geophysical Institute. "HAARP FAQ." January 9, 2010. www.gi.alaska.edu/haarp/faq.

TWA Flight 800

Barreveld, D. *The Spark That Killed 230 People: The Scary Details of the NTSB's Final Report of the Crash of TWA Flight 800.* Lincoln, NE: iUniverse, 2002.

Hall, J., J. Hammerschmidt, J. Goglia, G. Black, and C. Carmody. *NTSB Abstract AAR-00/03.* Washington, DC: National Transportation Safety Board, 2000.

Wald, M. "T.W.A. Crash Investigators Ridicule a Missile Theory and Pin Hopes on Research." *The New York Times*, March 14, 1997.

Malaysian Airlines MH370

Goodfellow, C. "A Startlingly Simple Theory about the Missing Malaysia Airlines Jet." *Wired.* March 18, 2014. www.wired.com/2014/03/mh370-electrical-fire/.

"MH370 Conspiracy Theories: The Truth Behind One of Aviation's Greatest Mysteries." *The Week.* January 18, 2018. www.theweek.co.uk/mh370/58037/mh370-conspiracy-theories-what-happened-to-the-missing-plane.

USCDornsife Spatial Sciences Institute. "The Search for Malaysia Airlines Flight #MH370." http://gis.usc.edu/blog/the-search-for-malaysia-airlines-flight-mh370/.

PART 8: CONSPIRACY THEORIES THAT TURNED OUT TO BE...TRUE?

Numbers Stations

Nieves, G. "Lawyer: Accused Spy to Plead Guilty." *The Miami Herald*, September 14, 2001.

Pierce, L. *Intercepting Numbers Stations.* Dorset, England: Interproducts, 1994.

Smolinski, C. "Spy Numbers Stations on Shortwave Radio." *Spy Numbers.* August 11, 2015. www.spynumbers.com/.

MKULTRA

Central Intelligence Agency. *Brainwashing from a Psychological Viewpoint.* Washington, DC: US Government Printing Office, 1956.

Gabbai, Lisbonne, and Pourquier. "Ergot Poisoning at Pont St. Esprit." *British Medical Journal* 2, no. 4732 (September 1951): 650–651.

Select Committee on Intelligence, and Subcommittee on Health and Scientific Research of the Committee on Human Resources. *Project MKULTRA: The CIA's Program of Research in Behavioral Modification.* Washington, DC: US Government Printing Office, 1977.

COINTELPRO

Blackstock, N. *COINTELPRO: The FBI's Secret War on Political Freedom.* New York: Monad Press, 1975.

Churchill, W., and J. Vander Wall. *The COINTELPRO Papers: Documents from the FBI's Secret Wars Against Domestic Dissent.* Boston: South End Press, 1990.

Medsger, B. *The Burglary: The Discovery of J. Edgar Hoover's Secret FBI.* New York: Vintage Books, 2014.

The Gulf of Tonkin

Ball, M. "Revisiting the Gulf of Tonkin Crisis: An Analysis of the Private Communication of President Johnson and His Advisers." *Discourse & Society* 2, no. 3 (1991): 281–296.

Hanyok, R. "Skunks, Bogies, Silent Hounds, and the Flying Fish: The Gulf of Tonkin Mystery, 2–4 August 1964." *Cryptologic Quarterly* 19, no. 4/20, no. 1 (Winter 2000/Spring 2001): 1–55.

Prados, J. "The Gulf of Tonkin Incident, 40 Years Later." National Security Archive. August 4, 2004. https://nsarchive2.gwu.edu/NSAEBB/NSAEBB132/index.htm.

Military Dolphins

Chapple, S. "The Pentagon's Deadly Pets." *Penthouse* 8, no. 10 (June 1977): 48–54.

Gasperini, W. "Uncle Sam's Dolphins." *Smithsonian* 34, no. 6 (September 2003): 28–30.

Space and Naval Warfare Systems Command. "US Navy Marine Mammal Program." May 21, 2011. www.public.navy.mil/spawar/Pacific/technology/Pages/mammals.aspx.

CIA Drugs for Guns

Kerry, J., B. Adams, and D. Moynihan. *Drugs, Law Enforcement, and Policy: A Report Prepared by the Subcommittee on Terrorism, Narcotics, and International Operations.* Washington, DC: US Government Printing Office, 1989.

"The Contras, Cocaine, and Covert Operations." The National Security Archive. January 10, 2018. https://nsarchive2.gwu.edu//NSAEBB/NSAEBB2/index.html.

Webb, G. *Dark Alliance: The CIA, the Contras, and the Crack Cocaine Explosion.* New York: Seven Stories Press, 1996.

Index

About the Author

Brian Dunning is a science writer who since 2006 has been the host and producer of the podcast *Skeptoid®: Critical Analysis of Pop Phenomena* (Skeptoid.com), applying critical thinking to urban legends and popular pseudoscientific subjects promoted by the mass media. *Skeptoid®* has a weekly audience of more than 150,000 listeners. Brian has lectured on conspiracy theories at universities and conferences nationwide and internationally, including an annual appearance at a national security course at American University in Washington, DC. He has appeared on numerous radio shows and TV documentaries, and also hosts the science video series *inFact with Brian Dunning*. He is a member of the National Association of Science Writers.

communal environment. (If everybody owns the environment, then it belongs to nobody, right?) But example is better than precept. Heed now the history of Black Mesa and Four Corners, which even utility executives who make the hard decisions now call "the school of horrors."

In the mid-1950s a group of the Southwest's major electric utilities, recognizing their region's phenomenal growth, started searching for a good spot to put power plants that would provide energy for the burgeoning cities, especially Los Angeles, Phoenix and Las Vegas. Since nuclear stations were still much too small and experimental to figure in these plans, the companies were concerned with fossil-fired facilities. What the utilities needed, then, was a place with adequate supplies of fuel and water. As for air pollution — a growing problem even then — they decided to go someplace where no one lived and, presumably, no one would complain.

The search ended successfully, as it were, in the wide open desert area where New Mexico, Arizona, Utah and Colorado all meet — at the "Four Corners." There were thick, untouched seams of coal lying close to the surface in the vicinity and, though water was scarce, the Colorado River and its tributaries could just slake the power plants' thirst. Moreover, the population was sparse and poor, mostly Navajo and Hopi Indians. These people, the utilities believed, would eagerly welcome economic development of their lands and the good things money would bring.

The utilities formed a consortium known as Western Energy Supply and Transmission (WEST) consisting of twenty-three public and investor-owned companies. Together, they planned what would be the U.S.'s biggest power complex to produce approximately 36,000 megawatts of electricity in the 1980s—more than twice the Tennessee Valley Authority's total. The heart of the complex would comprise six enormous plants in four states. Two of the monsters— Four Corners (2,075 megawatts) and San Juan (990 megawatts)—would be sited a few miles apart on the San Juan River near Farmington, New Mexico. Two others—Navajo (2,310 megawatts) and Kaiparowits (5,000 megawatts, minimum)—would stand on opposite sides of the man-made Lake Powell, one in Arizona and the other in Utah. The Mohave plant (2,310 megawatts) would be in nearby Nevada, downstream from Lake Powell on the Colorado River. The sixth, Huntington Canyon (2,000 megawatts), would be in central Utah on Huntington Creek.

To be sure, there was no dearth of legal problems standing in the way of implementing such an ambitious scheme. For one, much of the land and the coal under it belonged to the Indians. For another, the U.S. Department of the Interior and other federal agencies would have to approve road building, tapping the already overdroughted Colorado River Basin and stringing transmission lines through federally owned land. But those problems were surmountable. The states themselves actively wanted these additions to their tax bases. Representatives of the tribes, urged on by the U.S. Bureau of Indian Affairs, struck what sounded like advantageous deals with coal companies. The Interior Department contracted to supply cooling water to the coal companies at the surprisingly low price of seven dollars per acre-foot (according to one informed estimate, the "going" price to other users was twenty-eight dollars an acre-foot). Later on, Interior was to participate in the Navajo plant because it needed abundant power to pump water to central Arizona.

All these schemes and negotiations were carried out not exactly in a news blackout but as quietly and unobtrusively as possible. Correspondence between various federal agencies in 1969 reveals that most government employees did not even know for sure of the existence of the Navajo plant until months after Interior Secretary Stewart Udall had signed a water service contract with Navajo's operator, the Salt River Project. Meantime there had been no public hearings, no congressional hearings, no announcements. While such pervasive silence now raises troubling questions of just whom the federal agencies were representing—the people or the power consortium—at the time, it speeded implementation of the various aspects of the project.